® The Pocket Book Edition of the

S C O T T
1980 STAMP
CATALOGUE

® The Pocket Book Edition of the

SCOTT
1980 STAMP CATALOGUE

SCOTT PUBLISHING COMPANY

PUBLISHED BY POCKET BOOKS NEW YORK

Another *Original* publication of POCKET BOOKS

POCKET BOOKS, a Simon & Schuster division of
GULF & WESTERN CORPORATION
1230 Avenue of the Americas, New York, N.Y. 10020

ISBN: 0-671-83452-5

First Pocket Books printing December, 1979

10 9 8 7 6 5 4 3 2 1

CONTENTS

INTRODUCTION TO STAMP COLLECTING

A fascinating hobby, an engrossing avocation and a universal pastime, stamp collecting is pursued by millions. Young and old, rich and poor, cultured and uncultured, they are all involved in that king of indoor sport, "the paper chase."

It was 140 years ago that Rowland Hill's far-reaching postal reforms became a reality and the world's first adhesive postage stamp was put on sale throughout the post offices of Great Britain. The date was May 6, 1840. Not too long after, the world's first stamp collector came into being and a hobby was born that has continued to grow ever since.

Although for the next seven years there were only three stamps in England, the 1p black, 2p blue and 1p red, there were people who saved them. One apocryphal story has it that a stylish Victorian lady had a room papered with the ebon-hued "Penny Black." In 1850 there were reportedly collectors who were even more rabid. The Illustrated London News for May 8th of that year reports the dire tale of another Victorian damsel, this one in desperate need of help. Her collector father declared he would place her in a convent if she did not amass one million used postage stamps within a certain time. The story aroused concern and sympathy and the stamps poured in, "...many from persons of the highest rank, expressing the most kindly feeling."Shades of Rumpelstiltskin! Fortunately, few collectors have risen to the aberrative heights of those fabled fanatics. Stamp collecting, however, continued to spread, and as country after country began to issue stamps the fraternity flourished. Today, their numbers are legion, as are the number of stamp issuing countries.

Specialization can take many forms. There are those that collect the stamps of a single country. There are those that collect a single issue and those that collect a single stamp in all its nuances and variations. Some collect a particular type of postage stamp such as air mails, commemoratives, etc. Others specialize in cancellations and postmarks and collect their stamps on "cover," that is on the entire envelope. Most popular, however, is collecting by country- especially one's own country. The catalogue you now hold is designed to aid in forming just such a collection, it lists the stamps of the United States, Canada and the U.N. A simplified edition of the 1980 Scott Standard Postage Stamp Catalogue, it has many uses. We will go into them later. First, let us briefly discuss some of the ways of forming a collection.

Although the methods of collecting postage stamps are varied and many, anyone can enjoy them. One may begin by attempting to gather a single specimen of every stamp issued by a country. As one becomes more experienced, the collection may be enlarged to include the different types of each stamp such as perforation varieties, watermark varieties, different printings and color changes. The stamps may be collected on cover complete with all postal markings. Thus, the postal rates, cancellations, postmarks and any other postal information that helps speed a letter to its destination may be studied.

A very popular form of collecting practiced today is called "topical" collecting. Here, the subject depicted on the stamp is the paramount attraction. The topics or themes from which to choose are myriad. Animals, flowers, music and musicians, ships, birds and famous people on stamps make interesting collections as do transportation, exploration of space, artists and famous paintings. The list is endless.

Building such a collection is simple. Pick a topic that interests you, check it out on one of the many available lists of stamps dealing with that subject and begin. If your subject is broad enough, forming an interesting and meaningful collection should not be difficult.

Let us not forget another very popular form of collecting, the "First Day Cover." These are envelopes franked with a new stamp and cancelled on the first day of use, usually at a specially designated location. The envelope ordinarily contains a cachet commemorating the event or person for which the stamp was issued.

Collections may be limited to types of stamps. The postage stamps issued by most countries are divided into such categories as definitives, commemoratives, air mail stamps, special delivery stamps, postage due stamps, etc. Any of those groups provide the means for building a good collection.

Definitive stamps are those regular issues used on most of the mail sent out on a daily basis. Issued in a rising series of values that allows a mailer to meet any current postal rate, they range in the U.S. from one cent to five dollars. Printed in huge quantities, they are kept in service by the post office for long periods of time.

Commemoratives meet another need. They are stamps issued to celebrate an important event, honor a famous person or promote a special project. Such stamps are issued on a limited basis for a limited time. They are usually more colorful and of a larger size than the definitives, making them of special interest to the collector.

Although few air mail stamps are issued by the United States and Canada they remain highly popular among collectors. They, too, are subject to several ways of collecting. Besides amassing the actual stamps, enthusiasts eagerly pursue "First Flight Covers," "Airport Dedications" and even "Crash Covers."

Not as important, but often collected as a unit are the special delivery stamps which secure speedier delivery of a letter and postage due stamps which indicate that a letter did not carry enough postage to pay for its delivery, subjecting the recipient to a fee to make up the difference.

Let us move on to the tools of collecting. They are not many, but they are both useful and necessary. First a home for your collection is needed.

THE ALBUM

Stamps, to display them at their best, should be properly housed. A good album not only achieves this, but gives protection from dirt, loss and damage. When choosing one, however, make sure of three things. That the album is within your means, meets your special interests and is the best you can afford. There are many on the market and they are geared to fit every taste and pocketbook.

Loose-leaf albums are recommended. Not only will they allow for expansion of a collection, but the pages may be removed for mounting and for display. A special advantage of the loose-leaf album is that in a good many cases it may be kept up-to-date with supplements that are published annually on matching pages and are available at your stamp dealer.

MOUNTS AND HINGES

Along with the album one must have mounts and hinges. Let us consider the mount first. These days, when the never-hinged stamp has assumed some importance, the mount has become a necessary accessory. It is a must for mint stamps.

Most mounts consist of a pre-glued, clear plastic container that holds a stamp safely and can be affixed to an album page with minimum effort. They are available in sizes to fit any stamp, block or even whole envelopes.

Although the mount is important, the hinge is equally so. Many a stamp in the old days was ruined beyond redemption by being glued to an album page. Hinges are cheap and effective. The best ones are peelable and may be removed from a stamp or album page without leaving an unsightly mark or causing damage. They are perfect for less expensive stamps, used stamps and stamps that have previously been hinged. Using them is simple. Merely fold back about a quarter of the hinge, adhesive side out. Moisten the folded part and affix it to the back of the stamp. Then, holding the stamps with a pair of tongs, moisten the bottom part and place it and the stamp in its proper place on the album page.

STAMP TONGS

We mentioned tongs above. This simple, but important, accessory should always be used when handling a stamp. They cost little and will quickly pay for themselves. The ones with round ends are preferable, those with sharp ends may damage a stamp. Once you get used to using them you will find them easier to work with than your fingers. What's more, your stamps will be the better for it.

MAGNIFYING GLASS

A good magnifying glass for scrutinizing stamps in detail is another extremely useful philatelic tool. It lets you see flaws that are otherwise invisible to the naked eye. It makes minute parts of a design large enough to see. It saves wear and tear on the eyesight. It too pays for itself.

PERFORATION GAUGE and WATERMARK DETECTOR

As one becomes familiar with stamps he will discover that although many stamps appear to be exactly alike, they are not. The color and design may be identical, but there is a difference. The perforations around the edge of the stamp are not the same, nor is the watermark. To determine these differences a perforation gauge and a watermark detector are needed. Often, the perforations or the watermark found in the paper on which a stamp is printed are the only way to classify it properly.

The perforation gauge, printed on plastic or cardboard, contains a graded scale that measures the size of the perforations used for most stamps. Placing the stamp on the gauge and moving it up or down until the dots on the gauge and the teeth of the perforation mesh gives one the size of the perforation. Most gauges also contain a small millimeter rule that allows one to accurately determine the dimensions of the stamp.

Watermarks are not quite so easy to detect. They are a design or device impressed into the paper on which the stamp is printed. Occasionally a watermark may be seen by holding a stamp up to the light, but normally a watermark detector is necessary to bring it out. Many types of detectors exist, but the simplest and most useful is that old standby, the small black tray. The stamp is placed face down in it, some lighter fluid is poured over the stamp causing the watermark to become visible.

CONDITION

As collectors and stamp collecting become more sophisticated, "condition" becomes more and more important. "Condition," speaking philatelicly, means the state of a stamp - superb, mediocre or below average. Like anything else, a stamp in fine condition will always bring more than the same item in poor condition

A stamp when added to a collection should be the best obtainable. If it is unused, it should be well-centered and have a clean, fresh look. The gum should be intact. Stamps that have been hinged sell for less than those with pristine gum and stamps with part gum sell for much less.

Used stamps should be well-centered and lightly cancelled. They should not be faded or dirty. They should not have any thinning.

When buying a stamp labled, "superb," it should be of top quality, perfectly centered, brilliant in color and have perfect gum. Used copies should be fresh, lightly cancelled and sound in every respect.

When buying a stamp labeled, "fine," it should be without flaws, but with average centering. The gum may have light hinge marks. Used copies are not quite as fresh as, "superb," centering is average and the cancels are heavier.

A stamp listed as "good" or "average" is usually off-center, but attractive. It may have minor defects such as disturbed gum, tiny thins or heavy hinge marks. Used copies, except for the gum, fall into the same classification. Stamps that fall below these standards should be ignored.

THE CATALOGUE

The catalogue is one of the collector's most valued tools. Without it he is liable to be as lost as a sailor at sea without a compass. An illustrated and priced list of the postage stamps issued by every country of the world, it is a prime source of basic information pertaining to stamps and stamp collecting. Issued annually, it is the chief and handiest guide to what postage stamps exist. Its illustrations make it easy to identify one's stamps and are a guide to the fundamental elements of the hobby.

Scott's Standard Postage Stamp Catalogue is the leading general catalogue in the United States. It identifies every stamp and its major varieties by color, design and denomination. It gives the date of issue, the printing method, perforation size and watermark, if any, of each stamp where possible and the reason for its issuance. Every stamp is priced used and unused. In addition, every stamp has an identifying number. These are used by dealers and collectors as a quick method of identifying stamps they wish to buy or sell.

This "Pocket Book Edition" of the "Standard Catalogue" which you hold in your hand is a simplified version of the parent volume. Limited to the United States, Canada and the United Nations, it does not go into the massive detail that the larger one does. Nevertheless, it is a valuable and useful tool containing the basic information needed to identify and assign the stamps of these entities to your collection. Besides giving the current market value of each stamp it gives their philatelic details as well. As in the parent catalogue, the following style of listing is used.

The number in the first column is its Scott number or identifying number. The letter and number that come next (A41) indicate the design and refer to the illustration so designated. Following that is the denomination of the stamp and its color. Finally, the price, unused and used is shown.

Especially useful in this catalogue is the provision for making your own inventory and checklist. It allows one to keep a complete record of his holdings with a minimum of effort.

Above the columns of boxes are spaces in which a collector may indicate such designations as, "Mint," "Used," "Block," "Plate Block," "First Day Cover," or any other classification he desires. A mark in any of the boxes below makes a quickly visible checklist that instantly shows the status of his collection. A handy pocket inventory, it eliminates such chores as the compiling of buying lists.

Benjamin Franklin
A1
A3

George Washington
A2
A4

Reproductions. The letters R. W. H. & E. at the bottom of each stamp are less distinct on the reproductions than on the originals.

5c. On the originals the left side of the white shirt frill touches the oval on a level with the top of the "F" of "Five." On the reproductions it touches the oval about on a level with the top of the figure "5."

10c. On the reproductions, line of coat at left points to right tip of "X" and line of coat at right points to center of "S" of CENTS. On the originals, line of coat points to "T" of TEN and between "T" and "S" of CENTS. On the reproductions the eyes have a sleepy look, the line of the mouth is straighter, and in the curl of hair near the left cheek is a strong black dot, while the originals have only a faint one.

Franklin
A5

A5

ONE CENT.

Type I. Has complete curved lines outside the labels with "U.S. Postage" and "One Cent." The scrolls below the lower label are turned under, forming little balls. The ornaments at top are substantially complete.

Type Ib. Same as I but balls below the bottom label are not so clear. The plume-like scrolls at bottom are not complete.

A6

Type Ia. Same as I at bottom but top ornaments and outer line at top are partly cut away.

A7

Type II. The little balls of the bottom scrolls and the bottoms of the lower plume ornaments are missing. The side ornaments are complete.

A8

Type III. The top and bottom curved lines outside the labels are broken in the middle. The side ornaments are complete.

Type IIIa. Similar to type III with the outer line broken at top or bottom but not both.

A9

Type IV. Similar to type II, but with the curved lines outside the labels recut at top or bottom or both.

Prices for types I and III are for stamps showing the marked characteristics plainly. Copies of type I showing the balls indistinctly and of type III with the lines only slightly broken, sell for much lower prices.

UNITED STATES

Scott® No.	Illus No.	Description	Unused Price	Used Price	/ / / / / /
1847		**All Issues from 1847 to 1894 are Unwatermarked.**			
1	A1	5¢ red brown, *bluish*	2000.00	475.00	☐☐☐☐☐
2	A2	10¢ black, *bluish*	11000.00	1300.00	☐☐☐☐☐
1875		**REPRODUCTIONS.**	Bluish paper without gum.		
3	A3	5¢ red brown	900.00		☐☐☐☐☐
4	A4	10¢ black	1200.00		☐☐☐☐☐
1851-56					
5	A5	1¢ blue, Type I	70000.00	12000.00	☐☐☐☐☐
5A	A5	1¢ blue, Type Ib	5500.00	1350.00	☐☐☐☐☐
6	A6	1¢ blue, Type Ia	7250.00	2000.00	☐☐☐☐☐
7	A7	1¢ blue, Type II	300.00	55.00	☐☐☐☐☐
8	A8	1¢ blue, Type III	2850.00	750.00	☐☐☐☐☐
8A	A8	1¢ blue, Type IIIa	850.00	375.00	☐☐☐☐☐
9	A9	1¢ blue, Type IV ('52)	185.00	45.00	☐☐☐☐☐
10	A10	3¢ orange brown, Type I	750.00	40.00	☐☐☐☐☐
11	A10	3¢ dull red, Type I	70.00	4.50	☐☐☐☐☐
12	A11	5¢ red brown, Type I ('56)	4250.00	650.00	☐☐☐☐☐
13	A12	10¢ green, Type I ('55)	3750.00	400.00	☐☐☐☐☐
14	A13	10¢ green, Type II ('55)	750.00	160.00	☐☐☐☐☐
15	A14	10¢ green, Type III ('55)	725.00	150.00	☐☐☐☐☐
16	A15	10¢ green, Type IV ('55)	5250.00	800.00	☐☐☐☐☐
17	A16	12¢ black	900.00	125.00	☐☐☐☐☐
1857-61		*Perf. 15*			
18	A5	1¢ blue, Type I ('61)	425.00	225.00	☐☐☐☐☐
19	A6	1¢ blue, Type Ia	4750.00	1150.00	☐☐☐☐☐
20	A7	1¢ blue, Type II	265.00	67.50	☐☐☐☐☐
21	A8	1¢ blue, Type III	1600.00	525.00	☐☐☐☐☐
22	A8	1¢ blue, Type IIIa	325.00	100.00	☐☐☐☐☐
23	A9	1¢ blue, Type IV	1000.00	140.00	☐☐☐☐☐
24	A20	1¢ blue, Type V	62.50	15.00	☐☐☐☐☐
25	A10	3¢ rose, Type I	375.00	15.00	☐☐☐☐☐
26	A21	3¢ dull red, Type II	25.00	2.00	☐☐☐☐☐
26a	A21	3c dull red, Type IIa	65.00	10.00	☐☐☐☐☐
27	A11	5¢ brick red, Type I ('58)	3500.00	475.00	☐☐☐☐☐
28	A11	5¢ red brown, Type I	950.00	135.00	☐☐☐☐☐
28A	A11	5¢ Indian red, Type I ('58)	5000.00	550.00	☐☐☐☐☐
29	A11	5¢ brown, Type I ('59)	450.00	90.00	☐☐☐☐☐
30	A22	5¢ orange brown, Type II ('61)	400.00	525.00	☐☐☐☐☐
30A	A22	5¢ brown, Type II ('60)	235.00	62.50	☐☐☐☐☐
31	A12	10¢ green, Type I	2600.00	275.00	☐☐☐☐☐
32	A13	10¢ grn., Type II	700.00	75.00	☐☐☐☐☐
33	A14	10¢ grn., Type III	650.00	70.00	☐☐☐☐☐
34	A15	10¢ green, Type IV	6500.00	600.00	☐☐☐☐☐
35	A23	10¢ green, Type V ('59)	95.00	35.00	☐☐☐☐☐
36	A16	12¢ black, plate I	165.00	45.00	☐☐☐☐☐
36b	A16	12c black, plate III ('59)	125.00	50.00	☐☐☐☐☐

Washington
A10

Thomas Jefferson
A11

A13

Type II. The design is complete at the top.
The outer line at the bottom is broken in the middle.
The shells are partly cut away.

A10

THREE CENTS.

Type I. There is an outer frame line at top
and bottom.

A14

Type III. The outer lines are broken
above the top label and the "X" numerals.
The outer line at the bottom and the shells
are partly cut away, as in Type II.

A11

FIVE CENTS.

Type I. There are projections on all four sides.

A12

A15

Type IV. The outer lines have been recut at
top or bottom or both.

Types I, II, III and IV have complete ornaments
at the sides of the stamps and three pearls at each
outer edge of the bottom panel.

A12

TEN CENTS.

Type I. The "shells" at the lower corners are
practically complete. The outer line below the
label is very nearly complete. The outer lines are
broken above the middle of the top label and the
" X " in each upper corner.

A16

Franklin
A20

A23
(Two typical examples).

ONE CENT.

Type V. Similar to type III of 1851-56 but with side ornaments partly cut away.

A21

THREE CENTS.

Type II. The outer frame line has been removed at top and bottom. The side frame lines were recut so as to be continuous from the top to the bottom of the plate.

Type IIa. The side frame lines extend only to the top and bottom of the stamp design.

A22

A22

FIVE CENTS.

Type II. The projections at top and bottom are partly cut away.

TEN CENTS.

Type V. The side ornaments are slightly cut away. Usually only one pearl remains at each end of the lower label but some copies show two or three pearls at the right side. At the bottom the outer line is complete and the shells nearly so. The outer lines at top are complete except over the right " X ".

A17   **A18**

A19

TWELVE CENTS.

Plate I. Outer frame lines complete.

Plate III. Outer frame lines noticeably uneven or broken, sometimes partly missing.

A24a

A25

A25a

3c.   Ornaments at corners have been enlarged and end in a small ball.

A26a

A26

A27a

5c.   A leaflet has been added to the foliated ornaments at each corner.

A28a   A24

A27

A31a

A24

1c.   A dash has been added under the tip of the ornament at right of the numeral in upper left corner.

10c.   A heavy curved line has been cut below the stars and an outer line added to the ornaments above them.

Scott® No.	Illus No.	Description	Unused Price	Used Price	//////
37	A17	24¢ gray lilac ('60)	375.00	135.00 □□□□□	
38	A18	30¢ orange ('60)	450.00	185.00 □□□□□	
39	A19	90¢ blue ('60)	800.00	1500.00 □□□□□	
1875		**GOVERNMENT REPRINTS.**	Without Gum.		*Perf. 12.*
40	A5	1¢ bright blue	350.00	□□□□□	
41	A10	3¢ scarlet	2000.00	□□□□□	
42	A22	5¢ orange brown	575.00	□□□□□	
43	A12	10¢ blue green	1500.00	□□□□□	
44	A16	12¢ greenish black	1650.00	□□□□□	
45	A17	24¢ blackish violet	1750.00	□□□□□	
46	A18	30¢ yellow orange	1850.00	□□□□□	
47	A19	90¢ deep blue	3000.00	□□□□□	
1861					
55	A24a	1¢ indigo	16000.00	□□□□□	
56	A25a	3¢ brown rose	400.00	□□□□□	
57	A26a	5¢ brown	10000.00	□□□□□	
58	A27a	10¢ dark green	2500.00	□□□□□	
59	A28a	12¢ black	32500.00	□□□□□	
60	A29	24¢ dark violet	2750.00	□□□□□	
61	A30	30¢ red orange	13000.00	□□□□□	
62	A31a	90¢ dull blue	17000.00	□□□□□	

The paper of Nos. 55–62 is thin and semitransparent. That of the following issues is thicker and more opaque, except Nos. 62B, 70c, and 70d.
It is doubtful that Nos. 55–62 were regularly issued.

Scott® No.	Illus No.	Description	Unused Price	Used Price	//////
62B	A27a	10¢ dark green	2500.00	350.00 □□□□□	

No. 62B unused cannot be distinguished from No. 58 which does not exist used.

Scott® No.	Illus No.	Description	Unused Price	Used Price	//////
1861-62					
63	A24	1¢ blue	65.00	12.00 □□□□□	
64	A25	3¢ pink	1650.00	150.00 □□□□□	
64a	A25	3c pigeon blood pink		650.00 □□□□□	
64b	A25	3c rose pink	135.00	30.00 □□□□□	
65	A25	3¢ rose	25.00	.75 □□□□□	
66	A25	3¢ lake	950.00	□□□□□	
67	A26	5¢ buff	2000.00	185.00 □□□□□	
68	A27	10¢ yellow green	120.00	11.50 □□□□□	
69	A28	12¢ black	225.00	24.00 □□□□□	
70	A29	24¢ red lilac ('62)	300.00	32.50 □□□□□	
70a	A29	24c brown lilac	250.00	27.50 □□□□□	
70b	A29	24c steel blue	1350.00	85.00 □□□□□	
70c	A29	24c violet	1150.00	275.00 □□□□□	
70d	A29	24c grayish lilac	600.00	175.00 □□□□□	
71	A30	30¢ orange	265.00	35.00 □□□□□	
72	A31	90¢ blue	650.00	110.00 □□□□□	

Nos. 70c and 70d are on a thinner, harder and more transparent paper than Nos. 70, 70a, 70b, or the later No. 78,

A28

12c. Ovals and scrolls have been added to the corners.

A29

A30

A31

Grill

A31

90c. Parallel lines form an angle above the ribbon with "U. S. Postage"; between these lines a row of dashes has been added and a point of color to the apex of the lower pair.

A32

A33

A34

A35

A36

A37

A38

A39

A40

A41

A42

A43

A40

FIFTEEN CENTS. Type I. Picture unframed.

A40a

Type II. Picture framed.

Type III. Same as type I but without fringe of brown shading lines around central vignette.

18

Scott® No.	Illus No.	Description	Unused Price	Used Price	/ / / / / /
1861-66					
73	A32	2¢ black ('63)	75.00	13.50	☐☐☐☐☐
74	A25	3¢ scarlet	2500.00		☐☐☐☐☐
75	A26	5¢ red brown ('62)	650.00	110.00	☐☐☐☐☐
76	A26	5¢ brown ('63)	150.00	25.00	☐☐☐☐☐
77	A33	15¢ black ('66)	300.00	35.00	☐☐☐☐☐
78	A29	24¢ lilac ('63)	120.00	20.00	☐☐☐☐☐

Same as 1861-66 Issues.
Embossed with grills of various sizes.
Grill with Points Up

1867		A. Grill covering the entire stamp.		*Perf. 12·*	
79	A25	3¢ rose	1300.00	300.00	☐☐☐☐☐
80	A26	5¢ brown	35000.00		☐☐☐☐☐
80a	A26	5c dark brown		35000.00	☐☐☐☐☐
81	A30	30¢ orange		30000.00	☐☐☐☐☐

B. Grill about 18x15 mm.
(22 by 18 points.)

82	A25	3¢ rose		32500.00	☐☐☐☐☐

C. Grill about 13x16 mm.
(16 to 17 by 18 to 21 points.)

83	A25	3¢ rose	750.00	150.00	☐☐☐☐☐

Grill with Points Down.
D. Grill about 12x14 mm.
(15 by 17 to 18 points.)

84	A32	2¢ black	1250.00	425.00	☐☐☐☐☐
85	A25	3¢ rose	600.00	135.00	☐☐☐☐☐

Z. Grill about 11x14 mm.
(13 to 14 by 17 to 18 points.)

85A	A24	1¢ blue		90000.00	☐☐☐☐☐
85B	A32	2¢ black	600.00	140.00	☐☐☐☐☐
85C	A25	3¢ rose	1500.00	325.00	☐☐☐☐☐
85D	A27	10¢ green		22000.00	☐☐☐☐☐
85E	A28	12¢ black	850.00	250.00	☐☐☐☐☐
85F	A33	15¢ black		30000.00	☐☐☐☐☐

E. Grill about 11x13 mm.
(14 by 15 to 17 points.)

86	A24	1¢ blue	350.00	90.00	☐☐☐☐☐
87	A32	2¢ black	150.00	30.00	☐☐☐☐☐
88	A25	3¢ rose	95.00	4.00	☐☐☐☐☐
89	A27	10¢ green	600.00	75.00	☐☐☐☐☐
90	A28	12¢ black	650.00	75.00	☐☐☐☐☐
91	A33	15¢ black	1300.00	175.00	☐☐☐☐☐

F. Grill about 9x13 mm.
(11 to 12 by 15 to 17 points.)

92	A24	1¢ blue	135.00	35.00	☐☐☐☐☐
93	A32	2¢ black	65.00	12.50	☐☐☐☐☐
94	A25	3¢ red	40.00	2.00	☐☐☐☐☐
95	A26	5¢ brown	450.00	100.00	☐☐☐☐☐

A44

A45

A48

A49

A44

A48

A45

A49

A46

A50

A46

A51

A47

A50

A47

A51

Scott® No.	Illus No.	Description	Unused Price	Used Price	/ / / / / /
96	A27	10¢ yellow green	265.00	37.50	☐☐☐☐☐
97	A28	12¢ black	285.00	40.00	☐☐☐☐☐
98	A33	15¢ black	300.00	42.50	☐☐☐☐☐
99	A29	24¢ gray lilac	650.00	200.00	☐☐☐☐☐
100	A30	30¢ orange	775.00	140.00	☐☐☐☐☐
101	A31	90¢ blue	1700.00	450.00	☐☐☐☐☐

1875   Re-issue. Without Grill.   *Perf. 12.*

Scott® No.	Illus No.	Description	Unused Price	Used Price	/ / / / / /
102	A24	1¢ blue	275.00	400.00	☐☐☐☐☐
103	A32	2¢ black	1650.00	2000.00	☐☐☐☐☐
104	A25	3¢ brown red	2000.00	2500.00	☐☐☐☐☐
105	A26	5¢ brown	1100.00	1100.00	☐☐☐☐☐
106	A27	10¢ green	1450.00	1750.00	☐☐☐☐☐
107	A28	12¢ black	2000.00	2300.00	☐☐☐☐☐
108	A33	15¢ black	2000.00	2300.00	☐☐☐☐☐
109	A29	24¢ deep violet	2300.00	2500.00	☐☐☐☐☐
110	A30	30¢ brownish orange	2850.00	3000.00	☐☐☐☐☐
111	A31	90¢ blue	3600.00	4250.00	☐☐☐☐☐

These stamps can be distinguished from the 1861–66 issues by the shades and the paper which is hard and very white instead of yellowish. The gum is white and crackly.

G. Grill measuring 9½x9 mm.

1869   (12 by 11 to 11½ points)   *Perf. 12*

Scott® No.	Illus No.	Description	Unused Price	Used Price	/ / / / / /
112	A34	1¢ buff	150.00	37.50	☐☐☐☐☐
113	A35	2¢ brown	90.00	15.00	☐☐☐☐☐
114	A36	3¢ ultramarine	80.00	3.50	☐☐☐☐☐
115	A37	6¢ ultramarine	500.00	60.00	☐☐☐☐☐
116	A38	10¢ yellow	525.00	65.00	☐☐☐☐☐
117	A39	12¢ green	450.00	60.00	☐☐☐☐☐
118	A40	15¢ brown & blue, Type I	1000.00	150.00	☐☐☐☐☐
119	A40a	15¢ brown & blue, Type II	500.00	70.00	☐☐☐☐☐
119b	A40a	Center inverted	80000.00	10000.00	☐☐☐☐☐
120	A41	24¢ green & violet	1250.00	300.00	☐☐☐☐☐
120b	A41	Center invtd.	60000.00	10000.00	☐☐☐☐☐
121	A42	30¢ blue & car.	1100.00	125.00	☐☐☐☐☐
121b	A42	Flags invtd.	70000.00	30000.00	☐☐☐☐☐
122	A43	90¢ car. & black	4000.00	700.00	☐☐☐☐☐

1875   Re-issues. Without Grill. Hard White Paper.   *Perf. 12*

Scott® No.	Illus No.	Description	Unused Price	Used Price	/ / / / / /
123	A34	1¢ buff	225.00	125.00	☐☐☐☐☐
124	A35	2¢ brown	250.00	200.00	☐☐☐☐☐
125	A36	3¢ blue	2000.00	850.00	☐☐☐☐☐
126	A37	6¢ blue	575.00	300.00	☐☐☐☐☐
127	A38	10¢ yellow	900.00	550.00	☐☐☐☐☐
128	A39	12¢ green	950.00	600.00	☐☐☐☐☐
129	A40	15¢ brown & blue, Type III	900.00	375.00	☐☐☐☐☐
130	A41	24¢ green & vio.	900.00	300.00	☐☐☐☐☐

A52

A46a

3c. The under part of the upper tail of the left ribbon is heavily shaded.

A53

A47a

6c. The first four vertical lines of the shading in the lower part of the left ribbon have been strengthened.

A54

A48a

7c. Two small semi-circles are drawn around the ends of the lines which outline the ball in the lower right hand corner.

A44a

1c. In pearl at left of numeral "1" is a small cresent.

A45a

2c. Under the scroll at the left of "U. S." there is a small diagonal line. This mark seldom shows clearly. The stamp, No. 157, can be distinguished by its color.

A49a

10c. There is a small semi-circle in the scroll at the right end of the upper label.

Scott® No.	Illus No.	Description	Unused Price	Used Price	/ / / / / /
131	A42	30¢ blue & car.	1200.00	700.00 ☐☐☐☐☐
132	A43	90¢ car. & black	3000.00	3500.00 ☐☐☐☐☐

1880   Soft Porous Paper.

133	A34	1¢ buff	130.00	110.00 ☐☐☐☐☐
133a	A34	1c brn. orange	110.00	95.00 ☐☐☐☐☐

H. Grill about 10x12 mm. (11 to 13 by 14 to 16 points.) On all values, 1c to 90c.

I. Grill about 8½x10 mm. (10 to 11 by 10 to 13 points.) On 1, 2, 3, 6, 7c.

Two varieties of grill are known on this issue.

On the 1870–71 stamps the grill impressions are usually faint or incomplete. This is especially true of the H grill, which often shows only a few points.

Prices are for stamps showing well defined grills.

1870-71   White Wove Paper.   *Perf. 12.*

134	A44	1¢ ultramarine	275.00	25.00 ☐☐☐☐☐
135	A45	2¢ red brown	175.00	15.00 ☐☐☐☐☐
136	A46	3¢ green	110.00	3.50 ☐☐☐☐☐
137	A47	6¢ carmine	750.00	135.00 ☐☐☐☐☐
138	A48	7¢ vermilion ('71)	575.00	115.00 ☐☐☐☐☐
139	A49	10¢ brown	850.00	235.00 ☐☐☐☐☐
140	A50	12¢ dull violet	8500.00	1000.00 ☐☐☐☐☐
141	A51	15¢ orange	950.00	375.00 ☐☐☐☐☐
142	A52	24¢ purple		8000.00 ☐☐☐☐☐
143	A53	30¢ black	2400.00	600.00 ☐☐☐☐☐
144	A54	90¢ carmine	3250.00	400.00 ☐☐☐☐☐

1870-71   Without Grill. White Wove Paper. *Perf. 12.*

145	A44	1¢ ultramarine	70.00	4.00 ☐☐☐☐☐
146	A45	2¢ red brown	25.00	2.50 ☐☐☐☐☐
147	A46	3¢ green	40.00	.30 ☐☐☐☐☐
148	A47	6¢ carmine	100.00	5.50 ☐☐☐☐☐
149	A48	7¢ vermilion ('71)	175.00	25.00 ☐☐☐☐☐
150	A49	10¢ brown	95.00	5.50 ☐☐☐☐☐
151	A50	12¢ dull violet	300.00	22.50 ☐☐☐☐☐
152	A51	15¢ bright orange	250.00	25.00 ☐☐☐☐☐
153	A52	24¢ purple	285.00	30.00 ☐☐☐☐☐
154	A53	30¢ black	550.00	50.00 ☐☐☐☐☐
155	A54	90¢ carmine	625.00	80.00 ☐☐☐☐☐

1873   White Wove Paper, thin to thick Without Grill* *Perf. 12.*

156	A44a	1¢ ultramarine	25.00	1.10 ☐☐☐☐☐
157	A45a	2¢ brown	70.00	3.00 ☐☐☐☐☐
158	A46a	3¢ green	13.50	.10 ☐☐☐☐☐
159	A47a	6¢ dull pink	80.00	4.25 ☐☐☐☐☐
160	A48a	7¢ org. vermilion	200.00	25.00 ☐☐☐☐☐
161	A49a	10¢ brown	82.50	5.00 ☐☐☐☐☐
162	A50a	12¢ blackish violet	325.00	30.00 ☐☐☐☐☐

A50a

12c. The balls of the figure "2" are crescent shaped.

A51a

15c. In the lower part of the triangle in the upper left corner two lines have been made heavier forming a "V". This mark can be found on some of the Continental and American (1879) printings, but not all stamps show it.

Secret marks were added to the dies of the 24c, 30c and 90c but new plates were not made from them. The various printings of these stamps can be distinguished only by the shades and paper.

A55

A56

A44b

1c. The vertical lines in the upper part of the stamp have been so deepened that the background often appears to be solid. Lines of shading have been added to the upper arabesques.

A46b

3c. The shading at the sides of the central oval appears only about one-half the previous width. A short horizontal dash has been cut about 1mm. below the "TS" of "CENTS."

A47b

6c. On the original stamps four vertical lines can be counted from the edge of the panel to the outside of the stamp. On the re-engraved stamps there are but three lines in the same place.

A49b

10c. On the original stamps there are five vertical lines between the left side of the oval and the edge of the shield. There are only four lines on the re-engraved stamps. In the lower part of the latter, also, the horizontal lines of the background have been strengthened.

Scott® No.	Illus No.	Description	Unused Price	Used Price	//////

1873

163	A51a	15¢ yellow orange	275.00	25.00 □□□□□
165	A53	30¢ gray black	285.00	20.00 □□□□□
166	A54	90¢ rose carmine	650.00	90.00 □□□□□

* All values except 90c exist with experimental (J) grill, about 7x9½ mm.

Special Printing. **Without Gum**

1875 Hard, White Wove Paper. **Perf. 12**

167	A44a	1¢ ultramarine	4250.00	□□□□□
168	A45a	2¢ dark brown	2200.00	□□□□□
169	A46a	3¢ blue green	5500.00	□□□□□
170	A47a	6¢ dull rose	5500.00	□□□□□
171	A48a	7¢ reddish vermilion	1500.00	□□□□□
172	A49a	10¢ pale brown	4500.00	□□□□□
173	A50a	12¢ dark violet	1850.00	□□□□□
174	A51a	15¢ bright orange	5000.00	□□□□□
175	A52	24¢ dull purple	1400.00	□□□□□
176	A53	30¢ greenish blk.	4750.00	□□□□□
177	A54	90¢ vio. carmine	4750.00	□□□□□

1875 Yellowish Wove Paper. **Perf. 12.**

178	A45a	2¢ vermilion	85.00	2.00 □□□□□
179	A55	5¢ blue	80.00	5.00 □□□□□

Special Printing. **Without Gum.**

1875 Hard, White Wove Paper.

180	A45a	2¢ carmine vermilion	12500.00	□□□□□
181	A55	5¢ bright blue	20000.00	□□□□□

Same as 1870–75 Issues. Varying from Thin to Thick.
Soft Porous Paper. **Perf. 12**

1879

182	A44a	1¢ dk. ultramarine	55.00	.75 □□□□□
183	A45a	2¢ vermilion	25.00	.70 □□□□□
184	A46a	3¢ green	20.00	.08 □□□□□
185	A55	5¢ blue	85.00	4.00 □□□□□
186	A47a	6¢ pink	300.00	5.50 □□□□□
187	A49	10¢ brown (without secret mark)	350.00	6.50 □□□□□
188	A49a	10¢ brown (with secret mark)	200.00	6.50 □□□□□
189	A51a	15¢ red orange	77.50	7.50 □□□□□
190	A53	30¢ full black	225.00	10.00 □□□□□
191	A54	90¢ carmine	600.00	70.00 □□□□□

Special Printing. **Without Gum.**

1880 Soft Porous Paper. **Perf. 12.**

192	A44a	1¢ dark ultramarine	6250.00	□□□□□
193	A45a	2¢ black brown	3500.00	□□□□□
194	A46a	3¢ blue green	8000.00	□□□□□
195	A47a	6¢ dull rose	6000.00	□□□□□
196	A48a	7¢ scarlet vermilion	1750.00	□□□□□
197	A49a	10¢ deep brown	5750.00	□□□□□
198	A50a	12¢ blackish purple	3500.00	□□□□□

A57

A58

A59

A60

A61

A62

A63

A64

A65

A66

A67

A68

A69

A70

Scott® No.	Illus No.	Description	Unused Price	Used Price	/ / / / / /
1880					
199	A51a	15¢ orange	5500.00		☐☐☐☐☐
200	A52	24¢ dark violet	1600.00		☐☐☐☐☐
201	A53	30¢ greenish blk.	4500.00		☐☐☐☐☐
202	A54	90¢ dull carmine	4500.00		☐☐☐☐☐
203	A45a	2¢ scarlet vermilion	11000.00		☐☐☐☐☐
204	A55	5¢ deep blue	16000.00		☐☐☐☐☐
1882		*Perf. 12.*			
205	A56	5¢ yellow brown	52.50	2.50	☐☐☐☐☐
1882		Special Printing. Soft Porous Paper.	Without Gum.		
205C	A56	5¢ gray brown	13000.00		☐☐☐☐☐
1881-82					
206	A44b	1¢ gray blue	17.50	.35	☐☐☐☐☐
207	A46b	3¢ blue green	22.50	.08	☐☐☐☐☐
208	A47b	6¢ rose ('82)	140.00	25.00	☐☐☐☐☐
208a	A47b	6c brown red	110.00	35.00	☐☐☐☐☐
209	A49B	10¢ brown ('82)	32.50	1.65	☐☐☐☐☐
1883					
210	A57	2¢ red brown	13.50	.08	☐☐☐☐☐
211	A58	4¢ blue green	65.00	3.50	☐☐☐☐☐
		Special Printing. Soft Porous Paper.			
211B	A57	2¢ pale red brown	450.00		☐☐☐☐☐
211D	A58	4¢ deep blue green	10000.00		☐☐☐☐☐
1887-88					
212	A59	1¢ ultramarine	32.50	.40	☐☐☐☐☐
213	A57	2¢ green	8.00	.05	☐☐☐☐☐
214	A46b	3¢ vermilion	25.00	22.50	☐☐☐☐☐
215	A58	4¢ carmine	60.00	6.25	☐☐☐☐☐
216	A56	5¢ indigo	55.00	3.00	☐☐☐☐☐
217	A53	30¢ orange brown	225.00	50.00	☐☐☐☐☐
218	A54	90¢ purple	500.00	80.00	☐☐☐☐☐
1890-93					
219	A60	1¢ dull blue	11.00	.05	☐☐☐☐☐
219D	A61	2¢ lake	65.00	.35	☐☐☐☐☐
220	A61	2¢ carmine	8.50	.05	☐☐☐☐☐
220a	A61	Cap on left '2'	25.00	1.00	☐☐☐☐☐
220c	A61	Cap on both '2's'	75.00	4.00	☐☐☐☐☐
221	A62	3¢ purple	37.50	2.00	☐☐☐☐☐
222	A63	4¢ dark brown	35.00	1.25	☐☐☐☐☐
223	A64	5¢ chocolate	36.00	1.10	☐☐☐☐☐
224	A65	6¢ brown red	35.00	7.00	☐☐☐☐☐
225	A66	8¢ lilac ('93)	21.00	5.00	☐☐☐☐☐
226	A67	10¢ green	67.50	1.00	☐☐☐☐☐
227	A68	15¢ indigo	100.00	11.00	☐☐☐☐☐
228	A69	30¢ black	135.00	13.00	☐☐☐☐☐
229	A70	90¢ orange	250.00	52.50	☐☐☐☐☐

A71   A72   A73

A74   A75   A76

A77   A78   A79

A80   A81   A82

A83   A84   A85

A86

Wmk.190   Wmk.191

TWO CENTS.

Type I. The horizontal lines of the ground work run across the triangle and are of the same thickness within it as without.

Type II. The horizontal lines cross the triangle but are thinner within it than without.

Type III. The horizontal lines do not cross the double frame lines of the triangle. The lines within the triangle are thin, as in type II.

28

Scott® No.	Illus No.	Description	Unused Price	Used Price	//////
1893					
230	A71	1¢ deep blue	21.00	.25	☐☐☐☐☐
231	A72	2¢ brown violet	20.00	.06	☐☐☐☐☐
232	A73	3¢ green	45.00	10.00	☐☐☐☐☐
233	A74	4¢ ultramarine	60.00	4.50	☐☐☐☐☐
233a	A74	4c blue (error)	5250.00	1800.00	☐☐☐☐☐
234	A75	5¢ chocolate	75.00	5.00	☐☐☐☐☐
235	A76	6¢ purple	70.00	12.50	☐☐☐☐☐
236	A77	8¢ magenta	40.00	6.00	☐☐☐☐☐
237	A78	10¢ black brown	90.00	5.00	☐☐☐☐☐
238	A79	15¢ dark green	160.00	35.00	☐☐☐☐☐
239	A80	30¢ orange brown	240.00	55.00	☐☐☐☐☐
240	A81	50¢ slate blue	300.00	80.00	☐☐☐☐☐
241	A82	$1 salmon	925.00	325.00	☐☐☐☐☐
242	A83	$2 brown red	1000.00	300.00	☐☐☐☐☐
243	A84	$3 yellow green	1850.00	550.00	☐☐☐☐☐
244	A85	$4 crimson lake	2650.00	825.00	☐☐☐☐☐
245	A86	$5 black	2800.00	900.00	☐☐☐☐☐
1894		*Perf. 12.*	Unwmkd.		
246	A87	1¢ ultramarine	12.50	2.50	☐☐☐☐☐
247	A87	1¢ blue	27.50	1.25	☐☐☐☐☐
248	A88	2¢ pink, Type I	8.50	1.50	☐☐☐☐☐
249	A88	2¢ carmine lake, Type I	56.00	1.00	☐☐☐☐☐
250	A88	2¢ carmine, Type I	12.50	.15	☐☐☐☐☐
251	A88	2¢ carmine, Type II	110.00	2.00	☐☐☐☐☐
252	A88	2¢ carmine, Type III	45.00	2.00	☐☐☐☐☐
253	A89	3¢ purple	40.00	4.50	☐☐☐☐☐
254	A90	4¢ dark brown	42.50	1.35	☐☐☐☐☐
255	A91	5¢ chocolate	30.00	2.50	☐☐☐☐☐
256	A92	6¢ dull brown	57.50	9.00	☐☐☐☐☐
257	A93	8¢ violet brown	37.50	6.00	☐☐☐☐☐
258	A94	10¢ dark green	87.50	4.00	☐☐☐☐☐
259	A95	15¢ dark blue	160.00	27.50	☐☐☐☐☐
260	A96	50¢ orange	200.00	45.00	☐☐☐☐☐
261	A97	$1 black, Type I	600.00	135.00	☐☐☐☐☐
261A	A97	$1 black, Type II	900.00	250.00	☐☐☐☐☐
262	A98	$2 bright blue	1150.00	275.00	☐☐☐☐☐
263	A99	$5 dark green	2300.00	650.00	☐☐☐☐☐
1895	Wmkd.	USPS in Double lined Capitals. (191)			
264	A87	1¢ blue	3.25	.06	☐☐☐☐☐
265	A88	2¢ carmine, Type I	13.50	.30	☐☐☐☐☐
266	A88	2¢ carmine, Type II	16.50	1.25	☐☐☐☐☐
267	A88	2¢ carmine, Type III	2.25	.05	☐☐☐☐☐
268	A89	3¢ purple	15.00	.65	☐☐☐☐☐
269	A90	4¢ dark brown	15.00	.65	☐☐☐☐☐
270	A91	5¢ chocolate	15.00	1.10	☐☐☐☐☐
271	A92	6¢ dull brown	35.00	2.50	☐☐☐☐☐

A87   A88   A89   A90

A91   A92   A93   A94

A95   A96   A97   A98

A99

ONE DOLLAR.

Type I. The circles enclosing "$1" are broken where they meet the curved line below "One Dollar." The fifteen left vertical rows of impressions from plate 76 are Type I, the balance being Type II.

Type II. The circles are complete.

TEN CENTS

Type I. Tips of foliate ornaments do not impinge on white curved line below "TEN CENTS".

Type II. Tips of ornaments break curved line below "E" of "TEN" and "T" of "CENTS".

A100   A101   A102

A103   A104   A105

A106   A107   A108

Scott® No.	Illus No.	Description	Unused Price	Used Price	/ / / / / /
1895					
271a	A92	Wmkd. USIR	850.00	150.00	☐☐☐☐☐
272	A93	8¢ violet brown	12.50	.60	☐☐☐☐☐
272a	A93	Wmkd. USIR	400.00	35.00	☐☐☐☐☐
273	A94	10¢ dark green	28.50	1.00	☐☐☐☐☐
274	A95	15¢ dark blue	100.00	5.00	☐☐☐☐☐
275	A96	50¢ orange	140.00	11.00	☐☐☐☐☐
276	A97	$1 black, Type I	425.00	30.00	☐☐☐☐☐
276A	A97	$1 black, Type II	800.00	65.00	☐☐☐☐☐
277	A98	$2 bright blue	600.00	150.00	☐☐☐☐☐
278	A99	$5 dark green	1200.00	190.00	☐☐☐☐☐
1898					
279	A87	1¢ deep green	5.00	.06	☐☐☐☐☐
279B	A88	2¢ red, Type III	4.50	.05	☐☐☐☐☐
279e	A88	Booklet pane of 6	350.00	200.00	☐☐☐☐☐
280	A90	4¢ rose brown	13.50	.70	☐☐☐☐☐
281	A91	5¢ dark blue	15.00	.50	☐☐☐☐☐
282	A92	6¢ lake	20.00	1.50	☐☐☐☐☐
282C	A94	10¢ brown, Type I	75.00	1.50	☐☐☐☐☐
283	A94	10¢ orange brown, Type II	55.00	1.25	☐☐☐☐☐
284	A95	15¢ olive green	65.00	4.25	☐☐☐☐☐
1898					
285	A100	1¢ dk. yel. green	23.00	3.75	☐☐☐☐☐
286	A101	2¢ copper red	22.00	1.00	☐☐☐☐☐
287	A102	4¢ orange	110.00	14.00	☐☐☐☐☐
288	A103	5¢ dull blue	90.00	13.50	☐☐☐☐☐
289	A104	8¢ violet brown	140.00	25.00	☐☐☐☐☐
290	A105	10¢ gray violet	150.00	13.50	☐☐☐☐☐
291	A106	50¢ sage green	575.00	75.00	☐☐☐☐☐
292	A107	$1 black	1300.00	400.00	☐☐☐☐☐
293	A108	$2 org. brown	2000.00	575.00	☐☐☐☐☐
1901					
294	A109	1¢ green & black	17.50	3.50	☐☐☐☐☐
294a	A109	Center invtd.	6500.00	2000.00	☐☐☐☐☐
295	A110	2¢ car. & black	17.50	.75	☐☐☐☐☐
295a	A110	Center invtd.	30000.00	8000.00	☐☐☐☐☐
296	A111	4¢ deep red brown & black	95.00	12.00	☐☐☐☐☐
296a	A111	Center invtd.	9500.00		☐☐☐☐☐
296b	A111	Same as 'a' overprinted 'Specimen'	3750.00		☐☐☐☐☐
297	A112	5¢ ultramarine & black	95.00	12.50	☐☐☐☐☐
298	A113	8¢ brown violet & black	120.00	35.00	☐☐☐☐☐
299	A114	10¢ yellow brown & black	165.00	17.50	☐☐☐☐☐
1902-03		*Perf. 12*			
300	A115	1¢ blue green ('03)	5.50	.05	☐☐☐☐☐
300b	A115	Bklt. pane of 6	500.00	200.00	☐☐☐☐☐
301	A116	2¢ carmine ('03)	6.50	.05	☐☐☐☐☐
301c	A116	Booklet pane of 6	400.00	200.00	☐☐☐☐☐

A109

A110

A111

A112

A113

A114

A115

A116

A117

A118

A119

A120

A121

A122

A123

A124

A125

A126

A127

A128

A129

Scott® No.	Illus No.	Description	Unused Price	Used Price	/ / / / / /
1902-03					
302	A117	3¢ bright violet ('03)	35.00	1.85	☐☐☐☐☐
303	A118	4¢ brown ('03)	35.00	.90	☐☐☐☐☐
304	A119	5¢ blue ('03)	40.00	.85	☐☐☐☐☐
305	A120	6¢ claret ('03)	42.50	1.75	☐☐☐☐☐
306	A121	8¢ violet black	20.00	1.50	☐☐☐☐☐
307	A122	10¢ pale red brown ('03)	45.00	.75	☐☐☐☐☐
308	A123	13¢ purple black	20.00	7.00	☐☐☐☐☐
309	A124	15¢ olive green ('03)	125.00	4.50	☐☐☐☐☐
310	A125	50¢ orange ('03)	325.00	20.00	☐☐☐☐☐
311	A126	$1 black ('03)	625.00	32.50	☐☐☐☐☐
312	A127	$2 dk. bl. ('03)	800.00	125.00	☐☐☐☐☐
313	A128	$5 dark green ('03)	1550.00	425.00	☐☐☐☐☐
1906-08		*Imperf.*			
314	A115	1¢ blue green	21.00	12.50	☐☐☐☐☐
314A	A118	4¢ brown ('08)	10000.00	5000.00	☐☐☐☐☐
315	A119	5¢ blue ('08)	525.00	225.00	☐☐☐☐☐
		Coil Stamps.			
1908		*Perf. 12 Horizontally.*			
316	A115	1¢ bl. grn., pair	14500.00		☐☐☐☐☐
317	A119	5¢ blue, pair	3000.00		☐☐☐☐☐
		Perf. 12 Vertically.			
318	A115	1¢ blue grn., pair	2250.00		☐☐☐☐☐
1903		*Perf. 12.*			
319	A129	2¢ carmine	4.00	.04	☐☐☐☐☐
319g	A129	Booklet pane of 6	100.00	20.00	☐☐☐☐☐
1906		*Imperf.*			
320	A129	2¢ carmine	18.50	10.00	☐☐☐☐☐
		Coil Stamps.			
1908		*Perf. 12 Horizontally.*			
321	A129	2¢ car., pair	25000.00		☐☐☐☐☐
		Perf. 12 Vertically.			
322	A129	2¢ carmine, pair	3000.00		☐☐☐☐☐
1904					
323	A130	1¢ green	23.00	4.00	☐☐☐☐☐
324	A131	2¢ carmine	21.00	1.25	☐☐☐☐☐
325	A132	3¢ violet	67.50	20.00	☐☐☐☐☐
326	A133	5¢ dark blue	82.50	15.00	☐☐☐☐☐
327	A134	10¢ red brown	175.00	22.50	☐☐☐☐☐
1907					
328	A135	1¢ green	17.50	4.50	☐☐☐☐☐
329	A136	2¢ carmine	22.50	3.25	☐☐☐☐☐
330	A137	5¢ blue	105.00	23.50	☐☐☐☐☐
1908-09		Wmkd. USPS (191) *Perf. 12.*			
331	A138	1¢ green	4.50	.05	☐☐☐☐☐

A130

A131

A132

A133

A134

A135

A136

A137

Franklin

A138

Washington

A139

Washington

A140

Franklin

A148

A141

Scott® No.	Illus No.	Description	Unused Price	Used Price	//////
1908-09					
331a	A138	Booklet pane of 6	120.00	35.00	☐☐☐☐☐
332	A139	2¢ carmine	4.25	.05	☐☐☐☐☐
332a	A139	Bklt. pane of 6	100.00	35.00	☐☐☐☐☐
333	A140	3¢ deep violet, Type I	13.50	2.00	☐☐☐☐☐
334	A140	4¢ orange brown	15.00	.75	☐☐☐☐☐
335	A140	5¢ blue	21.00	1.00	☐☐☐☐☐
336	A140	6¢ red orange	26.00	3.75	☐☐☐☐☐
337	A140	8¢ olive green	15.00	1.75	☐☐☐☐☐
338	A140	10¢ yellow ('09)	35.00	.65	☐☐☐☐☐
339	A140	13¢ blue green ('09)	20.00	15.00	☐☐☐☐☐
340	A140	15¢ pale ultramarine ('09)	32.50	3.25	☐☐☐☐☐
341	A140	50¢ violet ('09)	160.00	8.00	☐☐☐☐☐
342	A140	$1 violet brown ('09)	275.00	40.00	☐☐☐☐☐
		Imperf.			
343	A138	1¢ green	6.25	2.50	☐☐☐☐☐
344	A139	2¢ carmine	8.00	1.25	☐☐☐☐☐
345	A140	3¢ deep violet, Type I ('09)	18.50	6.75	☐☐☐☐☐
346	A140	4¢ orange brown ('09)	42.50	10.00	☐☐☐☐☐
347	A140	5¢ blue ('09)	62.50	20.00	☐☐☐☐☐
		Coil Stamps.			
1908-10		*Perf. 12 Horizontally*			
348	A138	1¢ green	15.00	7.75	☐☐☐☐☐
349	A139	2¢ carmine ('09)	27.50	4.50	☐☐☐☐☐
350	A140	4¢ orange brown ('10)	75.00	35.00	☐☐☐☐☐
351	A140	5¢ blue ('09)	95.00	50.00	☐☐☐☐☐
1909		*Perf. 12 Vertically.*			
352	A138	1¢ green	35.00	11.00	☐☐☐☐☐
353	A139	2¢ carmine	30.00	4.25	☐☐☐☐☐
354	A140	4¢ orange brown	62.50	25.00	☐☐☐☐☐
355	A140	5¢ blue	85.00	40.00	☐☐☐☐☐
356	A140	10¢ yellow	750.00	200.00	☐☐☐☐☐
1909		*Bluish Paper Perf. 12.*			
357	A138	1¢ green	60.00	50.00	☐☐☐☐☐
358	A139	2¢ carmine	55.00	35.00	☐☐☐☐☐
359	A140	3¢ deep violet, Type I	800.00	550.00	☐☐☐☐☐
360	A140	4¢ orange brown	10000.00		☐☐☐☐☐
361	A140	5¢ blue	2250.00		☐☐☐☐☐
362	A140	6¢ red orange	600.00	375.00	☐☐☐☐☐
363	A140	8¢ olive green	10000.00		☐☐☐☐☐
364	A140	10¢ yellow	650.00	375.00	☐☐☐☐☐
365	A140	13¢ blue green	1350.00	500.00	☐☐☐☐☐
366	A140	15¢ pale ultra.	550.00	275.00	☐☐☐☐☐
1909		*Perf. 12.*			
367	A141	2¢ carmine	6.50	2.75	☐☐☐☐☐
		Imperf.			
368	A141	2¢ carmine	37.50	15.00	☐☐☐☐☐
		Bluish Paper. *Perf. 12.*			
369	A141	2¢ carmine	225.00	100.00	☐☐☐☐☐

A142

A143

A144

A145

A146

A147

TYPE I

THREE CENTS.

Type I. The top line of the toga rope is weak
and the rope shading lines are thin. The fifth line
from the left is missing.

The line between the lips is thin.

Used on both flat plate and rotary press printings.

Scott® No.	Illus No.	Description	Unused Price	Used Price	//////
1909		*Perf. 12*			
370	A142	2¢ carmine	8.75	2.00 ☐☐☐☐☐	
		Imperf.			
371	A142	2¢ carmine	50.00	15.00 ☐☐☐☐☐	
1909		*Perf. 12.*			
372	A143	2¢ carmine	8.75	2.75 ☐☐☐☐☐	
		Imperf.			
373	A143	2¢ carmine	60.00	15.00 ☐☐☐☐☐	
	Wmkd. USPS	in Single lined Capitals. (190)			
1910-11		*Perf. 12*			
374	A138	1¢ green	4.00	.06 ☐☐☐☐☐	
374a	A138	Bklt. pane of 6	110.00	30.00 ☐☐☐☐☐	
375	A139	2¢ carmine	3.75	.03 ☐☐☐☐☐	
375a	A139	Booklet pane of 6	100.00	25.00 ☐☐☐☐☐	
376	A140	3¢ deep violet, Type I ('11)	8.00	1.10 ☐☐☐☐☐	
377	A140	4¢ brown ('11)	11.50	.50 ☐☐☐☐☐	
378	A140	5¢ blue ('11)	11.50	.35 ☐☐☐☐☐	
379	A140	6¢ red org. ('11)	22.50	.50 ☐☐☐☐☐	
380	A140	8¢ olive grn. ('11)	65.00	8.00 ☐☐☐☐☐	
381	A140	10¢ yellow ('11)	60.00	2.75 ☐☐☐☐☐	
382	A140	15¢ pale ultra. ('11)	110.00	12.00 ☐☐☐☐☐	
1911		*Imperf.*			
383	A138	1¢ green	3.25	2.00 ☐☐☐☐☐	
384	A139	2¢ carmine	4.50	1.10 ☐☐☐☐☐	
		Coil Stamps.			
1910		*Perf. 12 Horizontally*			
385	A138	1¢ green	18.50	8.00 ☐☐☐☐☐	
386	A139	2¢ carmine	25.00	6.50 ☐☐☐☐☐	
1910-11		*Perf. 12 Vertically.*			
387	A138	1¢ green	47.50	12.00 ☐☐☐☐☐	
388	A139	2¢ carmine	375.00	40.00 ☐☐☐☐☐	
389	A140	3¢ deep violet, Type I ('11)	10000.00	2250.00 ☐☐☐☐☐	
1910		*Perf. 8½ Horizontally.*			
390	A138	1¢ green	3.25	1.85 ☐☐☐☐☐	
391	A139	2¢ carmine	35.00	4.50 ☐☐☐☐☐	
1910-13		*Perf. 8½ Vertically.*			
392	A138	1¢ green	18.50	10.00 ☐☐☐☐☐	
393	A139	2¢ carmine	40.00	4.50 ☐☐☐☐☐	
394	A140	3¢ deep violet, Type I ('11)	45.00	20.00 ☐☐☐☐☐	
395	A140	4¢ brown ('12)	47.50	17.50 ☐☐☐☐☐	
396	A140	5¢ blue ('13)	47.50	20.00 ☐☐☐☐☐	
1913		*Perf. 12.*			
397	A144	1¢ green	18.00	1.50 ☐☐☐☐☐	
398	A145	2¢ carmine	20.00	.50 ☐☐☐☐☐	
399	A146	5¢ blue	75.00	8.50 ☐☐☐☐☐	
400	A147	10¢ orange yellow	135.00	15.00 ☐☐☐☐☐	
400A	A147	10¢ orange	200.00	11.00 ☐☐☐☐☐	
1914-15		*Perf. 10.*			
401	A144	1¢ green	22.50	5.00 ☐☐☐☐☐	

TYPE I

TWO CENTS.

Type I. There is one shading line in the first curve of the ribbon above the left "2" and one in the second curve of the ribbon above the right "2."

The button of the toga has a faint outline.

The top line of the toga rope, from the button to the front of the throat, is also very faint.

The shading lines at the face terminate in front of the ear with little or no joining, to form a lock of hair.

Used on both flat and rotary press printings.

TYPE II

TWO CENTS.

Type II. Shading lines in ribbons as on type I.

The toga button, rope, and shading lines are heavy.

The shading lines of the face at the lock of hair end in a strong vertical curved line.

Used on rotary press printings only.

TYPE III

TWO CENTS.

Type III. Two lines of shading in the curves of the ribbons.

Other characteristics similar to type II.

Used on rotary press printings only.

Scott® No.	Illus No.	Description	Unused Price	Used Price	//////
1914-15					
402	A145	2¢ carmine ('15)	60.00	1.00	☐☐☐☐☐
403	A146	5¢ blue ('15)	190.00	11.00	☐☐☐☐☐
404	A147	10¢ orange ('15)	1100.00	45.00	☐☐☐☐☐
1912-14		Wmkd. USPS (190) *Perf. 12.*			
405	A140	1¢ green	3.50	.06	☐☐☐☐☐
405b	A140	Bklt. pane of 6	50.00	7.50	☐☐☐☐☐
406	A140	2¢ carmine, Type I	2.75	.03	☐☐☐☐☐
406a	A140	Bklt. pane of 6	60.00	17.50	☐☐☐☐☐
407	A140	7¢ black ('14)	45.00	5.00	☐☐☐☐☐
1912		*Imperf.*			
408	A140	1¢ green	.75	.35	☐☐☐☐☐
409	A140	2¢ carmine, Type I	.85	.35	☐☐☐☐☐
		Coil Stamps.			
1912		*Perf. 8½ Horizontally.*			
410	A140	1¢ green	4.25	2.00	☐☐☐☐☐
411	A140	2¢ carmine, Type I	4.75	2.00	☐☐☐☐☐
		Perf. 8½ Vertically.			
412	A140	1¢ green	17.50	3.25	☐☐☐☐☐
413	A140	2¢ car., Type I	35.00	.25	☐☐☐☐☐
1912-14		*Perf. 12*			
414	A148	8¢ pale olive grn.	17.50	1.10	☐☐☐☐☐
415	A148	9¢ salmon red ('14)	22.50	9.00	☐☐☐☐☐
416	A148	10¢ orange yellow	17.50	.15	☐☐☐☐☐
417	A148	12¢ claret brown ('14)	15.00	2.25	☐☐☐☐☐
418	A148	15¢ gray	35.00	2.25	☐☐☐☐☐
419	A148	20¢ ultra. ('14)	85.00	10.00	☐☐☐☐☐
420	A148	30¢ orange red ('14)	65.00	9.50	☐☐☐☐☐
421	A148	50¢ violet ('14)	350.00	11.00	☐☐☐☐☐
1912		Wmkd. USPS (191) *Perf. 12.*			
422	A148	50¢ violet	150.00	9.00	☐☐☐☐☐
423	A148	$1 violet brown	350.00	40.00	☐☐☐☐☐
1914-15		Wmkd. USPS (190) *Perf. 10*			
424	A140	1¢ green	2.00	.06	☐☐☐☐☐
424a	A140	Perf. 12 × 10	250.00	175.00	☐☐☐☐☐
424b	A140	Perf. 10 × 12		110.00	☐☐☐☐☐
424d	A140	Booklet pane of 6	3.00	.75	☐☐☐☐☐
425	A140	2¢ rose red, Type I	1.50	.04	☐☐☐☐☐
425d	A140	Perf. 12 × 10		200.00	☐☐☐☐☐
425e	A140	Booklet pane of 6	12.50	2.00	☐☐☐☐☐
426	A140	3¢ deep violet, Type I	6.50	.75	☐☐☐☐☐
427	A140	4¢ brown	23.00	.18	☐☐☐☐☐
428	A140	5¢ blue	12.50	.30	☐☐☐☐☐
428a	A140	Perf. 12 × 10		400.00	☐☐☐☐☐
429	A140	6¢ red orange	25.00	.75	☐☐☐☐☐
430	A140	7¢ black	47.50	3.25	☐☐☐☐☐

TYPE Ia

TYPE Ia

TWO CENTS.

Type Ia. Design characteristics similar to type I except that all lines of design are stronger.

The toga button, toga rope and rope shading lines are heavy. The latter characteristics are those of type II, which, however, occur only on impressions from rotary plates.

Used only on flat plates 10208 and 10209.

TYPE II

TYPE II

THREE CENTS.

Type II. The top line of the toga rope is strong and the rope shading lines are heavy and complete. The line between the lips is heavy.

Used on both flat plate and rotary press printings.

TYPE IV

TYPE IV

TWO CENTS.

Type IV. Top line of toga rope is broken. Shading lines in toga button are so arranged that the curving of the first and last form "ⅢD".

Line of color in left "2" is very thin and usually broken.

Used on offset printings only.

Scott® No.	Illus No.	Description	Unused Price	Used Price	/ / / / / /

1914-15

Scott® No.	Illus No.	Description	Unused Price	Used Price	
431	A148	8¢ pale olive grn.	17.50	1.10	☐☐☐☐☐
432	A148	9¢ salmon red	23.50	6.00	☐☐☐☐☐
433	A148	10¢ orange yellow	20.00	.06	☐☐☐☐☐
434	A148	11¢ dark green ('15)	11.00	4.00	☐☐☐☐☐
435	A148	12¢ claret brown	11.00	2.50	☐☐☐☐☐
437	A148	15¢ gray	65.00	5.25	☐☐☐☐☐
438	A148	20¢ ultramarine	125.00	2.75	☐☐☐☐☐
439	A148	30¢ orange red	165.00	8.50	☐☐☐☐☐
440	A148	50¢ violet ('15)	525.00	10.00	☐☐☐☐☐

1914 Coil Stamps. *Perf. 10 Horizontally*

441	A140	1¢ green	.85	.60	☐☐☐☐☐
442	A140	2¢ carmine, Type I	7.50	4.00	☐☐☐☐☐

Perf. 10 Vertically.

443	A140	1¢ green	15.00	3.50	☐☐☐☐☐
444	A140	2¢ car., Type I	27.50	.75	☐☐☐☐☐
445	A140	3¢ violet, Type I	165.00	65.00	☐☐☐☐☐
446	A140	4¢ brown	115.00	25.00	☐☐☐☐☐
447	A140	5¢ blue	40.00	12.50	☐☐☐☐☐

1915-16 Coil Stamps Rotary Press Printing *Perf. 10 Horizontally*

448	A140	1¢ green	4.00	1.75	☐☐☐☐☐
449	A140	2¢ red, Type I	900.00	85.00	☐☐☐☐☐
450	A140	2¢ car., Type III ('16)	8.50	1.50	☐☐☐☐☐

1914-16 *Perf. 10 Vertically.*

452	A140	1¢ green	7.50	1.20	☐☐☐☐☐
453	A140	2¢ red, Type I	110.00	3.75	☐☐☐☐☐
454	A140	2¢ car., Type II	120.00	15.00	☐☐☐☐☐
455	A140	2¢ car., Type III	9.50	.50	☐☐☐☐☐
456	A140	3¢ violet, Type I ('16)	200.00	55.00	☐☐☐☐☐
457	A140	4¢ brown ('16)	22.50	10.00	☐☐☐☐☐
458	A140	5¢ blue ('16)	22.50	10.00	☐☐☐☐☐

1914 *Imperf.*

459	A140	2¢ car., Type I	300.00	325.00	☐☐☐☐☐

1915 Wmk. 191 *Perf. 10*

460	A148	$1 violet black	600.00	42.50	☐☐☐☐☐

1915 Wmk. 190 *Perf. 11*

461	A140	2¢ pale carmine red, Type I	45.00	35.00	☐☐☐☐☐

1916-17 *Perf. 10. Unwmkd.*

462	A140	1¢ green	4.00	.20	☐☐☐☐☐
462a	A140	Booklet pane of 6	8.50	1.00	☐☐☐☐☐
463	A140	2¢ carmine, Type I	2.00	.06	☐☐☐☐☐
463a	A140	Booklet pane of 6	65.00	15.00	☐☐☐☐☐
464	A140	3¢ violet, Type I	45.00	8.00	☐☐☐☐☐
465	A140	4¢ orange brown	25.00	1.25	☐☐☐☐☐

TYPE V

TWO CENTS.

Type V. Top line of toga is complete.
Five vertical shading lines in toga button.

Line of color in left "2" is very thin and usually broken.

Shading dots on the nose and lip are as indicated on the diagram.

Used on offset printings only.

TYPE Va

TWO CENTS.

Type Va. Characteristics same as type V, except in shading dots of nose. Third row from bottom has 4 dots instead of 6. Overall height of type Va is 1/3 mm. less than type V.

Used on offset printings only.

TYPE VI

TWO CENTS.

Type VI. General characteristics same as type V, except that line of color in left "2" is very heavy.

Used on offset printings only.

Scott® No.	Illus No.	Description	Unused Price	Used Price	/ / / / / /
1916-17					
466	A140	5¢ blue	42.50	1.10	☐☐☐☐☐
467	A140	5¢ carmine (error in plate of 2c; '17)	625.00	350.00	☐☐☐☐☐
468	A140	6¢ red orange	60.00	5.50	☐☐☐☐☐
469	A140	7¢ black	75.00	10.00	☐☐☐☐☐
470	A148	8¢ olive green	35.00	5.00	☐☐☐☐☐
471	A148	9¢ salmon red	22.50	9.00	☐☐☐☐☐
472	A148	10¢ orange yellow	65.00	.75	☐☐☐☐☐
473	A148	11¢ dark green	16.50	9.50	☐☐☐☐☐
474	A148	12¢ claret brown	25.00	4.25	☐☐☐☐☐
475	A148	15¢ gray	100.00	8.50	☐☐☐☐☐
476	A148	20¢ light ultra.	150.00	9.50	☐☐☐☐☐
476A	A148	30¢ orange red			☐☐☐☐☐
477	A148	50¢ light violet ('17)	750.00	50.00	☐☐☐☐☐
478	A148	$1 violet black	600.00	12.00	☐☐☐☐☐
479	A127	$2 dark blue	425.00	21.00	☐☐☐☐☐
480	A128	$5 light green	325.00	25.00	☐☐☐☐☐
1916-17		*Imperf.*			
481	A140	1¢ green	.60	.50	☐☐☐☐☐
482	A140	2¢ carmine, Type I	1.00	.80	☐☐☐☐☐
482A	A140	2¢ carmine, Type Ia		4500.00	☐☐☐☐☐
483	A140	3¢ violet, Type I ('17)	12.00	5.50	☐☐☐☐☐
484	A140	3¢ violet, Type II	6.75	3.50	☐☐☐☐☐
485	A140	5¢ carmine (error in plate of 2c) ('17)	7000.00		☐☐☐☐☐
1916-19		Coil Stamps Rotary Press Printing	*Perf. 10 Horizontally.*		
486	A140	1¢ green ('18)	.60	.15	☐☐☐☐☐
487	A140	2¢ car., Type II	13.50	2.00	☐☐☐☐☐
488	A140	2¢ carmine, Type III ('19)	2.00	1.20	☐☐☐☐☐
489	A140	3¢ vio., Type I ('17)	2.50	1.00	☐☐☐☐☐
1916-22		*Perf. 10 Vertically.*			
490	A140	1¢ green	.35	.15	☐☐☐☐☐
491	A140	2¢ car., Type II	900.00	120.00	☐☐☐☐☐
492	A140	2¢ car., Type III	6.25	.15	☐☐☐☐☐
493	A140	3¢ vio., Type I ('17)	22.50	3.00	☐☐☐☐☐
494	A140	3¢ vio., Type II ('18)	13.50	.60	☐☐☐☐☐
495	A140	4¢ org. brown ('17)	11.50	2.75	☐☐☐☐☐
496	A140	5¢ blue ('19)	2.25	.60	☐☐☐☐☐
497	A148	10¢ orange yellow ('22)	18.50	6.50	☐☐☐☐☐
1917-19		*Perf. 11*			
498	A140	1¢ green	.25	.04	☐☐☐☐☐
498e	A140	Booklet pane of 6	1.75	.35	☐☐☐☐☐
498f	A140	Booklet pane of 30	450.00		☐☐☐☐☐
499	A140	2¢ rose, Type I	.25	.03	☐☐☐☐☐
499e	A140	Booklet pane of 6	2.00	.50	☐☐☐☐☐
499f	A140	Bklt. pane of 30	4750.00		☐☐☐☐☐

TYPE VII

TYPE VII

TWO CENTS.

Type VII. Line of color in left "2" is invariably continuous, clearly defined, and heavier than in type V or Va, but not as heavy as in type VI.

Additional vertical row of dots has been added to the upper lip.

Numerous additional dots have been added to hair on top of head.

Used on offset printings only.

TYPE III

TYPE III

THREE CENTS.

Type III. The top line of the toga rope is strong but the fifth shading line is missing as in type I.

Center shading line of the toga button consists of two dashes with a central dot.

The "P" and "O" of "POSTAGE" are separated by a line of color.

The frame line at the bottom of the vignette is complete.

Used on offset printings only.

TYPE IV

TYPE IV

THREE CENTS.

Type IV. Shading lines of toga rope are complete.

Second and fourth shading lines in toga button are broken in the middle and the third line is continuous with a dot in the center.

"P" and "O" of "POSTAGE" are joined.

Frame line at bottom of vignette is broken.

Used on offset printings only.

Scott® No.	Illus No.	Description	Unused Price	Used Price	//////
1917-19					
500	A140	2¢ dp. rose, Type Ia	205.00	85.00 □□□□□
501	A140	3¢ lt. violet, Type I	7.50	.08 □□□□□
501b	A140	Booklet pane of 6	65.00	15.00 □□□□□
502	A140	3¢ dk. vio., Type II	10.00	.15 □□□□□
502b	A140	Booklet pane of 6	30.00	10.00 □□□□□
503	A140	4¢ brown	9.00	.10 □□□□□
504	A140	5¢ blue	6.50	.08 □□□□□
505	A140	5¢ rose (error in plate of 2c)	425.00	225.00 □□□□□
506	A140	6¢ red orange	8.50	.12 □□□□□
507	A140	7¢ black	20.00	1.00 □□□□□
508	A148	8¢ olive bistre	9.00	.50 □□□□□
509	A148	9¢ salmon red	15.00	1.85 □□□□□
510	A148	10¢ orange yellow	15.00	.05 □□□□□
511	A148	11¢ light green	6.75	2.75 □□□□□
512	A148	12¢ claret brown	5.75	.30 □□□□□
513	A148	13¢ apple green ('19)	10.00	5.50 □□□□□
514	A148	15¢ gray	30.00	.60 □□□□□
515	A148	20¢ light ultra.	32.50	.12 □□□□□
516	A148	30¢ orange red	32.50	.65 □□□□□
517	A148	50¢ red violet	65.00	.35 □□□□□
518	A148	$1 violet brown	90.00	.75 □□□□□
1917		Wmkd. USPS (191)		*Perf. 11.*	
519	A139	2¢ carmine	125.00	100.00 □□□□□
1918					
523	A149	$2 orange red & black	900.00	125.00 □□□□□
524	A149	$5 deep green & black	350.00	20.00 □□□□□
1918-20		Offset Printing.		*Perf. 11*	
525	A140	1¢ gray green	1.50	.50 □□□□□
526	A140	2¢ carmine, Type IV ('20)	20.00	3.50 □□□□□
527	A140	2¢ carmine, Type V	15.00	1.00 □□□□□
528	A140	2¢ carmine, Type Va	5.25	.15 □□□□□
528A	A140	2¢ carmine, Type VI	32.50	.75 □□□□□
528B	A140	2¢ car., Type VII	13.50	.08 □□□□□
529	A140	3¢ violet, Type III	1.20	.10 □□□□□
530	A140	3¢ purple, Type IV	.70	.06 □□□□□
		Imperf.			
531	A140	1¢ green ('19)	7.50	6.25 □□□□□
532	A140	2¢ carmine rose, Type IV ('20)	27.50	15.00 □□□□□
533	A140	2¢ carmine, Type V	165.00	50.00 □□□□□
534	A140	2¢ carmine, Type Va	7.75	6.00 □□□□□
534A	A140	2¢ car., Type VI	25.00	15.00 □□□□□
534B	A140	2¢ carmine, Type VII	1100.00	275.00 □□□□□
535	A140	3¢ violet, Type IV	6.50	5.00 □□□□□
		Perf. 12½.			
536	A140	1¢ gray green	11.00	9.00 □□□□□

A149

A150

A151

A152

A153

A154

A155

A156

A157

A158

A159

A160

A161

A162

A163

A164

A165

A166

A167

A168

A169

Scott® No.	Illus No.	Description	Unused Price	Used Price	/ / / / / /
1919		*Perf. 11.*			
537	A150	3¢ violet	9.00	3.50	☐☐☐☐☐
1919		*Perf. 11x10.*			
538	A140	1¢ green	6.50	6.50	☐☐☐☐☐
539	A140	2¢ carmine rose, Type II	1100.00	450.00	☐☐☐☐☐
540	A140	2¢ carmine rose, Type III	6.50	6.50	☐☐☐☐☐
541	A140	3¢ violet, Type II	25.00	25.00	☐☐☐☐☐
1920		Size: 19 mm. by 22½–22¾ mm. *Perf. 10x11.*			
542	A140	1¢ green	3.50	.60	☐☐☐☐☐
1921		Size: 19x22½mm. *Perf. 10.*			
543	A140	1¢ green	.25	.06	☐☐☐☐☐
1923		Size: 19x22½mm. *Perf. 11*			
544	A140	1¢ green	5500.00	1000.00	☐☐☐☐☐
1921		Size: 19½–20 mm. by 22 mm. *Perf. 11*			
545	A140	1¢ green	90.00	65.00	☐☐☐☐☐
546	A140	2¢ carmine rose, Type III	60.00	45.00	☐☐☐☐☐
1920		*Perf. 11.*			
547	A149	$2 car. & black	325.00	20.00	☐☐☐☐☐
548	A151	1¢ green	6.00	2.50	☐☐☐☐☐
549	A152	2¢ carmine rose	9.50	2.00	☐☐☐☐☐
550	A153	5¢ deep blue	52.50	16.50	☐☐☐☐☐
1922-25		*Perf. 11*			
551	A154	½ olive brown ('25)	.15	.05	☐☐☐☐☐
552	A155	1¢ dp. green ('23)	2.00	.07	☐☐☐☐☐
553	A156	1½ yellow brown ('25)	2.50	.10	☐☐☐☐☐
554	A157	2¢ carmine ('23)	1.25	.03	☐☐☐☐☐
554c	A157	Booklet pane of 6	5.00	1.00	☐☐☐☐☐
555	A158	3¢ violet ('23)	18.50	.50	☐☐☐☐☐
556	A159	4¢ yellow brown ('23)	13.50	.08	☐☐☐☐☐
557	A160	5¢ dark blue	15.00	.06	☐☐☐☐☐
558	A161	6¢ red orange	32.50	.40	☐☐☐☐☐
559	A162	7¢ black ('23)	6.50	.40	☐☐☐☐☐
560	A163	8¢ olive grn. ('23)	40.00	.50	☐☐☐☐☐
561	A164	9¢ rose ('23)	10.00	.75	☐☐☐☐☐
562	A165	10¢ orange ('23)	15.00	.06	☐☐☐☐☐
563	A166	11¢ light blue	1.75	.12	☐☐☐☐☐
564	A167	12¢ brown violet ('23)	5.50	.08	☐☐☐☐☐
565	A168	14¢ blue ('23)	4.00	.30	☐☐☐☐☐
566	A169	15¢ gray	15.00	.06	☐☐☐☐☐
567	A170	20¢ carmine rose ('23)	20.00	.05	☐☐☐☐☐
568	A171	25¢ yellow green	17.50	.15	☐☐☐☐☐
569	A172	30¢ olive brown ('23)	30.00	.15	☐☐☐☐☐
570	A173	50¢ lilac	57.50	.08	☐☐☐☐☐
571	A174	$1 violet black ('23)	50.00	.25	☐☐☐☐☐
572	A175	$2 deep blue ('23)	150.00	6.50	☐☐☐☐☐
573	A176	$5 carmine & bl.	375.00	8.00	☐☐☐☐☐

A170   A171   A172

A173   A174   A175

A176   A177

Type I.   Type I.   Type II.

Type II.

Type I—No heavy hair lines at top center of head. Outline of left acanthus scroll generally faint at top and toward base at left side.

Type II—The heavy hair lines at top center of head; two being outstanding in the white area. Outline of left acanthus scroll very strong and clearly defined at top (under left edge of lettered panel) and at lower curve (above and to left of numeral oval). Type II is found only on Nos. 599A and 634A.

A178   A179   A180

Scott® No.	Illus No.	Description	Unused Price	Used Price	/ / / / / /
1923-26		*Imperf.*			
575	A155	1¢ green	5.00	3.00 ☐☐☐☐☐
576	A156	1½ yellow brown ('25)	1.25	1.00 ☐☐☐☐☐
577	A157	2¢ carmine	1.50	1.10 ☐☐☐☐☐
		Perf. 11x10.			
578	A155	1¢ green	45.00	45.00 ☐☐☐☐☐
579	A157	2¢ carmine	30.00	30.00 ☐☐☐☐☐
1923-26		*Perf. 10.*			
581	A155	1¢ green	3.25	.50 ☐☐☐☐☐
582	A156	1½ brown ('25)	3.00	.40 ☐☐☐☐☐
583	A157	2¢ carmine ('24)	1.20	.05 ☐☐☐☐☐
583a	A157	Bklt. pane of 6	70.00	25.00 ☐☐☐☐☐
584	A158	3¢ violet ('25)	18.50	1.25 ☐☐☐☐☐
585	A159	4¢ yellow brown ('25)	11.00	.25 ☐☐☐☐☐
586	A160	5¢ blue ('25)	11.50	.15 ☐☐☐☐☐
587	A161	6¢ red orange ('25)	5.00	.25 ☐☐☐☐☐
588	A162	7¢ black ('26)	6.50	4.00 ☐☐☐☐☐
589	A163	8¢ olive grn. ('26)	18.50	2.00 ☐☐☐☐☐
590	A164	9¢ rose ('26)	3.50	1.75 ☐☐☐☐☐
591	A165	10¢ orange ('25)	40.00	.06 ☐☐☐☐☐
		Perf. 11.			
594	A155	1¢ green	6000.00	1500.00 ☐☐☐☐☐
595	A157	2¢ carmine	110.00	95.00 ☐☐☐☐☐

Nos. 594–595 were made from coil waste of Nos. 597 and 599, and measure approximately 19¾x22¼mm.

		Perf. 11			
596	A155	1¢ green		11000.00 ☐☐☐☐☐

No. 596 measures approximately 19¼x 22¾mm. Most copies carry the Bureau precancel "Kansas City, Mo."

1923-29		Coil Stamps	*Perf. 10 Vertically*		
597	A155	1¢ green	.25	.06 ☐☐☐☐☐
598	A156	1½ brown ('25)	.75	.08 ☐☐☐☐☐
599	A157	2¢ car., Type I ('23)	.30	.04 ☐☐☐☐☐
599A	A157	2¢ car., Type II ('29)	130.00	7.00 ☐☐☐☐☐
600	A158	3¢ violet ('24)	7.00	.08 ☐☐☐☐☐
601	A159	4¢ yellow brown	3.00	.20 ☐☐☐☐☐
602	A160	5¢ dark blue ('24)	1.10	.10 ☐☐☐☐☐
603	A165	10¢ orange ('24)	2.50	.06 ☐☐☐☐☐
		Perf. 10 Horizontally			
604	A155	1¢ yellow green	.25	.08 ☐☐☐☐☐
605	A156	1½ yel. brown ('25)	.30	.12 ☐☐☐☐☐
606	A157	2¢ carmine	.30	.10 ☐☐☐☐☐
1923		Flat Plate Printing (19¼x22¼mm.)	*Perf. 11*		
610	A177	2¢ black	1.00	.10 ☐☐☐☐☐
		Imperf.			
611	A177	2¢ black	13.50	4.00 ☐☐☐☐☐

A181

A182

A183

A184

A185

A186

A187

A188

A190

A189

A191

A192

A193

Scott® No.	Illus No.	Description	Unused Price	Used Price	//////
1923		*Perf. 10*			
612	A177	2¢ black	21.00	1.50	☐☐☐☐☐
		Perf. 11 (19¼x22¾mm.)			
613	A177	2¢ black		9500.00	☐☐☐☐☐
1924					
614	A178	1¢ dark green	5.25	4.25	☐☐☐☐☐
615	A179	2¢ carmine rose	8.25	3.00	☐☐☐☐☐
616	A180	5¢ dark blue	45.00	16.50	☐☐☐☐☐
1925					
617	A181	1¢ deep green	5.00	4.00	☐☐☐☐☐
618	A182	2¢ carmine rose	9.50	5.50	☐☐☐☐☐
619	A183	5¢ dark blue	42.50	16.00	☐☐☐☐☐
620	A184	2¢ carmine & black	9.00	3.50	☐☐☐☐☐
621	A185	5¢ dark blue & blk.	32.50	15.00	☐☐☐☐☐
1925-26		*Perf. 11*			
622	A186	13¢ green ('26)	14.00	.50	☐☐☐☐☐
623	A187	17¢ black	18.50	.30	☐☐☐☐☐
1926					
627	A188	2¢ carmine rose	4.75	.60	☐☐☐☐☐
628	A189	5¢ gray lilac	11.00	4.50	☐☐☐☐☐
629	A190	2¢ carmine rose	2.75	2.00	☐☐☐☐☐
630	A190	2¢ carmine rose, sheet of 25	550.00	300.00	☐☐☐☐☐
		Imperf.			
631	A156	1½ yellow brown	1.35	1.15	☐☐☐☐☐
1926-34		*Perf. 11x10½.*			
632	A155	1¢ green ('27)	.15	.03	☐☐☐☐☐
632a	A155	Booklet pane of 6	1.00	.25	☐☐☐☐☐
633	A156	1½ yellow brown ('27)	1.25	.08	☐☐☐☐☐
634	A157	2¢ carmine, Type I	.15	.03	☐☐☐☐☐
634d	A157	Bklt. pane of 6	1.00	.15	☐☐☐☐☐
634A	A157	2¢ carmine, Type II ('28)	325.00	15.00	☐☐☐☐☐
635	A158	3¢ violet ('27)	.50	.04	☐☐☐☐☐
635a	A158	3c bright violet ('34)	.35	.04	☐☐☐☐☐
636	A159	4¢ yellow brown ('27)	2.50	.08	☐☐☐☐☐
637	A160	5¢ dark blue ('27)	2.50	.03	☐☐☐☐☐
638	A161	6¢ red orange ('27)	2.50	.03	☐☐☐☐☐
639	A162	7¢ black ('27)	2.50	.08	☐☐☐☐☐
640	A163	8¢ olive grn. ('27)	2.50	.05	☐☐☐☐☐
641	A164	9¢ orange red ('31)	2.50	.05	☐☐☐☐☐
642	A165	10¢ orange ('27)	4.00	.03	☐☐☐☐☐
1927					
643	A191	2¢ carmine rose	1.50	1.00	☐☐☐☐☐
644	A192	2¢ carmine rose	4.50	2.75	☐☐☐☐☐
1928					
645	A193	2¢ carmine rose	1.00	.50	☐☐☐☐☐
646	A157	2¢ carmine	1.35	1.20	☐☐☐☐☐
647	A157	2¢ carmine	6.00	4.50	☐☐☐☐☐

A194

A195

A196

A197

A198

A199

A200

A201

A202

A203

A204

A205

Scott® No.	Illus No.	Description	Unused Price	Used Price	//////
1928-29					
648	A160	5¢ dark blue	19.00	15.00 □□□□□
649	A194	2¢ carmine rose	1.20	1.00 □□□□□
650	A195	5¢ blue	5.75	4.00 □□□□□
651	A196	2¢ carmine & black	.80	.60 □□□□□
653	A154	½ olive brown	.05	.04 □□□□□
		Perf. 11.			
654	A197	2¢ carmine rose	.90	.75 □□□□□
		Perf. 11x10½.			
655	A197	2¢ carmine rose	.75	.25 □□□□□
		Coil Stamp (Rotary Press)			
		Perf. 10 Vertically.			
656	A197	2¢ carmine rose	22.50	1.50 □□□□□
1929					
657	A198	2¢ carmine rose	.70	.60 □□□□□
		Overprinted **Kans.**			
658	A155	1¢ green	1.50	1.35 □□□□□
659	A156	1½ brown	2.75	2.50 □□□□□
660	A157	2¢ carmine	2.25	.40 □□□□□
661	A158	3¢ violet	13.50	10.00 □□□□□
662	A159	4¢ yellow brown	14.50	5.00 □□□□□
663	A160	5¢ deep blue	10.00	7.00 □□□□□
664	A161	6¢ red orange	20.00	11.00 □□□□□
665	A162	7¢ black	20.00	17.50 □□□□□
666	A163	8¢ olive green	60.00	45.00 □□□□□
667	A164	9¢ light rose	10.00	7.50 □□□□□
668	A165	10¢ orange yellow	18.50	7.50 □□□□□
		Overprinted **Nebr.**			
669	A155	1¢ green	1.50	1.50 □□□□□
670	A156	1½ brown	2.00	1.85 □□□□□
671	A157	2¢ carmine	1.20	.65 □□□□□
672	A158	3¢ violet	10.00	6.75 □□□□□
673	A159	4¢ yellow brown	12.50	7.00 □□□□□
674	A160	5¢ deep blue	11.50	7.50 □□□□□
675	A161	6¢ red orange	27.50	16.50 □□□□□
676	A162	7¢ black	15.00	11.00 □□□□□
677	A163	8¢ olive green	25.00	17.50 □□□□□
678	A164	9¢ light rose	24.00	18.00 □□□□□
679	A165	10¢ orange yellow	70.00	15.00 □□□□□
680	A199	2¢ carmine rose	1.15	.90 □□□□□
681	A200	2¢ carmine rose	.75	.60 □□□□□
1930					
682	A201	2¢ carmine rose	.65	.45 □□□□□
683	A202	2¢ carmine rose	1.25	1.00 □□□□□
		Perf. 11x10½.			
684	A203	1½ brown	.20	.05 □□□□□
685	A204	4¢ brown	.40	.06 □□□□□
		Coil Stamps *Perf. 10 Vertically*			
686	A203	1½ brown	.50	.07 □□□□□

A206

A207

A208

A209

A210

A211

A212

A213

A214

A215

A216

A217

A218

A219

A220

A221

A222

A223

A224

A225

A226

A227

A228

Scott® No.	Illus No.	Description	Unused Price	Used Price	/ / / / / /
1930					
687	A204	4¢ brown	1.10	.25 □□□□□
1930					
688	A205	2¢ carmine rose	1.25	1.00 □□□□□
689	A206	2¢ carmine rose	.75	.50 □□□□□
1931					
690	A207	2¢ carmine rose	.30	.18 □□□□□
1931		*Perf. 11x10½.*			
692	A166	11¢ light blue	2.50	.10 □□□□□
693	A167	12¢ brown violet	5.00	.06 □□□□□
694	A186	13¢ yellow green	1.60	.10 □□□□□
695	A168	14¢ dark blue	3.50	.30 □□□□□
696	A169	15¢ gray	8.50	.06 □□□□□
		Perf. 10½x11.			
697	A187	17¢ black	4.00	.20 □□□□□
698	A170	20¢ carmine rose	11.00	.05 □□□□□
699	A171	25¢ blue green	8.25	.08 □□□□□
700	A172	30¢ brown	20.00	.07 □□□□□
701	A173	50¢ lilac	60.00	.07 □□□□□
1931					
702	A208	2¢ black & red	.15	.12 □□□□□
703	A209	2¢ carmine rose & black	.40	.25 □□□□□
1932					
704	A210	½ olive brown	.08	.05 □□□□□
705	A211	1¢ green	.13	.04 □□□□□
706	A212	1½ brown	.40	.06 □□□□□
707	A213	2¢ carmine rose	.10	.03 □□□□□
708	A214	3¢ deep violet	.50	.06 □□□□□
709	A215	4¢ light brown	.30	.06 □□□□□
710	A216	5¢ blue	2.25	.08 □□□□□
711	A217	6¢ red orange	5.00	.06 □□□□□
712	A218	7¢ black	.40	.12 □□□□□
713	A219	8¢ olive bistre	5.25	.70 □□□□□
714	A220	9¢ pale red	4.00	.25 □□□□□
715	A221	10¢ orange yellow	16.50	.10 □□□□□
716	A222	2¢ carmine rose	.35	.20 □□□□□
717	A223	2¢ carmine rose	.18	.08 □□□□□
718	A224	3¢ violet	.55	.06 □□□□□
719	A225	5¢ blue	.90	.20 □□□□□
1932		*Perf. 11x10½.*			
720	A226	3¢ deep violet	.15	.03 □□□□□
720b	A226	Booklet pane of 6	22.50	5.00 □□□□□
		Coil Stamps *Perf. 10 Vertically*			
721	A226	3¢ deep violet	1.85	.08 □□□□□
		Perf. 10 Horizontally.			
722	A226	3¢ deep violet	1.25	.20 □□□□□
		Perf. 10 Vertically.			
723	A161	6¢ deep orange	7.00	.20 □□□□□

A229

A230

A231

A232

A233

A234

A235

A236

A237

A238

Scott® No.	Illus No.	Description	Unused Price	Used Price	//////
1932					
724	A227	3¢ violet	.30	.15 ☐☐☐☐☐
725	A228	3¢ violet	.50	.25 ☐☐☐☐☐
1933					
726	A229	3¢ violet	.35	.15 ☐☐☐☐☐
727	A230	3¢ violet	.15	.10 ☐☐☐☐☐
728	A231	1¢ yellow green	.12	.06 ☐☐☐☐☐
729	A232	3¢ violet	.18	.04 ☐☐☐☐☐
730	A231	1¢ deep yellow green, sheet of twenty-five	45.00	30.00 ☐☐☐☐☐
730a	A231	Single stamp, imperf.	.75	.50 ☐☐☐☐☐
731	A232	3¢ deep violet, sheet of twenty-five	37.50	25.00 ☐☐☐☐☐
731a	A232	Single stamp, imperf.	.60	.50 ☐☐☐☐☐
732	A233	3¢ violet	.14	.03 ☐☐☐☐☐
733	A234	3¢ dark blue	.85	.70 ☐☐☐☐☐
734	A235	5¢ blue	.75	.30 ☐☐☐☐☐
1934					
735	A234	3¢ dark blue, sheet of six	20.00	16.00 ☐☐☐☐☐
735a	A234	Single stamp, imperf.	2.50	2.25 ☐☐☐☐☐
736	A236	3¢ carmine rose	.20	.15 ☐☐☐☐☐
1934		*Perf. 11x10½.*			
737	A237	3¢ deep violet	.15	.06 ☐☐☐☐☐
		Perf. 11.			
738	A237	3¢ deep violet	.20	.18 ☐☐☐☐☐
739	A238	3¢ deep violet	.20	.12 ☐☐☐☐☐
740	A239	1¢ green	.10	.06 ☐☐☐☐☐
741	A240	2¢ red	.15	.06 ☐☐☐☐☐
742	A241	3¢ deep violet	.20	.06 ☐☐☐☐☐
743	A242	4¢ brown	.40	.40 ☐☐☐☐☐
744	A243	5¢ blue	1.00	.75 ☐☐☐☐☐
745	A244	6¢ dark blue	1.40	.80 ☐☐☐☐☐
746	A245	7¢ black	1.00	.75 ☐☐☐☐☐
747	A246	8¢ sage green	2.00	1.75 ☐☐☐☐☐
748	A247	9¢ red orange	2.25	.65 ☐☐☐☐☐
749	A248	10¢ gray black	3.75	1.00 ☐☐☐☐☐
750	A241	3¢ deep violet, sheet of six	37.50	25.00 ☐☐☐☐☐
750a	A241	Single stamp, imperf.	4.00	3.50 ☐☐☐☐☐
751	A239	1¢ green, sheet of six	14.50	10.00 ☐☐☐☐☐
751a	A239	Single stamp, imperf.	2.00	1.50 ☐☐☐☐☐

Without Gum.

Note. In 1940 the P.O. Department offered to and did gum full sheets of Nos. 754 to 771 sent in by owners.

1935					
752	A230	3¢ violet	.15	.10 ☐☐☐☐☐
753	A234	3¢ dark blue	.50	.50 ☐☐☐☐☐
		Imperf.			
754	A237	3¢ deep violet	.60	.50 ☐☐☐☐☐
755	A238	3¢ deep violet	.60	.50 ☐☐☐☐☐

A240

A239

A241

A242

A243

A244

A245

A246

A247

A249

A248

A250

A252

A253

Scott® No.	Illus No.	Description	Unused Price	Used Price	//////
1935		*Imperf.*			
756	A239	1¢ green	.15	.15 □□□□□
757	A240	2¢ red	.20	.20 □□□□□
758	A241	3¢ deep violet	.40	.40 □□□□□
759	A242	4¢ brown	.90	.75 □□□□□
760	A243	5¢ blue	1.10	.90 □□□□□
761	A244	6¢ dark blue	1.50	1.10 □□□□□
762	A245	7¢ black	1.10	.90 □□□□□
763	A246	8¢ sage green	1.20	1.00 □□□□□
764	A247	9¢ red orange	1.20	1.00 □□□□□
765	A248	10¢ gray black	2.75	2.00 □□□□□
766	A231	1¢ yellow green, pane of 25	42.50	27.50 □□□□□
766a	A231	Single stamp	.75	.50 □□□□□
767	A232	3¢ violet, pane of 25	35.00	25.00 □□□□□
767a	A232	Single stamp	.60	.50 □□□□□
768	A234	3¢ dark blue, pane of six	20.00	16.00 □□□□□
768a	A234	Single stamp	2.50	2.25 □□□□□
769	A239	1¢ green, pane of six	12.00	8.50 □□□□□
769a	A239	Single stamp	1.60	1.40 □□□□□
770	A241	3¢ deep violet, pane of six	27.50	22.50 □□□□□
770a	A241	Single stamp	3.25	3.00 □□□□□
771	APSD1	16¢ dark blue	2.00	2.00 □□□□□
1935		*Perf. 11x10½,11*			
772	A249	3¢ violet	.12	.06 □□□□□
773	A250	3¢ purple	.12	.06 □□□□□
774	A251	3¢ purple	.12	.06 □□□□□
775	A252	3¢ purple	.12	.06 □□□□□
1936					
776	A253	3¢ purple	.12	.06 □□□□□
777	A254	3¢ purple	.12	.06 □□□□□
778		sheet of 4, imperf.	3.75	3.00 □□□□□
778a		A249 3c violet	.80	.60 □□□□□
778b		A250 3c violet	.80	.60 □□□□□
778c		A252 3c violet	.80	.60 □□□□□
778d		A253 3c violet	.80	.60 □□□□□
782	A255	3¢ purple	.12	.06 □□□□□
783	A256	3¢ purple	.12	.06 □□□□□
784	A257	3¢ dark violet	.10	.05 □□□□□
1936-37					
785	A258	1¢ green	.10	.06 □□□□□
786	A259	2¢ carmine ('37)	.15	.06 □□□□□
787	A260	3¢ purple ('37)	.20	.08 □□□□□
788	A261	4¢ gray ('37)	.65	.15 □□□□□
789	A262	5¢ ultramarine ('37)	.70	.15 □□□□□
790	A263	1¢ green	.10	.06 □□□□□
791	A264	2¢ carmine ('37)	.15	.06 □□□□□
792	A265	3¢ purple ('37)	.20	.08 □□□□□

A251

A255

A254

A256

A257

A258

A259

A260

A261

A262

A263

A264

A265

A266

A267

A268

A269

A269a

A270

A272

A273

A274

A275

A271

A277

A276

A278

Thomas Jefferson
A279

James Madison
A280

White House
A281

James Monroe
A282

John Q. Adams
A283

Andrew Jackson
A284

Martin
Van Buren
A285

William H.
Harrison
A286

John Tyler
A287

James K. Polk
A288

Zachary Taylor
A289

Millard Fillmore
A290

Franklin Pierce
A291

James Buchanan
A292

Abraham Lincoln
A293

Andrew Johnson
A294

Ulysses S.
Grant
A295

Rutherford B.
Hayes
A296

James A. Garfield
A297

Chester A. Arthur
A298

Grover
Cleveland
A299

Benjamin
Harrison
A300

William
McKinley
A301

Theodore
Roosevelt
A302

Scott® No.	Illus No.	Description	Unused Price	Used Price	//////
1936-37					
793	A266	4¢ gray ('37)	.65	.15 ☐☐☐☐☐
794	A267	5¢ ultra. ('37)	.70	.15 ☐☐☐☐☐
1937					
795	A268	3¢ red violet	.12	.06 ☐☐☐☐☐
796	A269	5¢ gray blue	.40	.25 ☐☐☐☐☐
797	A269a	10¢ blue green	1.25	.60 ☐☐☐☐☐
798	A270	3¢ bright red violet	.15	.07 ☐☐☐☐☐
799	A271	3¢ violet	.15	.07 ☐☐☐☐☐
800	A272	3¢ violet	.15	.07 ☐☐☐☐☐
801	A273	3¢ bright violet	.15	.07 ☐☐☐☐☐
802	A274	3¢ light violet	.15	.07 ☐☐☐☐☐
1938-54		*Perf. 11x10½.*			
803	A275	½ deep orange	.05	.03 ☐☐☐☐☐
804	A276	1¢ green	.06	.03 ☐☐☐☐☐
804b	A276	Bklt. pane of 6	1.75	.20 ☐☐☐☐☐
805	A277	1½ bistre brown	.06	.03 ☐☐☐☐☐
806	A278	2¢ rose carmine	.06	.03 ☐☐☐☐☐
806b	A278	Bklt. pane of 6	4.25	.50 ☐☐☐☐☐
807	A279	3¢ deep violet	.10	.03 ☐☐☐☐☐
807a	A279	Bklt. pane of 6	8.50	.50 ☐☐☐☐☐
808	A280	4¢ red violet	.30	.04 ☐☐☐☐☐
809	A281	4½ dark gray	.15	.06 ☐☐☐☐☐
810	A282	5¢ bright blue	.30	.03 ☐☐☐☐☐
811	A283	6¢ red orange	.35	.03 ☐☐☐☐☐
812	A284	7¢ sepia	.30	.05 ☐☐☐☐☐
813	A285	8¢ olive green	.40	.04 ☐☐☐☐☐
814	A286	9¢ rose pink	.45	.04 ☐☐☐☐☐
815	A287	10¢ brown red	.40	.03 ☐☐☐☐☐
816	A288	11¢ ultramarine	.65	.08 ☐☐☐☐☐
817	A289	12¢ bright violet	.90	.06 ☐☐☐☐☐
818	A290	13¢ blue green	.90	.08 ☐☐☐☐☐
819	A291	14¢ blue	.90	.10 ☐☐☐☐☐
820	A292	15¢ blue gray	.65	.03 ☐☐☐☐☐
821	A293	16¢ black	1.20	.25 ☐☐☐☐☐
822	A294	17¢ rose red	1.20	.12 ☐☐☐☐☐
823	A295	18¢ brown carmine	1.40	.08 ☐☐☐☐☐
824	A296	19¢ bright violet	1.20	.30 ☐☐☐☐☐
825	A297	20¢ brt. blue green	.95	.03 ☐☐☐☐☐
826	A298	21¢ dull blue	1.35	.10 ☐☐☐☐☐
827	A299	22¢ vermilion	1.35	.35 ☐☐☐☐☐
828	A300	24¢ gray black	2.25	.25 ☐☐☐☐☐
829	A301	25¢ deep red lilac	1.35	.03 ☐☐☐☐☐
830	A302	30¢ dp. ultra.	7.00	.05 ☐☐☐☐☐
831	A303	50¢ light red violet	10.50	.06 ☐☐☐☐☐
		Perf. 11.			
832	A304	$1 purple & black	16.50	.10 ☐☐☐☐☐
832b	A304	Wmkd. USIR ('51)	100.00	25.00 ☐☐☐☐☐

William
Howard Taft

A303

Woodrow
Wilson

A304

Warren G.
Harding

A305

Calvin
Coolidge

A306

A308

A307

A309

A311

A310

A312

A313

A314

A315

A316

A317

64

Scott® No.	Illus No.	Description	Unused Price	Used Price	//////
1938-54					
832c	A304	$1 red violet & black ('54)	12.50	.15	☐☐☐☐☐
833	A305	$2 yel. grn. & blk.	42.50	4.25	☐☐☐☐☐
834	A306	$5 car. & black	185.00	4.00	☐☐☐☐☐
1938					
835	A307	3¢ deep violet	.25	.08	☐☐☐☐☐
836	A308	3¢ red violet	.25	.10	☐☐☐☐☐
837	A309	3¢ bright violet	.25	.08	☐☐☐☐☐
838	A310	3¢ violet	.25	.08	☐☐☐☐☐
1939		Coil Stamps	Perf. 10 Vertically.		
839	A276	1¢ green	.20	.06	☐☐☐☐☐
840	A277	1½ bistre brown	.25	.06	☐☐☐☐☐
841	A278	2¢ rose carmine	.25	.05	☐☐☐☐☐
842	A279	3¢ deep violet	.50	.04	☐☐☐☐☐
843	A280	4¢ red violet	6.25	.20	☐☐☐☐☐
844	A281	4½ dark gray	.50	.20	☐☐☐☐☐
845	A282	5¢ bright blue	4.00	.35	☐☐☐☐☐
846	A283	6¢ red orange	1.10	.20	☐☐☐☐☐
847	A287	10¢ brown red	12.50	.40	☐☐☐☐☐
		Perf. 10 Horizontally			
848	A276	1¢ green	.60	.12	☐☐☐☐☐
849	A277	1½ bistre brown	.85	.20	☐☐☐☐☐
850	A278	2¢ rose carmine	2.00	.20	☐☐☐☐☐
851	A279	3¢ deep violet	2.00	.25	☐☐☐☐☐
1939					
852	A311	3¢ bright purple	.12	.06	☐☐☐☐☐
853	A312	3¢ deep purple	.15	.06	☐☐☐☐☐
854	A313	3¢ bright red violet	.25	.10	☐☐☐☐☐
855	A314	3¢ violet	.22	.08	☐☐☐☐☐
856	A315	3¢ deep red violet	.22	.08	☐☐☐☐☐
857	A316	3¢ violet	.12	.08	☐☐☐☐☐
858	A317	3¢ rose violet	.12	.08	☐☐☐☐☐
1940					
859	A318	1¢ bright blue green	.08	.06	☐☐☐☐☐
860	A319	2¢ rose carmine	.10	.08	☐☐☐☐☐
861	A320	3¢ bright red violet	.12	.06	☐☐☐☐☐
862	A321	5¢ ultramarine	.35	.30	☐☐☐☐☐
863	A322	10¢ dark brown	2.50	2.00	☐☐☐☐☐
864	A323	1¢ bright blue green	.12	.08	☐☐☐☐☐
865	A324	2¢ rose carmine	.10	.08	☐☐☐☐☐
866	A325	3¢ bright red violet	.18	.06	☐☐☐☐☐
867	A326	5¢ ultramarine	.35	.25	☐☐☐☐☐
868	A327	10¢ dark brown	3.50	2.50	☐☐☐☐☐
869	A328	1¢ bright blue green	.09	.08	☐☐☐☐☐
870	A329	2¢ rose carmine	.10	.06	☐☐☐☐☐
871	A330	3¢ bright red violet	.30	.06	☐☐☐☐☐
872	A331	5¢ ultramarine	.50	.35	☐☐☐☐☐

Washington Irving	James Fenimore Cooper	Ralph Waldo Emerson	Louisa May Alcott
A318	A319	A320	A321

Samuel L. Clemens (Mark Twain)
A322

Henry W. Longfellow	John Greenleaf Whittier	James Russell Lowell	Walt Whitman
A323	A324	A325	A326

James Whitcomb Riley
A327

Horace Mann	Mark Hopkins	Charles W. Eliot	Frances E. Willard
A328	A329	A330	A331

Booker T. Washington
A332

John James
Audubon
A333

Dr. Crawford
W. Long
A334

Luther Burbank
A335

Dr. Walter Reed
A336

Jane Addams
A337

Stephen Collins
Foster
A338

John Philip
Sousa
A339

Victor
Herbert
A340

Edward
MacDowell
A341

Ethelbert Nevin
A342

Gilbert Charles
Stuart
A343

James A. McNeill
Whistler
A344

Augustus
Saint-Gaudens
A345

Daniel Chester
French
A346

Frederic Remington— **A347**

Eli Whitney
A348

Samuel F. B. Morse
A349

Cyrus Hall
McCormick
A350

Elias
Howe
A351

A353

A352

A355

A356

A354

A361

A357

A358

A359

A360

A362

A363

A364

A366

A367

68

Scott® No.	Illus No.	Description	Unused Price	Used Price	/ / / / / /
1940					
873	A332	10¢ dark brown	2.00	1.75 □□□□□
874	A333	1¢ bright blue green	.08	.06 □□□□□
875	A334	2¢ rose carmine	.10	.06 □□□□□
876	A335	3¢ bright red violet	.10	.06 □□□□□
877	A336	5¢ ultramarine	.30	.25 □□□□□
878	A337	10¢ dark brown	2.00	1.75 □□□□□
879	A338	1¢ bright blue green	.08	.06 □□□□□
880	A339	2¢ rose carmine	.10	.06 □□□□□
881	A340	3¢ bright red violet	.15	.06 □□□□□
882	A341	5¢ ultramarine	.50	.30 □□□□□
883	A342	10¢ dark brown	4.50	2.00 □□□□□
884	A343	1¢ bright blue green	.08	.06 □□□□□
885	A344	2¢ rose carmine	.10	.06 □□□□□
886	A345	3¢ bright red violet	.10	.06 □□□□□
887	A346	5¢ ultramarine	.40	.22 □□□□□
888	A347	10¢ dark brown	2.50	2.25 □□□□□
889	A348	1¢ bright blue green	.12	.08 □□□□□
890	A349	2¢ rose carmine	.10	.06 □□□□□
891	A350	3¢ bright red violet	.20	.06 □□□□□
892	A351	5¢ ultramarine	1.25	.40 □□□□□
893	A352	10¢ dark brown	10.50	3.25 □□□□□
894	A353	3¢ henna brown	.50	.20 □□□□□
895	A354	3¢ light violet	.45	.15 □□□□□
896	A355	3¢ bright violet	.20	.08 □□□□□
897	A356	3¢ brown violet	.20	.08 □□□□□
898	A357	3¢ violet	.20	.08 □□□□□
899	A358	1¢ bright blue green	.05	.04 □□□□□
900	A359	2¢ rose carmine	.06	.03 □□□□□
901	A360	3¢ bright violet	.12	.03 □□□□□
902	A361	3¢ deep violet	.25	.15 □□□□□
1941					
903	A362	3¢ light violet	.22	.10 □□□□□
1942					
904	A363	3¢ violet	.15	.12 □□□□□
905	A364	3¢ violet	.10	.03 □□□□□
906	A365	5¢ bright blue	.50	.30 □□□□□
1943					
907	A366	2¢ rose carmine	.08	.04 □□□□□
908	A367	1¢ bright blue green	.06	.05 □□□□□
1943-44					
909	A368	5¢ Poland Multicolored	.35	.20 □□□□□
910	A368	5¢ Czechoslovakia Multicolored	.20	.15 □□□□□
911	A368	5¢ Norway Multicolored	.15	.12 □□□□□

A365

A368

A369

A370

A371

A372

A373

A374

A375

A377

A376

A378

A379

A380

A381

A382

A383

70

Scott® No.	Illus No.	Description	Unused Price	Used Price	//////
1943-44					
912	A368	5¢ Luxembourg Multicolored	.15	.12 □□□□□
913	A368	5¢ Netherlands Multicolored	.15	.12 □□□□□
914	A368	5¢ Belgium Multicolored	.15	.12 □□□□□
915	A368	5¢ France Multicolored	.15	.10 □□□□□
916	A368	5¢ Greece Multicolored	.50	.25 □□□□□
917	A368	5¢ Yugoslavia Multicolored	.35	.20 □□□□□
918	A368	5¢ Albania Multicolored	.25	.20 □□□□□
919	A368	5¢ Austria Multicolored	.25	.20 □□□□□
920	A368	5¢ Denmark Multicolored	.25	.25 □□□□□
921	A368	5¢ Korea Multicolored	.28	.25 □□□□□
1944					
922	A369	3¢ violet	.12	.10 □□□□□
923	A370	3¢ violet	.12	.10 □□□□□
924	A371	3¢ bright red violet	.12	.10 □□□□□
925	A372	3¢ deep violet	.12	.10 □□□□□
926	A373	3¢ deep violet	.12	.10 □□□□□
1945					
927	A374	3¢ bright red violet	.10	.08 □□□□□
928	A375	5¢ ultramarine	.12	.08 □□□□□
929	A376	3¢ yellow green	.10	.05 □□□□□
1945-46					
930	A377	1¢ blue green	.05	.05 □□□□□
931	A378	2¢ carmine rose	.08	.08 □□□□□
932	A379	3¢ purple	.10	.06 □□□□□
933	A380	5¢ bright blue ('46)	.12	.08 □□□□□
1945					
934	A381	3¢ olive	.10	.05 □□□□□
935	A382	3¢ blue	.10	.05 □□□□□
936	A383	3¢ bright blue green	.10	.05 □□□□□
937	A384	3¢ purple	.10	.04 □□□□□
938	A385	3¢ dark blue	.10	.05 □□□□□
1946					
939	A386	3¢ blue green	.10	.05 □□□□□
940	A387	3¢ dark violet	.10	.04 □□□□□
941	A388	3¢ dark violet	.10	.05 □□□□□
942	A389	3¢ deep blue	.10	.05 □□□□□
943	A390	3¢ violet brown	.10	.05 □□□□□
944	A391	3¢ brown violet	.10	.05 □□□□□

A384

A385

A386

A387

A388

A389

A390

A391

A392

A393

A394

A399

A395

A396

A397

A398

A401

A400

A402

72

A403

A404

A405

A406

A407

A408

A409

A410

A411

A412

A413

A414

A415

A416

A417

A418

A419

A420

A421

A422

A423

A424

A425

A426

A427

A428

A429

A430

A432

A433

A431

A434

A435

A436

Scott® No.	Illus No.	Description	Unused Price	Used Price	/ / / / / /
1947					
945	A392	3¢ bright red violet	.10	.05 ☐☐☐☐☐
946	A393	3¢ purple	.10	.05 ☐☐☐☐☐
947	A394	3¢ deep blue	.10	.05 ☐☐☐☐☐
948	A395	Sheet of two	2.00	.65 ☐☐☐☐☐
948a		A1 5c blue	.35	.20 ☐☐☐☐☐
948b		A2 10c brown orange	.50	.20 ☐☐☐☐☐
949	A396	3¢ brown violet	.10	.05 ☐☐☐☐☐
950	A397	3¢ dark violet	.10	.05 ☐☐☐☐☐
951	A398	3¢ blue green	.10	.05 ☐☐☐☐☐
952	A399	3¢ bright green	.10	.05 ☐☐☐☐☐
1948					
953	A400	3¢ bright red violet	.10	.05 ☐☐☐☐☐
954	A401	3¢ dark violet	.10	.05 ☐☐☐☐☐
955	A402	3¢ brown violet	.10	.05 ☐☐☐☐☐
956	A403	3¢ gray black	.10	.05 ☐☐☐☐☐
957	A404	3¢ dark violet	.10	.05 ☐☐☐☐☐
958	A405	5¢ deep blue	.15	.10 ☐☐☐☐☐
959	A406	3¢ dark violet	.10	.05 ☐☐☐☐☐
960	A407	3¢ bright red violet	.10	.06 ☐☐☐☐☐
961	A408	3¢ blue	.10	.05 ☐☐☐☐☐
962	A409	3¢ rose pink	.10	.05 ☐☐☐☐☐
963	A410	3¢ deep blue	.10	.06 ☐☐☐☐☐
964	A411	3¢ brown red	.12	.10 ☐☐☐☐☐
965	A412	3¢ bright red violet	.15	.08 ☐☐☐☐☐
966	A413	3¢ blue	.25	.10 ☐☐☐☐☐
967	A414	3¢ rose pink	.10	.08 ☐☐☐☐☐
968	A415	3¢ sepia	.12	.08 ☐☐☐☐☐
969	A416	3¢ orange yellow	.12	.08 ☐☐☐☐☐
970	A417	3¢ violet	.12	.08 ☐☐☐☐☐
971	A418	3¢ brt. rose carmine	.12	.08 ☐☐☐☐☐
972	A419	3¢ dark brown	.12	.08 ☐☐☐☐☐
973	A420	3¢ violet brown	.12	.10 ☐☐☐☐☐
974	A421	3¢ blue green	.12	.08 ☐☐☐☐☐
975	A422	3¢ bright red violet	.12	.08 ☐☐☐☐☐
976	A423	3¢ henna brown	.25	.08 ☐☐☐☐☐
977	A424	3¢ rose pink	.12	.08 ☐☐☐☐☐
978	A425	3¢ bright blue	.12	.08 ☐☐☐☐☐
979	A426	3¢ carmine	.12	.08 ☐☐☐☐☐
980	A427	3¢ bright red violet	.12	.08 ☐☐☐☐☐
1949					
981	A428	3¢ blue green	.10	.05 ☐☐☐☐☐
982	A429	3¢ ultramarine	.10	.05 ☐☐☐☐☐
983	A430	3¢ green	.10	.05 ☐☐☐☐☐
984	A431	3¢ aquamarine	.10	.05 ☐☐☐☐☐
985	A432	3¢ bright rose car.	.10	.05 ☐☐☐☐☐
986	A433	3¢ bright red violet	.10	.05 ☐☐☐☐☐

A437

A438

A439

A440

A441

A442

A443

A444

A445

A446

A447

A448

A449

A450

A451

A452

A453

Scott® No.	Illus No.	Description	Unused Price	Used Price	/ / / / / /
1950					
987	A434	3¢ yellow green	.10	.05 ☐☐☐☐☐
988	A435	3¢ bright red violet	.10	.05 ☐☐☐☐☐
989	A436	3¢ bright blue	.10	.05 ☐☐☐☐☐
990	A437	3¢ deep green	.10	.05 ☐☐☐☐☐
991	A438	3¢ light violet	.10	.05 ☐☐☐☐☐
992	A439	3¢ bright red violet	.10	.05 ☐☐☐☐☐
993	A440	3¢ violet brown	.10	.05 ☐☐☐☐☐
994	A441	3¢ violet	.10	.05 ☐☐☐☐☐
995	A442	3¢ sepia	.10	.06 ☐☐☐☐☐
996	A443	3¢ bright blue	.10	.05 ☐☐☐☐☐
997	A444	3¢ yellow orange	.10	.05 ☐☐☐☐☐
1951					
998	A445	3¢ gray	.10	.05 ☐☐☐☐☐
999	A446	3¢ light olive green	.10	.05 ☐☐☐☐☐
1000	A447	3¢ blue	.10	.05 ☐☐☐☐☐
1001	A448	3¢ blue violet	.10	.05 ☐☐☐☐☐
1002	A449	3¢ violet brown	.10	.05 ☐☐☐☐☐
1003	A450	3¢ violet	.10	.05 ☐☐☐☐☐
1952					
1004	A451	3¢ carmine rose	.10	.05 ☐☐☐☐☐
1005	A452	3¢ blue green	.10	.05 ☐☐☐☐☐
1006	A453	3¢ bright blue	.10	.05 ☐☐☐☐☐
1007	A454	3¢ deep blue	.10	.05 ☐☐☐☐☐
1008	A455	3¢ deep violet	.10	.03 ☐☐☐☐☐
1009	A456	3¢ blue green	.10	.05 ☐☐☐☐☐
1010	A457	3¢ bright blue	.10	.05 ☐☐☐☐☐
1011	A458	3¢ blue green	.10	.05 ☐☐☐☐☐
1012	A459	3¢ violet blue	.10	.05 ☐☐☐☐☐
1013	A460	3¢ deep blue	.10	.05 ☐☐☐☐☐
1014	A461	3¢ violet	.10	.05 ☐☐☐☐☐
1015	A462	3¢ violet	.10	.05 ☐☐☐☐☐
1016	A463	3¢ deep blue & carmine	.10	.05 ☐☐☐☐☐
1953					
1017	A464	3¢ bright blue	.10	.05 ☐☐☐☐☐
1018	A465	3¢ chocolate	.10	.05 ☐☐☐☐☐
1019	A466	3¢ green	.10	.05 ☐☐☐☐☐
1020	A467	3¢ violet brown	.10	.05 ☐☐☐☐☐
1021	A468	5¢ green	.15	.10 ☐☐☐☐☐
1022	A469	3¢ rose violet	.10	.05 ☐☐☐☐☐
1023	A470	3¢ yellow green	.10	.05 ☐☐☐☐☐
1024	A471	3¢ deep blue	.10	.05 ☐☐☐☐☐
1025	A472	3¢ violet	.10	.05 ☐☐☐☐☐
1026	A473	3¢ blue violet	.10	.05 ☐☐☐☐☐
1027	A474	3¢ bright red violet	.10	.05 ☐☐☐☐☐

A454

A455

A456

A457

A458

A459

A460

A461

A462

A463

A464

A465

A466

A467

A468

A469

A470

A471

Scott® No.	Illus No.	Description	Unused Price	Used Price	//////
1953					
1028	A475	3¢ copper brown	.10	.05 ☐☐☐☐☐
1954					
1029	A476	3¢ blue	.10	.05 ☐☐☐☐☐
1954-68		*Perf. 11x10½, 10½x11 , 11.*			
1030	A477	½ red orange ('55)	.05	.03 ☐☐☐☐☐
1031	A478	1¢ dark green	.05	.03 ☐☐☐☐☐
1031A	A478a	1¼ turquoise ('60)	.05	.05 ☐☐☐☐☐
1032	A479	1½ brown car. ('56)	.05	.04 ☐☐☐☐☐
1033	A480	2¢ carmine rose	.05	.03 ☐☐☐☐☐
1034	A481	2½ gray blue ('59)	.08	.05 ☐☐☐☐☐
1035	A482	3¢ deep violet	.08	.03 ☐☐☐☐☐
1035a	A482	Booklet pane of 6	3.00	.50 ☐☐☐☐☐
1035b	A482	Tagged ('66)	.25	.20 ☐☐☐☐☐
1036	A483	4¢ red violet	.10	.03 ☐☐☐☐☐
1036a	A483	Booklet pane of 6 ('58)	2.00	.50 ☐☐☐☐☐
1036b	A483	Tagged ('63)	.50	.16 ☐☐☐☐☐
1037	A484	4½ blue green ('59)	.12	.08 ☐☐☐☐☐
1038	A485	5¢ deep blue	.12	.03 ☐☐☐☐☐
1039	A486	6¢ carmine ('55)	.20	.03 ☐☐☐☐☐
1040	A487	7¢ rose car. ('56)	.20	.03 ☐☐☐☐☐
1041	A488	8¢ dk. viol. bl. & car.	.35	.06 ☐☐☐☐☐
1042	A489	8¢ dk. viol. blue & car. rose ('58)	.20	.03 ☐☐☐☐☐
1042A	A489a	8¢ brown ('61)	.25	.03 ☐☐☐☐☐
1043	A490	9¢ rose lilac ('56)	.25	.04 ☐☐☐☐☐
1044	A491	10¢ rose lake ('56)	.30	.03 ☐☐☐☐☐
1044b	A491	Tagged ('66)	.60	.35 ☐☐☐☐☐
1044A	A491a	11¢ car. & dark vio. bl. ('61)	.30	.06 ☐☐☐☐☐
1044c	A491a	Tagged ('67)	1.00	.80 ☐☐☐☐☐
1045	A492	12¢ red ('59)	.45	.05 ☐☐☐☐☐
1045a	A492	Tagged ('68)	.45	.15 ☐☐☐☐☐
1046	A493	15¢ rose lake ('58)	.60	.03 ☐☐☐☐☐
1046a	A493	Tagged ('66)	.65	.22 ☐☐☐☐☐
1047	A494	20¢ ultra. ('56)	.70	.03 ☐☐☐☐☐
1048	A495	25¢ green ('58)	1.50	.03 ☐☐☐☐☐
1049	A496	30¢ black ('55)	1.75	.08 ☐☐☐☐☐
1050	A497	40¢ brn. red ('55)	2.75	.10 ☐☐☐☐☐
1051	A498	50¢ brt. pur. ('55)	3.25	.04 ☐☐☐☐☐
1052	A499	$1 purple ('55)	9.50	.06 ☐☐☐☐☐
1053	A500	$5 black ('56)	125.00	2.50 ☐☐☐☐☐
		Coil Stamps			
1954-73		*Perf. 10 Vertically Perf. 10 Horizontally*			
1054A	A478a	1¼ turquoise ('60)	.45	.10 ☐☐☐☐☐
1055	A480	2¢ rose carmine	.10	.05 ☐☐☐☐☐
1055a	A480	Tagged ('68)	.10	.05 ☐☐☐☐☐
1056	A481	2½ gray blue ('59)	.55	.07 ☐☐☐☐☐
1057	A482	3¢ deep violet	.15	.03 ☐☐☐☐☐

A472

A473

A474

A475

A476

A477

A478

A478a

A479

A480

A481

A482

A483

A484

A485

A486

A487

A488

A489

A489a

A490

A491

Scott® No.	Illus No.	Description	Unused Price	Used Price	//////
1954-73					
1057b	A482	Tagged ('66)	.75	.25 ☐☐☐☐☐
1058	A483	4¢ red violet ('58)	.15	.04 ☐☐☐☐☐
1059	A484	4½ bl. green ('59)	2.50	.10 ☐☐☐☐☐
1059A	A495	25¢ green ('65)	.70	.20 ☐☐☐☐☐
1059b	A495	Tagged ('73)	.70	.10 ☐☐☐☐☐
1954					
1060	A507	3¢ violet	.10	.05 ☐☐☐☐☐
1061	A508	3¢ brown orange	.10	.05 ☐☐☐☐☐
1062	A509	3¢ violet brown	.10	.05 ☐☐☐☐☐
1063	A510	3¢ violet brown	.10	.05 ☐☐☐☐☐
1955					
1064	A511	3¢ violet brown	.10	.05 ☐☐☐☐☐
1065	A512	3¢ green	.10	.05 ☐☐☐☐☐
1066	A513	8¢ deep blue	.20	.12 ☐☐☐☐☐
1067	A514	3¢ purple	.10	.05 ☐☐☐☐☐
1068	A515	3¢ green	.10	.05 ☐☐☐☐☐
1069	A516	3¢ blue	.10	.05 ☐☐☐☐☐
1070	A517	3¢ deep blue	.15	.05 ☐☐☐☐☐
1071	A518	3¢ light brown	.10	.05 ☐☐☐☐☐
1072	A519	3¢ rose carmine	.10	.05 ☐☐☐☐☐
1956					
1073	A520	3¢ bright carmine	.10	.05 ☐☐☐☐☐
1074	A521	3¢ deep blue	.10	.05 ☐☐☐☐☐
1075	A522	Sheet of two	6.00	3.50 ☐☐☐☐☐
1075a		3c deep violet, Type A482	1.35	.80 ☐☐☐☐☐
1075b		8c dark violet blue & carmine, Type A488	1.75	1.10 ☐☐☐☐☐
1076	A523	3¢ deep violet	.10	.05 ☐☐☐☐☐
1077	A524	3¢ rose lake	.12	.05 ☐☐☐☐☐
1078	A525	3¢ brown	.12	.05 ☐☐☐☐☐
1079	A526	3¢ blue green	.12	.05 ☐☐☐☐☐
1080	A527	3¢ dark blue green	.10	.05 ☐☐☐☐☐
1081	A528	3¢ black brown	.10	.05 ☐☐☐☐☐
1082	A529	3¢ deep blue	.10	.05 ☐☐☐☐☐
1083	A530	3¢ *orange*	.10	.05 ☐☐☐☐☐
1084	A531	3¢ violet	.10	.05 ☐☐☐☐☐
1085	A532	3¢ dark blue	.10	.05 ☐☐☐☐☐
1957					
1086	A533	3¢ rose red	.10	.05 ☐☐☐☐☐
1087	A534	3¢ red lilac	.10	.05 ☐☐☐☐☐
1088	A535	3¢ dark blue	.10	.05 ☐☐☐☐☐
1089	A536	3¢ red lilac	.10	.05 ☐☐☐☐☐
1090	A537	3¢ bright ultramarine	.10	.05 ☐☐☐☐☐
1091	A538	3¢ blue green	.10	.05 ☐☐☐☐☐
1092	A539	3¢ dark blue	.18	.05 ☐☐☐☐☐
1093	A540	3¢ rose lake	.10	.05 ☐☐☐☐☐

A491a

A492

A493

A494

A495

A496

A497

A498

A499

A500

A507

A509

A508

A510

A511

A512

A513

A514

Scott® No.	Illus No.	Description	Unused Price	Used Price	//////
1957					
1094	A541	4¢ dark blue & deep carmine	.10	.05	□□□□□
1095	A542	3¢ deep violet	.10	.05	□□□□□
1096	A543	8¢ carmine, ultramarine & ochre	.22	.15	□□□□□
1097	A544	3¢ rose lake	.10	.05	□□□□□
1098	A545	3¢ blue, ochre & green	.10	.05	□□□□□
1099	A546	3¢ black	.10	.05	□□□□□
1958					
1100	A547	3¢ green	.10	.05	□□□□□
1104	A551	3¢ deep claret	.10	.05	□□□□□
1105	A552	3¢ purple	.10	.05	□□□□□
1106	A553	3¢ green	.10	.05	□□□□□
1107	A554	3¢ black & red orange	.15	.05	□□□□□
1108	A555	3¢ light green	.10	.05	□□□□□
1109	A556	3¢ bright greenish blue	.10	.05	□□□□□
1110	A557	4¢ olive bistre	.10	.05	□□□□□
1111	A557	8¢ carmine, ultramarine & ochre	.25	.15	□□□□□
1112	A558	4¢ reddish purple	.10	.05	□□□□□
1958-59					
1113	A559	1¢ green ('59)	.05	.05	□□□□□
1114	A560	3¢ purple ('59)	.10	.06	□□□□□
1115	A561	4¢ sepia	.10	.05	□□□□□
1116	A562	4¢ dark blue ('59)	.10	.05	□□□□□
1958					
1117	A563	4¢ green	.10	.05	□□□□□
1118	A563	8¢ carmine, ultramarine & ochre	.22	.12	□□□□□
1119	A564	4¢ black	.10	.05	□□□□□
1120	A565	4¢ carmine rose	.10	.05	□□□□□
1121	A566	4¢ dark carmine rose	.10	.05	□□□□□
1122	A567	4¢ green, yellow & brown	.10	.05	□□□□□
1123	A568	4¢ blue	.10	.05	□□□□□
1959					
1124	A569	4¢ blue green	.10	.05	□□□□□
1125	A570	4¢ blue	.10	.05	□□□□□
1126	A570	8¢ carmine, ultramarine & ochre	.20	.12	□□□□□
1127	A571	4¢ blue	.10	.05	□□□□□
1128	A572	4¢ bright greenish blue	.13	.05	□□□□□
1129	A573	8¢ rose lake	.20	.12	□□□□□
1130	A574	4¢ black	.10	.05	□□□□□
1131	A575	4¢ red & dark blue	.10	.05	□□□□□
1132	A576	4¢ ochre, dark blue & deep carmine	.10	.05	□□□□□
1133	A577	4¢ blue, green & ochre	.10	.05	□□□□□

A516

A515

A517

A518

A519

A520

A521

Souvenir Sheet.

A523

A522

A524

A525

A526

A527

A528

84

Scott® No.	Illus No.	Description	Unused Price	Used Price	//////
1959					
1134	A578	4¢ brown	.10	.05 ☐☐☐☐☐
1135	A579	4¢ green	.10	.05 ☐☐☐☐☐
1136	A580	4¢ gray	.10	.05 ☐☐☐☐☐
1137	A580	8¢ carmine, ultramarine & ochre	.20	.12 ☐☐☐☐☐
1138	A581	4¢ rose lake	.10	.05 ☐☐☐☐☐
1960-61					
1139	A582	4¢ dark violet blue & carmine	.18	.05 ☐☐☐☐☐
1140	A583	4¢ olive bistre & green	.18	.05 ☐☐☐☐☐
1141	A584	4¢ gray & verm.	.18	.05 ☐☐☐☐☐
1142	A585	4¢ carmine & dark blue	.18	.05 ☐☐☐☐☐
1143	A586	4¢ magenta & green	.18	.05 ☐☐☐☐☐
1144	A587	4¢ green & brown ('61)	.18	.05 ☐☐☐☐☐
1960					
1145	A588	4¢ red, dark blue & dark bistre	.10	.05 ☐☐☐☐☐
1146	A589	4¢ dull blue	.10	.05 ☐☐☐☐☐
1147	A590	4¢ blue	.10	.05 ☐☐☐☐☐
1148	A590	8¢ carmine, ultramarine & ochre	.20	.12 ☐☐☐☐☐
1149	A591	4¢ gray black	.10	.05 ☐☐☐☐☐
1150	A592	4¢ dark blue, brown orange & green	.10	.05 ☐☐☐☐☐
1151	A593	4¢ blue	.10	.05 ☐☐☐☐☐
1152	A594	4¢ deep violet	.10	.05 ☐☐☐☐☐
1153	A595	4¢ dark blue & red	.10	.05 ☐☐☐☐☐
1154	A596	4¢ sepia	.10	.05 ☐☐☐☐☐
1155	A597	4¢ dark blue	.10	.05 ☐☐☐☐☐
1156	A598	4¢ green	.10	.05 ☐☐☐☐☐
1157	A599	4¢ green & rose red	.10	.05 ☐☐☐☐☐
1158	A600	4¢ blue & pink	.10	.05 ☐☐☐☐☐
1159	A601	4¢ blue	.10	.05 ☐☐☐☐☐
1160	A601	8¢ carmine, ultramarine & ochre	.20	.12 ☐☐☐☐☐
1161	A602	4¢ dull violet	.10	.05 ☐☐☐☐☐
1162	A603	4¢ dark blue	.10	.05 ☐☐☐☐☐
1163	A604	4¢ indigo, slate & rose red	.10	.05 ☐☐☐☐☐
1164	A605	4¢ dark blue & carmine	.10	.05 ☐☐☐☐☐
1165	A606	4¢ blue	.10	.05 ☐☐☐☐☐
1166	A606	8¢ carmine, ultra. & ochre	.20	.12 ☐☐☐☐☐
1167	A607	4¢ dark blue & bright red	.10	.05 ☐☐☐☐☐
1168	A608	4¢ green	.10	.05 ☐☐☐☐☐
1169	A608	8¢ carmine, ultra. & ochre	.20	.12 ☐☐☐☐☐
1170	A609	4¢ dull violet	.10	.05 ☐☐☐☐☐
1171	A610	4¢ deep claret	.10	.05 ☐☐☐☐☐
1172	A611	4¢ dull violet	.10	.05 ☐☐☐☐☐

A529

A530

A531

A532

A534

A533

A535

A537

A536

A538

A539

A540

A541

A542

A543

A544

86

A545

A546

A547

A551

A552

A553

A554

A555

A556

A557

A558

A559

A561

A560

A562

A564

A563

A565

A566

A568

A567

A569

A570

A572

A571

A573

A574

A578

A575

A577

A576

A580

A579

A581

The UNITED STATES
Observe good
faith and justice
toward all nations
G. Washington
AMERICA
Credo

A582

The UNITED STATES
Fear to do ill,
and you need fear
Nought else.
AMERICA
Credo

A583

The UNITED STATES
I have sworn
Hostility against every
form of TYRANNY
over the mind of man
Th. Jefferson
AMERICA
Credo

A584

VIII OLYMPIC
WINTER GAMES
CALIFORNIA 1960
4c
UNITED STATES POSTAGE

A589

The UNITED STATES
And this be our
Motto, in GOD
is our TRUST
F.S. Key
AMERICA
Credo

A585

The UNITED STATES
Those who Deny
freedom to others
Deserve it not
for Themselves.
A. Lincoln
AMERICA
Credo

A586

The UNITED STATES
Give me
LIBERTY
or give me
DEATH
P. Henry
AMERICA
Credo

A587

BOY SCOUTS OF AMERICA
1910 · 1960
U·S·POSTAGE
4c

A588

CHAMPION OF LIBERTY
4c
UNITED STATES POSTAGE

A590

WORLD REFUGEE YEAR
UNITED STATES POSTAGE

A591

WATER CONSERVATION
UNITED STATES POSTAGE
4c

A592

SEATO
UNITY
PEACE
PROGRESS
4c U.S. POSTAGE

A593

THE AMERICAN WOMAN
U.S.POSTAGE
4c

A594

JULY 4, 1960
4c
U.S. POSTAGE

A595

1860-1960 PONY EXPRESS
UNITED STATES POSTAGE
4c

A596

EMPLOY THE HANDICAPPED
4c
UNITED STATES POSTAGE

A597

89

A598

A599

A600

A604

A608

A603

A601

A613

A605

A606

A602

A609

A610

A611

A612

A607

A614

1960

1173	A612	4¢ deep violet	.55	.12 □□□□□

1961

1174	A613	4¢ red orange	.10	.05 □□□□□
1175	A613	8¢ carmine, ultra. & ochre	.20	.12 □□□□□
1176	A614	4¢ blue, slate & brown orange	.10	.05 □□□□□
1177	A615	4¢ dull violet	.10	.05 □□□□□

1961-65

1178	A616	4¢ light green	.18	.05 □□□□□
1179	A617	4¢ *peach blossom* ('62)	.15	.05 □□□□□
1180	A618	5¢ gray & blue ('63)	.15	.05 □□□□□
1181	A619	5¢ dk. red & blk. ('64)	.15	.05 □□□□□
1182	A620	5¢ Prussian bl. & black ('65)	.18	.05 □□□□□

1961

1183	A621	4¢ brown, dark red & green, *yellow*	.10	.05 □□□□□
1184	A622	4¢ blue green	.10	.05 □□□□□
1185	A623	4¢ blue	.10	.05 □□□□□
1186	A624	4¢ ultramarine, *grayish*	.10	.05 □□□□□
1187	A625	4¢ multicolored	.15	.05 □□□□□
1188	A626	4¢ blue	.10	.05 □□□□□
1189	A627	4¢ brown	.10	.05 □□□□□
1190	A628	4¢ blue, green, orange & black	.10	.05 □□□□□

1962

1191	A629	4¢ lt. blue, maroon & bistre	.10	.05 □□□□□
1192	A630	4¢ carmine, violet blue & green	.16	.05 □□□□□
1193	A631	4¢ dk. blue & yel.	.20	.10 □□□□□
1194	A632	4¢ blue & bistre	.10	.05 □□□□□
1195	A633	4¢ *buff*	.10	.05 □□□□□
1196	A634	4¢ red & dk. blue	.10	.05 □□□□□
1197	A635	4¢ blue, dk. slate green & red	.10	.05 □□□□□
1198	A636	4¢ slate	.10	.05 □□□□□
1199	A637	4¢ rose red	.10	.05 □□□□□
1200	A638	4¢ violet	.15	.05 □□□□□
1201	A639	4¢ *yellow bister*	.10	.05 □□□□□
1202	A640	4¢ dk. bl. & red brn.	.10	.05 □□□□□
1203	A641	4¢ blk., brn. & yel.	.12	.05 □□□□□
1204	A641	4¢ blk., brn. & yellow (yel. inverted)	.18	.08 □□□□□
1205	A642	4¢ green & red	.10	.03 □□□□□
1206	A643	4¢ blue grn. & blk.	.10	.05 □□□□□
1207	A644	4¢ multicolored	.15	.05 □□□□□

1963-66

1208	A645	5¢ blue & red	.12	.03 □□□□□
1208a	A645	Tagged ('66)	.20	.05 □□□□□

1962-66   *Perf. 11x10½*

1209	A646	1¢ green ('63)	.05	.03 □□□□□

A616

A615

A617

A618

A619

A621

A622

A620

A623

A624

A625

A626

A627

A628

A629

A631

A630

A633

A632

A634

A637

A636

A640

A638

A635

A639

A642

A645

A663

A646

A650

A644

A643

A641

A662

A664

A665

A666

A667

A668

A669

A670

A671

A675

A670

A676

A680

A672

A678

A679

A673

A677

A674

A681

A682

94

Scott® No.	Illus No.	Description	Unused Price	Used Price	//////
1962-66					
1209a	A646	Tagged ('66)	.06	.05 ☐☐☐☐☐
1213	A650	5¢ dk. blue gray	.12	.03 ☐☐☐☐☐
1213a	A650	Bklt. pane 5+ label	2.00	.75 ☐☐☐☐☐
1213b	A650	Tagged ('63)	.50	.30 ☐☐☐☐☐
1213c	A650	As 'a,' tagged ('63)	1.25	.50 ☐☐☐☐☐
		Coil Stamps *Perf. 10 Vertically*			
1225	A646	1¢ green ('63)	.12	.03 ☐☐☐☐☐
1225a	A646	Tagged ('66)	.18	.05 ☐☐☐☐☐
1229	A650	5¢ dk. blue gray	.50	.03 ☐☐☐☐☐
1229a	A650	Tagged ('63)	.75	.06 ☐☐☐☐☐
1963					
1230	A662	5¢ dk. car. & brown	.12	.05 ☐☐☐☐☐
1231	A663	5¢ green, buff & red	.12	.05 ☐☐☐☐☐
1232	A664	5¢ grn., red & blk.	.12	.05 ☐☐☐☐☐
1233	A665	5¢ dk. blue, black & red	.12	.05 ☐☐☐☐☐
1234	A666	5¢ ultra. & green	.12	.05 ☐☐☐☐☐
1235	A667	5¢ blue green	.12	.05 ☐☐☐☐☐
1236	A668	5¢ bright purple	.12	.05 ☐☐☐☐☐
1237	A669	5¢ Pruss. bl. & blk.	.20	.05 ☐☐☐☐☐
1238	A670	5¢ gray, dk. blue & red	.12	.05 ☐☐☐☐☐
1239	A671	5¢ bluish blk. & red	.12	.05 ☐☐☐☐☐
1240	A672	5¢ dk. bl., bluish blk. & red	.12	.03 ☐☐☐☐☐
1240a	A672	Tagged	1.00	.40 ☐☐☐☐☐
1241	A673	5¢ dark blue & multicolored	.15	.05 ☐☐☐☐☐
1964					
1242	A674	5¢ black	.12	.05 ☐☐☐☐☐
1243	A675	5¢ indigo, red brn. & olive	.15	.05 ☐☐☐☐☐
1244	A676	5¢ blue green	.15	.05 ☐☐☐☐☐
1245	A677	5¢ brn., grn., yel. grn. & olive	.12	.05 ☐☐☐☐☐
1246	A678	5¢ blue gray	.12	.05 ☐☐☐☐☐
1247	A679	5¢ bright ultra.	.12	.05 ☐☐☐☐☐
1248	A680	5¢ red, yellow & blue	.12	.05 ☐☐☐☐☐
1249	A681	5¢ dk. blue & red	.12	.05 ☐☐☐☐☐
1250	A682	5¢ blk. brown, *tan*	.12	.05 ☐☐☐☐☐
1251	A683	5¢ green	.12	.05 ☐☐☐☐☐
1252	A684	5¢ red, black & bl.	.12	.05 ☐☐☐☐☐
1253	A685	5¢ multicolored	.12	.05 ☐☐☐☐☐
1254	A686	5¢ grn., car. & blk.	1.00	.05 ☐☐☐☐☐
1254a	A686	Tagged	1.50	.50 ☐☐☐☐☐
1255	A687	5¢ car., grn. & blk.	1.00	.05 ☐☐☐☐☐
1255a	A687	Tagged	1.50	.50 ☐☐☐☐☐
1256	A688	5¢ car., grn. & blk.	1.00	.05 ☐☐☐☐☐
1256a	A688	Tagged	1.50	.50 ☐☐☐☐☐
1257	A689	5¢ blk., grn. & car.	1.00	.05 ☐☐☐☐☐
1257a	A689	Tagged	1.50	.50 ☐☐☐☐☐

A684

A683

A685

A686

A687

A688

A689

A690

A691

A692

A696

A694

A695

A697

A693

A698

Scott® No.	Illus No.	Description	Unused Price	Used Price	/ / / / / /
1964					
1257b		Block of 4, # 1254-1257	4.50	.40 ☐☐☐☐☐
1257c		Block of 4, tagged	6.50	3.00 ☐☐☐☐☐
1258	A690	5¢ blue green	.12	.05 ☐☐☐☐☐
1259	A691	5¢ ultra. black & dull red	.12	.05 ☐☐☐☐☐
1260	A692	5¢ red lilac	.12	.05 ☐☐☐☐☐
1965					
1261	A693	5¢ dp. carm., vio. blue & gray	.12	.05 ☐☐☐☐☐
1262	A694	5¢ maroon & black	.12	.05 ☐☐☐☐☐
1263	A695	5¢ black, purple & red orange	.12	.05 ☐☐☐☐☐
1264	A696	5¢ black	.12	.05 ☐☐☐☐☐
1265	A697	5¢ blk., yel. ocher & red lilac	.12	.05 ☐☐☐☐☐
1266	A698	5¢ dull bl. & blk.	.12	.05 ☐☐☐☐☐
1267	A699	5¢ red, black & dark blue	.12	.05 ☐☐☐☐☐
1268	A700	5¢ maroon, *tan*	.12	.05 ☐☐☐☐☐
1269	A701	5¢ rose red	.12	.05 ☐☐☐☐☐
1270	A702	5¢ black & blue	.12	.05 ☐☐☐☐☐
1271	A703	5¢ red, yel. & blk.	.12	.05 ☐☐☐☐☐
1272	A704	5¢ emerald, black & red	.12	.05 ☐☐☐☐☐
1273	A705	5¢ blk, brn. & olive	.18	.05 ☐☐☐☐☐
1274	A706	11¢ black, carmine & bister	.45	.16 ☐☐☐☐☐
1275	A707	5¢ pale blue, black, car. & vio. blue	.12	.05 ☐☐☐☐☐
1276	A708	5¢ car., dk. olive green & bister	.12	.03 ☐☐☐☐☐
1276a	A708	Tagged	.50	.15 ☐☐☐☐☐
1965-78		*Perf. 11x10½, 10½x11*			
1278	A710	1¢ green, tagged ('68)	.03	.03 ☐☐☐☐☐
1278a	A710	Booklet pane of 8 ('68)	1.00	.25 ☐☐☐☐☐
1278b	A710	Bklt. pane of 4 + 2 labels ('71)	.75	.20 ☐☐☐☐☐
1278c	A710	Untagged (Bureau precanceled)		.07 ☐☐☐☐☐
1279	A711	1¼ lt. green ('67)	.20	.05 ☐☐☐☐☐
1280	A712	2¢ dk. blue gray, tagged ('66)	.04	.03 ☐☐☐☐☐
1280a	A712	Booklet pane of 5 + label ('68)	1.20	.40 ☐☐☐☐☐
1280b	A712	Untagged (Bureau precanceled)		.10 ☐☐☐☐☐
1280c	A712	Booklet pane of 6 ('71)	1.00	.35 ☐☐☐☐☐
1281	A713	3¢ violet, tagged ('67)	.06	.03 ☐☐☐☐☐
1281a	A713	Untagged (Bureau precanceled)		.12 ☐☐☐☐☐
1282	A714	4¢ black	.08	.03 ☐☐☐☐☐
1282a	A714	Tagged	.08	.03 ☐☐☐☐☐
1283	A715	5¢ blue ('66)	.10	.03 ☐☐☐☐☐
1283a	A715	Tagged ('66)	.10	.03 ☐☐☐☐☐

A700

A706

A701

A703

A702

A705

A704

A708

A707

A699

A710

A711

A712

A713

A714

A715

A715a
Redrawn

A716

A717

Scott® No.	Illus No.	Description	Unused Price	Used Price	//////
1965-78					
1283B	A715a	5¢ blue, tagged ('67)	.12	.03 □□□□□
1283d	A715a	Untagged (Bureau precanceled)		.15 □□□□□
1284	A716	6¢ gray brown ('66)	.12	.03 □□□□□
1284a	A716	Tagged ('66)	.12	.03 □□□□□
1284b	A716	Booklet pane of 8 ('67)	1.50	.50 □□□□□
1284c	A716	Booklet pane of 5 + label ('68)	1.25	.50 □□□□□
1285	A717	8¢ violet ('66)	.16	.05 □□□□□
1285a	A717	Tagged ('66)	.16	.04 □□□□□
1286	A718	10¢ lilac, tagged ('67)	.20	.03 □□□□□
1286b	A718	Untagged (Bureau precanceled)		.20 □□□□□
1286A	A718a	12¢ black, tagged ('68)	.24	.03 □□□□□
1286c	A718a	Untagged (Bureau precanceled)		.25 □□□□□
1287	A719	13¢ brown, tagged ('67)	.26	.05 □□□□□
1287a	A719	Untagged (Bureau precanceled)		.25 □□□□□
1288	A720	15¢ rose claret, tagged ('68)	.30	.06 □□□□□
1288a	A720	Untagged (Bureau precanceled)		.30 □□□□□
		Perf. 10			
1288B	A720	15c dk. rose claret (from bklt. pane) ('78)	.30	.05 □□□□□
1288c	A720	Booklet pane of 8	2.40	□□□□□
		Perf. 11x10½, 10½x11			
1289	A721	20¢ dp. olive ('67)	.40	.06 □□□□□
1289a	A721	Tagged ('73)	.40	.06 □□□□□
1290	A722	25¢ rose lake ('67)	.50	.03 □□□□□
1290a	A722	Tagged ('73)	.50	.03 □□□□□
1291	A723	30¢ red lilac ('68)	.60	.08 □□□□□
1291a	A723	Tagged ('73)	.60	.06 □□□□□
1292	A724	40¢ bl. black ('68)	.80	.10 □□□□□
1292a	A724	Tagged ('73)	.80	.08 □□□□□
1293	A725	50¢ rose magenta ('68)	1.00	.04 □□□□□
1293a	A725	Tagged ('73)	1.00	.04 □□□□□
1294	A726	$1 dull purple ('67)	2.00	.08 □□□□□
1294a	A726	Tagged ('73)	2.00	.08 □□□□□
1295	A727	$5 gray black ('66)	10.00	2.00 □□□□□
1295a	A727	Tagged ('73)	10.00	2.00 □□□□□
1966-78		Coil Stamps Tagged *Perf. 10 Horiz.*			
1297	A713	3¢ violet ('75)	.06	.03 □□□□□
1297b	A713	Untagged (Bureau precanceled)		.12 □□□□□
1298	A716	6¢ gray brown ('67)	.40	.05 □□□□□

A718

A718a

A719

A720

A721

A723

A722

A724

A725

A726

A727

A727a

A730

A732

A731

A728

A729

A734

A733

A735

Scott® No.	Illus No.	Description	Unused Price	Used Price	//////
1966-78		*Perf. 10 Vertically*			
1299	A710	1¢ green ('68)	.06	.03 ☐☐☐☐☐
1299a	A710	Untagged (Bureau precanceled)		.07 ☐☐☐☐☐
1303	A714	4¢ black	.15	.03 ☐☐☐☐☐
1303a	A714	Untagged (Bureau precanceled)		.15 ☐☐☐☐☐
1304	A715	5¢ blue	.15	.03 ☐☐☐☐☐
1304a	A715	Untagged (Bureau precanceled)		.15 ☐☐☐☐☐
1305	A727a	6¢ gray brown ('68)	.20	.03 ☐☐☐☐☐
1305b	A727a	Untagged (Bureau precanceled)		.20 ☐☐☐☐☐
1305C	A726	$1 dull purple ('73)	2.25	.20 ☐☐☐☐☐
1966					
1306	A728	5¢ black, crimson & dark blue	.15	.05 ☐☐☐☐☐
1307	A729	5¢ org. brn. & blk.	.15	.05 ☐☐☐☐☐
1308	A730	5¢ yellow, ocher & violet blue	.12	.05 ☐☐☐☐☐
1309	A731	5¢ multicolored	.12	.05 ☐☐☐☐☐
1310	A732	5¢ multicolored	.12	.05 ☐☐☐☐☐
1311	A733	5¢ multicolored	.40	.15 ☐☐☐☐☐
1312	A734	5¢ car., dk. & lt. bl.	.12	.05 ☐☐☐☐☐
1313	A735	5¢ red	.15	.05 ☐☐☐☐☐
1314	A736	5¢ yel., blk. & grn.	.12	.05 ☐☐☐☐☐
1314a	A736	Tagged	.30	.15 ☐☐☐☐☐
1315	A737	5¢ blk., bister, red & ultra	.12	.05 ☐☐☐☐☐
1315a	A737	Tagged	.30	.15 ☐☐☐☐☐
1316	A738	5¢ blk., pink & blue	.12	.05 ☐☐☐☐☐
1316a	A738	Tagged	.30	.15 ☐☐☐☐☐
1317	A739	5¢ grn., red & black	.12	.05 ☐☐☐☐☐
1317a	A739	Tagged	.30	.15 ☐☐☐☐☐
1318	A740	5¢ emerald, pink & black	.15	.05 ☐☐☐☐☐
1318a	A740	Tagged	.30	.15 ☐☐☐☐☐
1319	A741	5¢ verm., yel., blue & green	.12	.05 ☐☐☐☐☐
1319a	A741	Tagged	.30	.15 ☐☐☐☐☐
1320	A742	5¢ red, dk. blue, lt. blue & black	.12	.05 ☐☐☐☐☐
1320a	A742	Tagged	.30	.15 ☐☐☐☐☐
1321	A743	5¢ multicolored	.12	.03 ☐☐☐☐☐
1321a	A743	Tagged	.25	.10 ☐☐☐☐☐
1322	A744	5¢ multicolored	.20	.05 ☐☐☐☐☐
1322a	A744	Tagged	.45	.15 ☐☐☐☐☐
1967					
1323	A745	5¢ multicolored	.12	.05 ☐☐☐☐☐
1324	A746	5¢ multicolored	.12	.05 ☐☐☐☐☐
1325	A747	5¢ multicolored	.12	.05 ☐☐☐☐☐
1326	A748	5¢ bl., red & black	.12	.05 ☐☐☐☐☐

A737

A736

A738

A739

A741

A743

A745

A740

A747

A744

A742

A746

A749

A748

A751

A750

A752

Scott® No.	Illus No.	Denom	Description	Unused Price	Used Price	//////
1967						
1327	A749	5¢	red, blk. & grn.	.12	.05 □□□□□
1328	A750	5¢	dk. red brown, lemon & yel.	.12	.05 □□□□□
1329	A751	5¢	red, blue, black & carmine	.12	.05 □□□□□
1330	A752	5¢	grn., blk. & yel.	.12	.05 □□□□□
1331	A753	5¢	multicolored	1.75	.25 □□□□□
1331a			Pair, # 1331-1332	5.50	2.00 □□□□□
1332	A754	5¢	multicolored	1.75	.25 □□□□□
1333	A755	5¢	dark blue, light blue & black	.15	.05 □□□□□
1334	A756	5¢	blue	.15	.05 □□□□□
1335	A757	5¢	gold & multi.	.18	.05 □□□□□
1336	A758	5¢	multicolored	.12	.04 □□□□□
1337	A759	5¢	brt. greenish bl., grn. & red brn.	.15	.05 □□□□□
1968-71			*Perf. 11*			
1338	A760	6¢	dk. blue, red & green	.12	.03 □□□□□
			Perf. 11x10½			
1338D	A760	6¢	dk. blue, red & green ('70)	.12	.03 □□□□□
1338F	A760	8¢	multi. ('71)	.16	.03 □□□□□
1969-71			*Coil stamps Perf. 10 Vert.*			
1338A	A760	6¢	dk. blue, red & green	.12	.03 □□□□□
1338G	A760	8¢	multi. ('71)	.16	.03 □□□□□
1968						
1339	A761	6¢	multicolored	.18	.05 □□□□□
1340	A762	6¢	blue, rose red & white	.18	.05 □□□□□
1341	A763	$1	sepia, dk. blue, ocher & brown red	3.75	2.00 □□□□□
1342	A764	6¢	ultra. & org. red	.18	.05 □□□□□
1343	A765	6¢	chalky blue, black & red	.18	.05 □□□□□
1344	A766	6¢	blk., yel. & org.	.18	.05 □□□□□
1345	A767	6¢	dark blue	.80	.35 □□□□□
1346	A768	6¢	dk. blue & red	.80	.35 □□□□□
1347	A769	6¢	dark blue & olive green	.80	.35 □□□□□
1348	A770	6¢	dk. blue & red	.80	.35 □□□□□
1349	A771	6¢	dark blue, yellow & red	.80	.35 □□□□□
1350	A772	6¢	dk. blue & red	.80	.35 □□□□□
1351	A773	6¢	dk. blue, olive green & red	.80	.35 □□□□□
1352	A774	6¢	dk. blue & red	.80	.35 □□□□□
1353	A775	6¢	dk. blue, yellow & red	.80	.35 □□□□□
1354	A776	6¢	dark blue, red & yellow	.80	.35 □□□□□
1354a			Strip of 10, Nos. 1345-1354	10.00	6.50 □□□□□
1355	A777	6¢	multicolored	.20	.05 □□□□□
1356	A778	6¢	blk., apple grn. & org. brown	.20	.05 □□□□□
1357	A779	6¢	yellow, dp. yel., maroon & blk.	.20	.05 □□□□□

A753

A754

A755

A757

A756

A758

A759

A760

A761

A764

A762

A765

A769

A766

A763

6¢ U.S. POSTAGE — LIBERTY — FORT MOULTRIE FLAG 1776	6¢ U.S. POSTAGE — U.S. FLAG 1795-1818 (FT. McHENRY FLAG)	6¢ U.S. POSTAGE — 76 — BENNINGTON FLAG 1777
A767	**A768**	**A770**

6¢ U.S. POSTAGE — HOPE — RHODE ISLAND FLAG 1775	6¢ U.S. POSTAGE — FIRST STARS AND STRIPES 1777	6¢ U.S. POSTAGE — BUNKER HILL FLAG 1776
A771	**A772**	**A773**

6¢ U.S. POSTAGE — GRAND UNION FLAG 1776	6¢ U.S. POSTAGE — PHILADELPHIA LIGHT HORSE FLAG 1775	6¢ U.S. POSTAGE — DONT TREAD ON ME — FIRST NAVY JACK 1775
A774	**A775**	**A776**

WALT DISNEY — UNITED STATES 6¢

A777

Marquette explores — 6¢ — UNITED STATES

A778

leif erikson — U.S. POSTAGE — 6¢

A781

UNITED STATES 6¢ — John Trumbull — AMERICAN PAINTER

A783

UNITED STATES 6¢ POSTAGE — DANIEL BOONE 1734

A779

UNITED STATES POSTAGE — 6¢ — ARKANSAS RIVER NAVIGATION

A780

CHRISTMAS 6¢ — NATIONAL GALLERY OF ART — UNITED STATES

A785

CHEROKEE STRIP — UNITED STATES POSTAGE 6¢

A782

Chief Joseph National Portrait Gallery — United States Postage 6¢

A786

WATERFOWL CONSERVATION — 6¢ — UNITED STATES

A784

105

A787

A788

A789

A790

A795

A791

A792

A793

A796

A794

A797

A798

A799

A800

A801

Scott® No.	Illus No.	Description	Unused Price	Used Price	/ / / / / /
1968					
1358	A780	6¢ brt. blue, dark blue & black	.20	.05 ☐☐☐☐☐
1359	A781	6¢ lt. gray brown & blk. brown	.20	.05 ☐☐☐☐☐
1360	A782	6¢ brown	.20	.05 ☐☐☐☐☐
1361	A783	6¢ multicolored	.25	.05 ☐☐☐☐☐
1362	A784	6¢ black & multi.	.30	.05 ☐☐☐☐☐
1363	A785	6¢ multicolored	.20	.04 ☐☐☐☐☐
1363a	A785	Untagged	.20	.04 ☐☐☐☐☐
1364	A786	6¢ black & multi.	.30	.05 ☐☐☐☐☐
1969					
1365	A787	6¢ multicolored	2.00	.15 ☐☐☐☐☐
1366	A788	6¢ multicolored	2.00	.15 ☐☐☐☐☐
1367	A789	6¢ multicolored	2.00	.15 ☐☐☐☐☐
1368	A790	6¢ multicolored	2.00	.15 ☐☐☐☐☐
1368a		Block of 4, # 1365-1368	8.50	2.50 ☐☐☐☐☐
1369	A791	6¢ red, blue & black	.20	.05 ☐☐☐☐☐
1370	A792	6¢ multicolored	.25	.05 ☐☐☐☐☐
1371	A793	6¢ blk., bl. & ocher	.30	.06 ☐☐☐☐☐
1372	A794	6¢ multicolored	.20	.05 ☐☐☐☐☐
1373	A795	6¢ multicolored	.20	.05 ☐☐☐☐☐
1374	A796	6¢ multicolored	.20	.05 ☐☐☐☐☐
1375	A797	6¢ multicolored	.20	.05 ☐☐☐☐☐
1376	A798	6¢ multicolored	2.75	.15 ☐☐☐☐☐
1377	A799	6¢ multicolored	2.75	.15 ☐☐☐☐☐
1378	A800	6¢ multicolored	2.75	.15 ☐☐☐☐☐
1379	A801	6¢ multicolored	2.75	.15 ☐☐☐☐☐
1379a		Block of 4, # 1376-1379	12.00	2.50 ☐☐☐☐☐
1380	A802	6¢ green	.20	.05 ☐☐☐☐☐
1381	A803	6¢ yellow, red, black & green	.25	.05 ☐☐☐☐☐
1382	A804	6¢ red & green	.25	.05 ☐☐☐☐☐
1383	A805	6¢ blue, black & red	.20	.05 ☐☐☐☐☐
1384	A806	6¢ dk. grn. & multi.	.18	.03 ☐☐☐☐☐
1384a	A806	Precanceled	.30	.06 ☐☐☐☐☐
1385	A807	6¢ multicolored	.18	.05 ☐☐☐☐☐
1386	A808	6¢ multicolored	.18	.05 ☐☐☐☐☐
1970					
1387	A809	6¢ multicolored	.30	.12 ☐☐☐☐☐
1388	A810	6¢ multicolored	.30	.12 ☐☐☐☐☐
1389	A811	6¢ multicolored	.30	.12 ☐☐☐☐☐
1390	A812	6¢ multicolored	.30	.12 ☐☐☐☐☐
1390a		Block of 4, # 1387-1390	1.35	.75 ☐☐☐☐☐
1391	A813	6¢ black & multi.	.18	.05 ☐☐☐☐☐
1392	A814	6¢ *light brown*	.18	.05 ☐☐☐☐☐
1970-74		*Perf. 11x10½, 10½x11; 11 (#1394)*		**Tagged**
1393	A815	6¢ dk. blue gray	.12	.03 ☐☐☐☐☐
1393a	A815	Booklet pane of 8	1.00	.50 ☐☐☐☐☐

A802

A803

A807

A806

A804

A805

A808

AMERICAN BALD EAGLE

A809

AFRICAN ELEPHANT HERD

A810

HAIDA CEREMONIAL CANOE

A811

THE AGE OF REPTILES

A812

A813

A814

EISENHOWER·USA
Dot between "R"
and "U"
A815

EISENHOWER USA
No dot between
"R" and "U"
A815a

A816

A817

A817a

A818

A818a

A818b

A820

A819

A821

A822

A823

A824

A825

A826

A827

A828

A829

A830

A831

A832

A835

A836

A833

A834

A837

A838

A839

A840

Scott® No.	Illus No.	Description	Unused Price	Used Price	/ / / / / /
1970-74					
1393b	A815	Booklet pane of 5 + label	.85	.35 □□□□□
1393c	A815	Untagged (Bureau precanceled)		.10 □□□□□
1393D	A816	7¢ brt. blue ('72)	.14	.03 □□□□□
1393e	A816	Untagged (Bureau precanceled)		.10 □□□□□
1394	A815a	8¢ black, red & blue gray ('71)	.16	.03 □□□□□
1395	A815	8¢ dp. claret ('71)	.16	.03 □□□□□
1395a	A815	Booklet pane of 8	1.50	1.25 □□□□□
1395b	A815	Booklet pane of 6	1.00	.75 □□□□□
1395c	A815	Booklet pane of 4 + 2 labels ('72)	1.00	.50 □□□□□
1395d	A815	Booklet pane of 7 + label ('72)	1.25	1.00 □□□□□
1396	A817	8¢ multi. ('71)	.25	.03 □□□□□
1397	A817a	14¢ gray brown ('72)	.28	.03 □□□□□
1397a	A817a	Untagged (Bureau precanceled)		.25 □□□□□
1398	A818	16¢ brown ('71)	.32	.03 □□□□□
1398a	A818	Untagged (Bureau precanceled)		.25 □□□□□
1399	A818a	18¢ violet ('74)	.36	.06 □□□□□
1400	A818b	21¢ green ('73)	.42	.06 □□□□□
		Coil Stamps; *Perf. 10 Vert.*			
1401	A815	6¢ dark blue gray	.20	.03 □□□□□
1401a	A815	Untagged (Bureau precanceled)		.10 □□□□□
1402	A815	8¢ deep claret ('71)	.22	.03 □□□□□
1402b	A815	Untagged (Bureau precanceled)		.10 □□□□□
1970					
1405	A819	6¢ blk. & olive bister	.18	.05 □□□□□
1406	A820	6¢ blue	.18	.05 □□□□□
1407	A821	6¢ bis., black & red	.18	.05 □□□□□
1408	A822	6¢ gray	.18	.05 □□□□□
1409	A823	6¢ yellow & multi.	.18	.05 □□□□□
1410	A824	6¢ multicolored	.85	.13 □□□□□
1411	A825	6¢ multicolored	.85	.13 □□□□□
1412	A826	6¢ multicolored	.85	.13 □□□□□
1413	A827	6¢ multicolored	.85	.13 □□□□□
1413a	A827	Block of 4, # 1410-1413		□□□□□
1414	A828	6¢ multicolored	.20	.03 □□□□□
1414a	A828	Precanceled	.35	.08 □□□□□
1415	A829	6¢ multicolored	1.10	.10 □□□□□
1415a	A829	Precanceled	1.75	.15 □□□□□

A841

A842

A843

A844

A845

A846

A847

A848

A849

A850

A851

A852

A853

Scott® No.	Illus No.	Description	Unused Price	Used Price	////////
1970					
1416	A830	6¢ multicolored	1.10	.10 □□□□□
1416a	A830	Precanceled	1.75	.15 □□□□□
1417	A831	6¢ multicolored	1.10	.10 □□□□□
1417a	A831	Precanceled	1.75	.15 □□□□□
1418	A832	6¢ multicolored	1.10	.10 □□□□□
1418a	A832	Precanceled	1.75	.15 □□□□□
1418b		Block of 4, # 1415-1418	4.50	.90 □□□□□
1418c		As 'b,' precanceled	8.00	1.25 □□□□□
1419	A833	6¢ black, verm. & ultra.	.18	.05 □□□□□
1420	A834	6¢ black, orange, yellow, brown, magenta & blue	.18	.05 □□□□□
1421	A835	6¢ multicolored	.30	.10 □□□□□
1421a		Pair, # 1421-1422	.70	.30 □□□□□
1422	A836	6¢ dark blue, black & red	.30	.10 □□□□□
1971					
1423	A837	6¢ multicolored	.18	.05 □□□□□
1424	A838	6¢ black, red & dark blue	.18	.05 □□□□□
1425	A839	6¢ lt. blue, scarlet & indigo	.18	.05 □□□□□
1426	A840	8¢ multicolored	.20	.05 □□□□□
1427	A841	8¢ multicolored	.30	.10 □□□□□
1428	A842	8¢ multicolored	.30	.10 □□□□□
1429	A843	8¢ multicolored	.30	.10 □□□□□
1430	A844	8¢ multicolored	.30	.10 □□□□□
1430a		Block of 4, # 1427-1430	1.30	.85 □□□□□
1431	A845	8¢ red & dk. blue	.25	.05 □□□□□
1432	A846	8¢ red, blue, gray & black	.85	.05 □□□□□
1433	A847	8¢ multicolored	.22	.05 □□□□□
1434	A848	8¢ blk., bl., yel. & red	.25	.10 □□□□□
1434a		Pair, # 1434-1435	.60	.35 □□□□□
1435	A849	8¢ blk., bl., yel. & red	.25	.10 □□□□□
1436	A850	8¢ multi., *greenish*	.18	.05 □□□□□
1437	A851	8¢ multicolored		□□□□□
1438	A852	8¢ bl., dp. bl. & blk.	.18	.05 □□□□□
1439	A853	8¢ multicolored	.18	.05 □□□□□
1440	A854	8¢ blk. brn. & ocher	.28	.12 □□□□□
1441	A855	8¢ blk. brn. & ocher	.28	.12 □□□□□
1442	A856	8¢ blk. brn. & ocher	.28	.12 □□□□□
1443	A857	8¢ blk. brn. & ocher	.28	.12 □□□□□
1443a		Block of 4, # 1440-1443		□□□□□
1444	A858	8¢ gold & multi.	.18	.03 □□□□□
1445	A859	8¢ dk. green, red & multicolored	.18	.03 □□□□□
1972					
1446	A860	8¢ black, brown & light blue	.18	.05 □□□□□
1447	A861	8¢ dk. blue, lt. blue & red	.18	.05 □□□□□
1448	A862	2¢ black & multi.	.06	.06 □□□□□

A854

A855

A856

A857

A862

A863

A858

A864

A865

A860

A859

A867

A861

A866

A868

Scott® No.	Illus No.	Description	Unused Price	Used Price	//////
1972					
1449	A863	2¢ black & multi.	.06	.06 □□□□□
1450	A864	2¢ black & multi.	.06	.06 □□□□□
1451	A865	2¢ black & multi.	.06	.06 □□□□□
1451a		Block of 4, # 1448-1451	.25	.30 □□□□□
1452	A866	6¢ black & multi.	.16	.04 □□□□□
1453	A867	8¢ blk., blue, brn. & multi	.18	.05 □□□□□
1454	A868	15¢ black & multi.	.35	.22 □□□□□
1455	A869	8¢ black & multi.	.16	.05 □□□□□
1456	A870	8¢ deep brown	.30	.08 □□□□□
1457	A871	8¢ deep brown	.30	.08 □□□□□
1458	A872	8¢ deep brown	.30	.08 □□□□□
1459	A873	8¢ deep brown	.30	.08 □□□□□
1459a		Block of 4, # 1456-1459		□□□□□
1460	A874	6¢ multicolored	.12	.04 □□□□□
1461	A875	8¢ multicolored	.16	.05 □□□□□
1462	A876	15¢ multicolored	.30	.18 □□□□□
1463	A877	8¢ yellow & black	.16	.05 □□□□□
1464	A878	8¢ multicolored	.22	.08 □□□□□
1465	A879	8¢ multicolored	.22	.08 □□□□□
1466	A880	8¢ multicolored	.22	.08 □□□□□
1467	A881	8¢ multicolored	.22	.08 □□□□□
1467a		Block of 4, # 1464-1467		□□□□□
1468	A882	8¢ multicolored	.16	.05 □□□□□
1469	A883	8¢ yellow, orange & dark brown	.16	.05 □□□□□
1470	A884	8¢ black & multi.	.16	.05 □□□□□
1471	A885	8¢ multicolored	.16	.03 □□□□□
1472	A886	8¢ multicolored	.16	.03 □□□□□
1473	A887	8¢ black & multi.	.16	.05 □□□□□
1474	A888	8¢ dk. blue green, blk. & brown	.16	.05 □□□□□
1973					
1475	A889	8¢ red, emerald & violet blue	.16	.05 □□□□□
1476	A890	8¢ ultra., greenish black & red	.20	.05 □□□□□
1477	A891	8¢ black, verm. & ultramarine	.20	.05 □□□□□
1478	A892	8¢ multicolored	.20	.05 □□□□□
1479	A893	8¢ multicolored	.20	.05 □□□□□
1480	A894	8¢ black & multi.	.22	.10 □□□□□
1481	A895	8¢ black & multi.	.22	.10 □□□□□
1482	A896	8¢ black & multi.	.22	.10 □□□□□
1483	A897	8¢ black & multi.	.22	.10 □□□□□
1483a		Block of 4, # 1480-1483	.95	.70 □□□□□
1484	A898	8¢ dp. grn. & multi.	.16	.05 □□□□□
1485	A899	8¢ Prus. blue & multicolored	.16	.05 □□□□□

Family Planning

UNITED STATES 8¢

A869

COLONIAL AMERICAN CRAFTSMEN

BICENTENNIAL ERA

UNITED STATES POSTAGE 8 CENTS

A870

COLONIAL AMERICAN CRAFTSMEN

BICENTENNIAL ERA

UNITED STATES POSTAGE 8 CENTS

A871

COLONIAL AMERICAN CRAFTSMEN

BICENTENNIAL ERA

UNITED STATES POSTAGE 8 CENTS

A872

COLONIAL AMERICAN CRAFTSMEN

BICENTENNIAL ERA

UNITED STATES POSTAGE 8 CENTS

A873

XX OLYMPIC SUMMER GAMES MUNICH 1972

A874

XI OLYMPIC WINTER GAMES SAPPORO 1972

A875

XX OLYMPIC SUMMER GAMES MUNICH 1972

A876

P.T.A. 1897 1972 8¢
Parent Teacher Association u.s.

A877

FUR SEAL
UNITED STATES
•WILDLIFE CONSERVATION•

A878

UNITED STATES
CARDINAL
•WILDLIFE CONSERVATION•

A879

•WILDLIFE CONSERVATION•
BROWN PELICAN
UNITED STATES

A880

•WILDLIFE CONSERVATION•
UNITED STATES
BIGHORN SHEEP

A881

A883

A882

A884

A885

A887

A886

A888

A889

A890

A891

A892

A893

A894   A895
A896   A897

A898

A899

A900

A901

A902

Scott® No.	Illus No.	Description	Unused Price	Used Price	//////
1973					
1486	A900	8¢ yellow brown & multicolored	.16	.05 ☐☐☐☐☐
1487	A901	8¢ dp. brn. & multi.	.16	.05 ☐☐☐☐☐
1488	A902	8¢ black & orange	.16	.05 ☐☐☐☐☐
1489	A903	8¢ multicolored	.20	.12 ☐☐☐☐☐
1490	A904	8¢ multicolored	.20	.12 ☐☐☐☐☐
1491	A905	8¢ multicolored	.20	.12 ☐☐☐☐☐
1492	A906	8¢ multicolored	.20	.12 ☐☐☐☐☐
1493	A907	8¢ multicolored	.20	.12 ☐☐☐☐☐
1494	A908	8¢ multicolored	.20	.12 ☐☐☐☐☐
1495	A909	8¢ multicolored	.20	.12 ☐☐☐☐☐
1496	A910	8¢ multicolored	.20	.12 ☐☐☐☐☐
1497	A911	8¢ multicolored	.20	.12 ☐☐☐☐☐
1498	A912	8¢ multicolored	.20	.12 ☐☐☐☐☐
1498a		Strip of 10, Nos. 1489-1498	2.25	1.75 ☐☐☐☐☐
1499	A913	8¢ car. rose, black & blue	.16	.05 ☐☐☐☐☐
1500	A914	6¢ lilac & multi.	.12	.10 ☐☐☐☐☐
1501	A915	8¢ tan & multi.	.16	.05 ☐☐☐☐☐
1502	A916	15¢ gray green & multicolored	.30	.20 ☐☐☐☐☐
1503	A917	8¢ black & multi.	.16	.05 ☐☐☐☐☐
1973-74					
1504	A918	8¢ multi.	.16	.05 ☐☐☐☐☐
1505	A919	10¢ multi. ('74)	.20	.05 ☐☐☐☐☐
1506	A920	10¢ multi. ('74)	.20	.05 ☐☐☐☐☐
1973					
1507	A921	8¢ tan & multi.	.16	.03 ☐☐☐☐☐
1508	A922	8¢ green & multi.	.16	.03 ☐☐☐☐☐
1973-74		Tagged *Perf. 11x10½*			
1509	A923	10¢ red & blue	.20	.03 ☐☐☐☐☐
1510	A924	10¢ blue	.20	.03 ☐☐☐☐☐
1510a	A924	Untagged (Bureau precanceled)		.20 ☐☐☐☐☐
1510b	A924	Bklt. pane of 5 + label	1.00	.30 ☐☐☐☐☐
1510c	A924	Bklt. pane of 8	1.60	.30 ☐☐☐☐☐
1510d	A924	Bklt. pane of 6 ('74)	1.20	.30 ☐☐☐☐☐
1511	A925	10¢ multicolored	.20	.03 ☐☐☐☐☐
		Coil Stamps *Perf. 10 Vert.*			
1518	A926	6.3¢ brick red	.13	.07 ☐☐☐☐☐
1518a	A926	Untagged (Bureau precanceled)		.13 ☐☐☐☐☐
1519	A923	10¢ red & blue	.20	.03 ☐☐☐☐☐
1520	A924	10¢ blue	.20	.03 ☐☐☐☐☐
1520a	A924	Untagged (Bureau precanceled)		.20 ☐☐☐☐☐
1974					
1525	A928	10¢ red & dk. blue	.20	.05 ☐☐☐☐☐

U.S. POSTAL SERVICE 8¢

A903

U.S. POSTAL SERVICE 8¢

A904

U.S. POSTAL SERVICE 8¢

A905

U.S. POSTAL SERVICE 8¢

A906

U.S. POSTAL SERVICE 8¢

A907

U.S. POSTAL SERVICE 8¢

A908

U.S. POSTAL SERVICE 8¢

A909

U.S. POSTAL SERVICE 8¢

A910

U.S. POSTAL SERVICE 8¢

A911

U.S. POSTAL SERVICE 8¢

A912

Harry S. Truman

U.S. Postage 8 cents A913

A914

A915

A916

120

A917

A918

A919

A920

A921

A922

A923

A924

A925

A926

A929

A928

A930

A931

A932

A933

A934

A935

A936

A937

A938

A939

A940

Scott® No.	Illus No.	Description	Unused Price	Used Price	/ / / / / /

1974

Scott® No.	Illus No.	Description	Unused Price	Used Price	
1526	A929	10¢ black	.20	.05 ☐☐☐☐☐
1527	A930	10¢ multicolored	.20	.05 ☐☐☐☐☐
1528	A931	10¢ yel. & multi.	.20	.05 ☐☐☐☐☐
1529	A932	10¢ multicolored	.20	.05 ☐☐☐☐☐
1530	A933	10¢ multicolored	.20	.10 ☐☐☐☐☐
1531	A934	10¢ multicolored	.20	.10 ☐☐☐☐☐
1532	A935	10¢ multicolored	.20	.10 ☐☐☐☐☐
1533	A936	10¢ multicolored	.20	.10 ☐☐☐☐☐
1534	A937	10¢ multicolored	.20	.10 ☐☐☐☐☐
1535	A938	10¢ multicolored	.20	.10 ☐☐☐☐☐
1536	A939	10¢ multicolored	.20	.10 ☐☐☐☐☐
1537	A940	10¢ multicolored	.20	.10 ☐☐☐☐☐
1537a		Block or strip of 8, # 1530-1537	1.60	1.75 ☐☐☐☐☐
1538	A941	10¢ lt. bl. & multi.	.20	.10 ☐☐☐☐☐
1539	A942	10¢ lt. bl. & multi.	.20	.10 ☐☐☐☐☐
1540	A943	10¢ lt. bl. & multi.	.20	.10 ☐☐☐☐☐
1541	A944	10¢ lt. bl. & multi.	.20	.10 ☐☐☐☐☐
1541a		Block of 4, # 1538-1541	.80	.60 ☐☐☐☐☐
1542	A945	10¢ green & multi.	.20	.05 ☐☐☐☐☐
1543	A946	10¢ dk. blue & red	.20	.10 ☐☐☐☐☐
1544	A947	10¢ gray, dark blue & red	.20	.10 ☐☐☐☐☐
1545	A948	10¢ gray, dark blue & red	.20	.10 ☐☐☐☐☐
1546	A949	10¢ red & dk. blue	.20	.10 ☐☐☐☐☐
1546a		Block of 4, # 1543-1546	.80	.60 ☐☐☐☐☐
1547	A950	10¢ multicolored	.20	.05 ☐☐☐☐☐
1548	A951	10¢ dk. blue, black, org. & yellow	.20	.05 ☐☐☐☐☐
1549	A952	10¢ brn. red & dk. brown	.20	.05 ☐☐☐☐☐
1550	A953	10¢ multicolored	.20	.03 ☐☐☐☐☐
1551	A954	10¢ multicolored	.20	.03 ☐☐☐☐☐
1552	A955	10¢ multicolored	.25	.08 ☐☐☐☐☐

Unused price of No. 1552 is for copy on rouletted paper backing as issued. Used price is for copy on piece, with or without postmark. Die cutting includes crossed slashes through dove, applied to prevent removal and re-use of stamp. The stamp will separate into layers if soaked. No. 1552 is untagged.

1975

Scott® No.	Illus No.	Description	Unused Price	Used Price	
1553	A956	10¢ multicolored	.20	.05 ☐☐☐☐☐
1554	A957	10¢ multicolored	.20	.05 ☐☐☐☐☐
1555	A958	10¢ multicolored	.20	.05 ☐☐☐☐☐
1556	A959	10¢ violet blue, yellow & red	.20	.05 ☐☐☐☐☐
1557	A960	10¢ blk., red, ultra. & bister	.20	.05 ☐☐☐☐☐
1558	A961	10¢ multicolored	.20	.05 ☐☐☐☐☐
1559	A962	8¢ multicolored	.16	.13 ☐☐☐☐☐
1560	A963	10¢ multicolored	.20	.05 ☐☐☐☐☐
1561	A964	10¢ multicolored	.20	.05 ☐☐☐☐☐

A941

A942

A943

A944

A946

A947

A948

A949

A945

A951

A950

Scott® No.	Illus No.	Description	Unused Price	Used Price	//////
1975					
1562	A965	18¢ multicolored	.36	.20 ☐☐☐☐☐
1563	A966	10¢ multicolored	.20	.05 ☐☐☐☐☐
1564	A967	10¢ multicolored	.20	.05 ☐☐☐☐☐
1565	A968	10¢ multicolored	.20	.08 ☐☐☐☐☐
1566	A969	10¢ multicolored	.20	.08 ☐☐☐☐☐
1567	A970	10¢ multicolored	.20	.08 ☐☐☐☐☐
1568	A971	10¢ multicolored	.20	.08 ☐☐☐☐☐
1568a		Block of 4, # 1565-1568	.80	.50 ☐☐☐☐☐
1569	A972	10¢ multicolored	.20	.10 ☐☐☐☐☐
1569a		Pair, # 1569-1570	.40	.25 ☐☐☐☐☐
1570	A973	10¢ multicolored	.20	.10 ☐☐☐☐☐
1571	A974	10¢ blue, orange & dark blue	.20	.05 ☐☐☐☐☐
1572	A975	10¢ multicolored	.20	.08 ☐☐☐☐☐
1573	A976	10¢ multicolored	.20	.08 ☐☐☐☐☐
1574	A977	10¢ multicolored	.20	.08 ☐☐☐☐☐
1575	A978	10¢ multicolored	.20	.08 ☐☐☐☐☐
1575a		Block of 4, # 1572-1575	.80	.50 ☐☐☐☐☐
1576	A979	10¢ grn., Prus. bl. & rose brn.	.20	.05 ☐☐☐☐☐
1577	A980	10¢ multicolored	.20	.08 ☐☐☐☐☐
1577a		Pair, # 1577-1578	.40	.20 ☐☐☐☐☐
1578	A981	10¢ multicolored	.20	.08 ☐☐☐☐☐
1975		*Perf. 11*			
1579	A982	10¢ multicolored	.20	.03 ☐☐☐☐☐
1580	A983	10¢ multicolored	.20	.03 ☐☐☐☐☐
1580b	A983	Perf. 10½ ✕ 11	.50	.05 ☐☐☐☐☐
1975-79		*Perf. 11x10½*			
1581	A984	1¢ dark blue, *greenish* ('77)	.03	.03 ☐☐☐☐☐
1581a	A984	Untagged (Bureau precanceled)		.05 ☐☐☐☐☐
1582	A985	2¢ red brown, *greenish* ('77)	.04	.03 ☐☐☐☐☐
1582a	A985	Untagged (Bureau precanceled)		.06 ☐☐☐☐☐
1584	A987	3¢ olive, *greenish* ('77)	.06	.03 ☐☐☐☐☐
1584a	A987	Untagged (Bureau precanceled)		.06 ☐☐☐☐☐
1585	A988	4¢ rose magenta, *cream* ('77)	.08	.04 ☐☐☐☐☐
1585a	A988	Untagged (Bureau precanceled)		.08 ☐☐☐☐☐
1590	A994	9¢ slate grn. ('77)	.25	.20 ☐☐☐☐☐
1590a	A994	Perf. 10	15.00	5.00 ☐☐☐☐☐
1591	A994	9¢ slate green, *gray*	.18	.03 ☐☐☐☐☐
1591a	A994	Untagged (Bureau precanceled)		.18 ☐☐☐☐☐
1592	A995	10¢ vio., *gray* ('77)	.20	.03 ☐☐☐☐☐
1593	A996	11¢ orange, *gray*	.22	.03 ☐☐☐☐☐
1595	A998	13¢ brown	.26	.03 ☐☐☐☐☐
1595a	A998	Booklet pane of 6	1.60	.50 ☐☐☐☐☐
1595b	A998	Booklet pane of 7 + label	1.80	.50 ☐☐☐☐☐
1595c	A998	Booklet pane of 8	2.10	.50 ☐☐☐☐☐
1595d	A998	Booklet pane of 5 + label ('76)	1.30	.50 ☐☐☐☐☐

A952

A953

A954

A955

A956

A958

A957

A959

A960

A962

A963

A964

A965

A961

A966

US Bicentennial IOc

A967

A968

A969

A970

A971

A972

A973

A974

A979

A975

A976

A977

A978

A980

A981

A982

A983

128

A984

A985

A987

A988

A994

A995

A996

A998

A999

A1001

A1002

A1006

A1007

A1008

A1009

A101J

A1013

A1013a

A1014

A1015

A1016

A1017

A1018

A1018a

A1019

A1020

A1021

A1022

Scott® No.	Illus No.	Description	Unused Price	Used Price	//////
1975-79					
1596	A999	13¢ multicolored	.26	.03	☐☐☐☐☐
		Perf. 11			
1597	A1001	15¢ gray, dk. blue & red ('78)	.30	.03	☐☐☐☐☐
		Perf. 11x10½			
1598	A1001	15¢ gray, dk. blue & red ('78)	.30	.03	☐☐☐☐☐
1598a	A1001	Booklet pane of 8	2.40		☐☐☐☐☐
1599	A1002	16¢ blue ('78)	.32	.03	☐☐☐☐☐
1603	A1006	24¢ red, blue	.48	.06	☐☐☐☐☐
1604	A1007	28¢ brn., blue ('78)	.56	.08	☐☐☐☐☐
1605	A1008	29¢ blue, blue ('78)	.58	.08	☐☐☐☐☐
1606	A1009	30¢ grn., *blue* ('79)	.60	.08	☐☐☐☐☐
1608	A1011	50¢ brn., red & yel., *tan* ('79)	1.00	.10	☐☐☐☐☐
1610	A1013	$1 brn., red & yel., *tan* ('79)	2.00	.25	☐☐☐☐☐
1611	A1013a	$2 dk. green & org., *buff* ('78)	4.00	1.00	☐☐☐☐☐
1612	A1014	$5 yel., org. & brn., *tan* ('79)	10.00		☐☐☐☐☐
		Coil Stamps **Perf. 10 Vertically**			
1614	A1015	7.7c brown, *brt. yellow* ('76)	.16	.08	☐☐☐☐☐
1614a	A1015	Untagged (Bureau precanceled)		.16	☐☐☐☐☐
1615	A1016	7.9c carmine, *yellow* ('76)	.16	.08	☐☐☐☐☐
1615a	A1016	Untagged (Bureau precanceled)		.16	☐☐☐☐☐
1615C	A1017	8.4c dk. blue *yellow* ('78)	.18	.08	☐☐☐☐☐
1615d	A1017	Untagged (Bureau precanceled)		.16	☐☐☐☐☐
1616	A994	9¢ slate green, *gray*	.18	03	☐☐☐☐☐
1616b	A994	Untagged (Bureau precanceled)		.18	☐☐☐☐☐
1617	A995	10¢ vio., *gray* ('77)	.20	.03	☐☐☐☐☐
1617a	A995	Untagged (Bureau precanceled)		.25	☐☐☐☐☐
1618	A998	13¢ brown	.26	.03	☐☐☐☐☐
1618a	A998	Untagged (Bureau precanceled)		.25	☐☐☐☐☐
1618C	A1001	15c gray,dk. blue & red ('78)	.30	.08	☐☐☐☐☐
1619	A1002	16¢ blue ('78)	.32	.03	☐☐☐☐☐
1975-77		*Perf. 11x10½*			
1622	A1018	13¢ dark blue & red ('77)	.26	.03	☐☐☐☐☐
1623	A1018a	13¢ blue & red ('77)	.26	.03	☐☐☐☐☐
1623a	A1018a	Booklet pane of 8 (1 # 1590 and 7 # 1623)	2.00		☐☐☐☐☐
1623b	A1018a	Perf. 10	1.00	.50	☐☐☐☐☐
1623c	A1018a	Booklet pane of 8 (1 # 1590a + 7 # 1623b)	50.00		☐☐☐☐☐
		Coil Stamp **Perf. 10 Vertically**			
1625	A1018	13¢ dk. bl. & red	.26	.03	☐☐☐☐☐
1976					
1629	A1019	13¢ multicolored			☐☐☐☐☐
1630	A1020	13¢ multicolored	.26	.08	☐☐☐☐☐
1631	A1021	13¢ multicolored	.26	.08	☐☐☐☐☐
1631a		Strip of 3, # 1629-1631	.78	.40	☐☐☐☐☐
1632	A1022	13¢ dark blue, red & ultra.	.26	.06	☐☐☐☐☐

State Flags A1023-A1072

A1073

A1074

A1075

132

1976

Scott® No.	Illus No.	Description	Unused Price	Used Price
1633	A1023	13¢ Delaware	.45	.30 □□□□□
1634	A1024	13¢ Pennsylvania	.45	.30 □□□□□
1635	A1025	13¢ New Jersey	.45	.30 □□□□□
1636	A1026	13¢ Georgia	.45	.30 □□□□□
1637	A1027	13¢ Connecticut	.45	.30 □□□□□
1638	A1028	13¢ Massachusetts	.45	.30 □□□□□
1639	A1029	13¢ Maryland	.45	.30 □□□□□
1640	A1030	13¢ South Carolina	.45	.30 □□□□□
1641	A1031	13¢ New Hampshire	.45	.30 □□□□□
1642	A1032	13¢ Virginia	.45	.30 □□□□□
1643	A1033	13¢ New York	.45	.30 □□□□□
1644	A1034	13¢ North Carolina	.45	.30 □□□□□
1645	A1035	13¢ Rhode Island	.45	.30 □□□□□
1646	A1036	13¢ Vermont	.45	.30 □□□□□
1647	A1037	13¢ Kentucky	.45	.30 □□□□□
1648	A1038	13¢ Tennessee	.45	.30 □□□□□
1649	A1039	13¢ Ohio	.45	.30 □□□□□
1650	A1040	13¢ Louisiana	.45	.30 □□□□□
1651	A1041	13¢ Indiana	.45	.30 □□□□□
1652	A1042	13¢ Mississippi	.45	.30 □□□□□
1653	A1043	13¢ Illinois	.45	.30 □□□□□
1654	A1044	13¢ Alabama	.45	.30 □□□□□
1655	A1045	13¢ Maine	.45	.30 □□□□□
1656	A1046	13¢ Missouri	.45	.30 □□□□□
1657	A1047	13¢ Arkansas	.45	.30 □□□□□
1658	A1048	13¢ Michigan	.45	.30 □□□□□
1659	A1049	13¢ Florida	.45	.30 □□□□□
1660	A1050	13¢ Texas	.45	.30 □□□□□
1661	A1051	13¢ Iowa	.45	.30 □□□□□
1662	A1052	13¢ Wisconsin	.45	.30 □□□□□
1663	A1053	13¢ California	.45	.30 □□□□□
1664	A1054	13¢ Minnesota	.45	.30 □□□□□
1665	A1055	13¢ Oregon	.45	.30 □□□□□
1666	A1056	13¢ Kansas	.45	.30 □□□□□
1667	A1057	13¢ West Virginia	.45	.30 □□□□□
1668	A1058	13¢ Nevada	.45	.30 □□□□□
1669	A1059	13¢ Nebraska	.45	.30 □□□□□
1670	A1060	13¢ Colorado	.45	.30 □□□□□
1671	A1061	13¢ North Dakota	.45	.30 □□□□□
1672	A1062	13¢ South Dakota	.45	.30 □□□□□
1673	A1063	13¢ Montana	.45	.30 □□□□□
1674	A1064	13¢ Washington	.45	.30 □□□□□
1675	A1065	13¢ Idaho	.45	.30 □□□□□
1676	A1066	13¢ Wyoming	.45	.30 □□□□□
1677	A1067	13¢ Utah	.45	.30 □□□□□
1678	A1068	13¢ Oklahoma	.45	.30 □□□□□
1679	A1069	13¢ New Mexico	.45	.30 □□□□□

Surrender of Cornwallis at Yorktown, by John Trumbull— **A1076**

Declaration of Independence, by John Trumbull— **A1077**

Scott® No.	Illus No.	Description	Unused Price	Used Price	////////
1976					
1680	A1070	13¢ *Arizona*	.45	.30 ☐☐☐☐☐
1681	A1071	13¢ *Alaska*	.45	.30 ☐☐☐☐☐
1682	A1072	13¢ *Hawaii*	.45	.30 ☐☐☐☐☐
1682a		Sheet of 50	25.00	☐☐☐☐☐
1976					
1683	A1073	13¢ blk., purple & red, *tan*	.26	.06 ☐☐☐☐☐
1684	A1074	13¢ blue & multi.	.26	.06 ☐☐☐☐☐
1685	A1075	13¢ multicolored	.26	.06 ☐☐☐☐☐
1686	A1076	13¢ sheet of 5	4.50	☐☐☐☐☐
1687	A1077	18¢ sheet of 5	6.00	☐☐☐☐☐
1688	A1078	24¢ sheet of 5	7.50	☐☐☐☐☐
1689	A1079	31¢ sheet of 5	9.00	☐☐☐☐☐
1690	A1080	13¢ ultra. & multi.	.26	.06 ☐☐☐☐☐
1691	A1081	13¢ multicolored	.26	.08 ☐☐☐☐☐
1692	A1082	13¢ multicolored	.26	.08 ☐☐☐☐☐
1693	A1083	13¢ multicolored	.26	.08 ☐☐☐☐☐
1694	A1084	13¢ multicolored	.26	.08 ☐☐☐☐☐
1694a		Strip of 4, # 1691-1694	1.10	.50 ☐☐☐☐☐
1695	A1085	13¢ multicolored	.26	.06 ☐☐☐☐☐
1696	A1086	13¢ multicolored	.26	.06 ☐☐☐☐☐
1697	A1087	13¢ multicolored	.26	.06 ☐☐☐☐☐
1698	A1088	13¢ multicolored	.26	.06 ☐☐☐☐☐
1698a		Block of 4, # 1695-1698	1.10	☐☐☐☐☐
1699	A1089	13¢ multicolored	.26	.06 ☐☐☐☐☐
1700	A1090	13¢ black & gray	.26	.06 ☐☐☐☐☐
1701	A1091	13¢ multicolored	.26	.03 ☐☐☐☐☐
1702	A1092	13¢ multicolored	.26	.03 ☐☐☐☐☐
1703	A1092	13¢ multicolored	.26	.03 ☐☐☐☐☐

No. 1702 has overall tagging. Lettering at base is black and usually ½mm. below design. As a rule, no "snowflaking" in sky or pond. Pane of 50 has margins on 4 sides with slogans.

No. 1703 has block tagging the size of printed area. Lettering at base is gray black and usually ¾mm. below design. "Snowflaking" generally in sky and pond. Pane has margin only at right or left, and no slogans.

1977					
1704	A1093	13¢ multicolored	.26	.06 ☐☐☐☐☐
1705	A1094	13¢ blk. & multi.	.26	.06 ☐☐☐☐☐
1706	A1095	13¢ multicolored	.26	.06 ☐☐☐☐☐
1707	A1096	13¢ multicolored	.26	.06 ☐☐☐☐☐
1708	A1097	13¢ multicolored	.26	.06 ☐☐☐☐☐
1709	A1098	13¢ multicolored	.26	.06 ☐☐☐☐☐
1709a		Block or strip of 4, # 1706-1709	1.05	.25 ☐☐☐☐☐
1710	A1099	13¢ multicolored	.26	.06 ☐☐☐☐☐

Washington Crossing the Delaware
From a Painting by Emanuel Leutze / Eastman Johnson

**Washington Crossing the Delaware, by
Emanuel Leutze/Eastman Johnson— A1078**

Washington Reviewing His Ragged Army at Valley Forge
From a Painting by William T. Trego

**Washington Reviewing Army at Valley Forge,
by William T. Trego— A1079**

A1080

JULY 4,1776 · JULY 4,1776 · JULY 4,1776 · JULY 4,1776

Declaration of Independence, by John Trumbull

A1081   A1082   A1083   A1084

A1085   A1086

A1089

A1087   A1088

A1090

A1091

US Bicentennial 13c

A1093

A1092   A1094

Zia Museum of New Mexico
Pueblo Art USA 13c

A1095

San Ildefonso Denver Art Museum
Pueblo Art USA 13c

A1096

Hopi Heard Museum Phoenix
Pueblo Art USA 13c

A1097

Acoma School of American Research
Pueblo Art USA 13c

A1098

USA·13c

50th Anniversary Solo Transatlantic Flight

A1099

COLORADO

13c
usa

THE CENTENNIAL STATE

A1100

Lafayette

US Bicentennial 13c

A1105

Swallowtail

USA 13c *Papilio oregonius*

A1101

Checkerspot

USA 13c *Euphydryas phaeton*

A1102

Dogface

USA 13c *Colias eurydice*

A1103

Orange-Tip

USA 13c *Anthocaris midea*

A1104

Scott® No.	Illus No.	Description	Unused Price	Used Price	/ / / / / /
1977					
1711	A1100	13¢ multicolored	.26	.06 ☐☐☐☐☐
1712	A1101	13¢ tan & multi.	.26	.06 ☐☐☐☐☐
1713	A1102	13¢ tan & multi.	.26	.06 ☐☐☐☐☐
1714	A1103	13¢ tan & multi.	.26	.06 ☐☐☐☐☐
1715	A1104	13¢ tan & multi.	.26	.06 ☐☐☐☐☐
1715a		Block of 4, # 1712-1715	1.05	.25 ☐☐☐☐☐
1716	A1105	13¢ bl., blk. & red	.26	.06 ☐☐☐☐☐
1717	A1106	13¢ multicolored	.26	.06 ☐☐☐☐☐
1718	A1107	13¢ multicolored	.26	.06 ☐☐☐☐☐
1719	A1108	13¢ multicolored	.26	.06 ☐☐☐☐☐
1720	A1109	13¢ multicolored	.26	.06 ☐☐☐☐☐
1720a		Block of 4, # 1717-1720	1.05	.25 ☐☐☐☐☐
1721	A1110	13¢ blue	.26	.06 ☐☐☐☐☐
1722	A1111	13¢ multicolored	.26	.06 ☐☐☐☐☐
1723	A1112	13¢ multicolored	.26	.06 ☐☐☐☐☐
1723a		Pair, # 1723-1724	.52	.12 ☐☐☐☐☐
1724	A1113	13¢ multicolored	.26	.06 ☐☐☐☐☐
1725	A1114	13¢ blk. & multi.	.26	.06 ☐☐☐☐☐
1726	A1115	13¢ red & brown, *cream*	.26	.06 ☐☐☐☐☐
1727	A1116	13¢ multicolored	.26	.06 ☐☐☐☐☐
1728	A1117	13¢ multicolored	.26	.06 ☐☐☐☐☐
1729	A1118	13¢ multicolored	.26	.03 ☐☐☐☐☐
1730	A1119	13¢ multicolored	.26	.03 ☐☐☐☐☐
1978					
1731	A1120	13¢ black & brn.	.26	.06 ☐☐☐☐☐
1732	A1121	13¢ dark blue	.26	.06 ☐☐☐☐☐
1732a		Pair, # 1732-1733	.55	.20 ☐☐☐☐☐
1733	A1122	13¢ green	.26	.06 ☐☐☐☐☐
1734	A1123	13¢ brn. & bl. grn., *bister*	.26	.03 ☐☐☐☐☐
1735	A1124	(.15) orange (Perf. 11)	.30	.03 ☐☐☐☐☐
1736	A1124	(.15) orange (Perf. 11×10½)	.30	.03 ☐☐☐☐☐
1738	A1126	15¢ multicolored	.30	.06 ☐☐☐☐☐
1742	A1124	(.15) orange (Perf. 10 Vert.)	.30	.03 ☐☐☐☐☐
1744	A1133	13¢ multicolored	.26	.06 ☐☐☐☐☐
1745	A1134	13¢ multicolored	.26	.06 ☐☐☐☐☐
1746	A1135	13¢ multicolored	.26	.06 ☐☐☐☐☐
1747	A1136	13¢ multicolored	.26	.06 ☐☐☐☐☐
1748	A1137	13¢ multicolored	.26	.06 ☐☐☐☐☐
1748a		Block of 4, # 1745-1748	1.05	.30 ☐☐☐☐☐
1749	A1138	13¢ multicolored	.26	.06 ☐☐☐☐☐
1750	A1139	13¢ multicolored	.26	.06 ☐☐☐☐☐
1751	A1140	13¢ multicolored	.26	.06 ☐☐☐☐☐
1752	A1141	13¢ multicolored	.26	.06 ☐☐☐☐☐
1752a		Block of 4, # 1749-1752	1.05	.30 ☐☐☐☐☐
1753	A1142	13¢ bl., blk. & red	.26	.06 ☐☐☐☐☐
1754	A1143	13¢ brown	.26	.06 ☐☐☐☐☐

A1106

A1107

A1108

A1109

A1110

A1112

A1111

A1114

A1113

A1115

A1116

A1117

A1118

A1120

A1119

Alaska 1778
Captⁿ JAMES COOK
13c USA **A1121**

Captⁿ JAMES COOK   13c USA
Hawaii 1778

A1122

A1134   **A1135**

13c   13c

Folk Art USA Quilts   Folk Art USA Quilts

13c   13c

Folk Art USA: Quilts   Folk Art USA: Quilts

A1136   **A1137**

USA 13c

A1123   **A1138**

A
US Postage

A1124

13c
USA

A1126

USA Dance Ballet
13c

USA Dance Folk
13c

USA Dance Theater
13c

USA Dance Modern
13c

A1138   **A1139**

A1140   **A1141**

Harriet Tubman
Black Heritage USA 13c

A1133

French Alliance
1778

US Bicentennial 13c

A1142

EARLY CANCER DETECTION
PAP TEST
USA 13c
Dr. George Papanicolaou

A1143

A1144

A1146

A1145

A1149

A1150

A1148

A1151

A1152

A1147

A1153

 A1154

A1155

A1156

A1157

A1159

A1158

A1160

A1161

A1162

A1163

A1164 A1165

A1166 A1167

A1168 Jefferson 1743-1826 Virginia Rotunda
Architecture USA 15c

A1169 Latrobe 1764-1820 Baltimore Cathedral
Architecture USA 15c

A1170 Bulfinch 1763-1844 Boston State House
Architecture USA 15c

A1171 Strickland 1788-1854 Philadelphia Exchange
Architecture USA 15c

A1172 *Endangered Flora* — PERSISTENT TRILLIUM — 15c USA

A1173 *Endangered Flora* — HAWAIIAN WILD BROADBEAN — 15c USA

A1174 *Endangered Flora* — CONTRA COSTA WALLFLOWER — 15c USA

A1175 *Endangered Flora* — ANTIOCH DUNES EVENING PRIMROSE — 15c USA

USA 15c
Seeing For Me
A1176

Scott® No.	Illus No.	Description	Unused Price	Used Price	/ / / / / /
1755	A1144	13¢ multicolored	.26	.06 ☐☐☐☐☐
1756	A1145	15¢ multicolored	.30	.06 ☐☐☐☐☐
1757	A1146	13¢ Block of 8, multicolored	2.25	— ☐☐☐☐☐
1757a	A1146	*Cardinal*	.26	.10 ☐☐☐☐☐
1757b	A1146	*Mallard*	.26	.10 ☐☐☐☐☐
1757c	A1146	*Canada goose*	.26	.10 ☐☐☐☐☐
1757d	A1146	*Blue jay*	.26	.10 ☐☐☐☐☐
1757e	A1146	*Moose*	.26	.10 ☐☐☐☐☐
1757f	A1146	*Chipmunk*	.26	.10 ☐☐☐☐☐
1757g	A1146	*Red fox*	.26	.10 ☐☐☐☐☐
1757h	A1146	*Raccoon*	.26	.10 ☐☐☐☐☐
1758	A1147	15¢ multicolored	.30	.06 ☐☐☐☐☐
1759	A1148	15¢ multicolored	.30	.06 ☐☐☐☐☐
1760	A1149	15¢ multicolored	.30	.06 ☐☐☐☐☐
1761	A1150	15¢ multicolored	.30	.06 ☐☐☐☐☐
1762	A1151	15¢ multicolored	.30	.06 ☐☐☐☐☐
1763	A1152	15¢ multicolored	.30	.06 ☐☐☐☐☐
1763a		Block of 4	1.25	.30 ☐☐☐☐☐
1764	A1153	15¢ multicolored	.30	.06 ☐☐☐☐☐
1765	A1154	15¢ multicolored	.30	.06 ☐☐☐☐☐
1766	A1155	15¢ multicolored	.30	.06 ☐☐☐☐☐
1767	A1156	15¢ multicolored	.30	.06 ☐☐☐☐☐
1767a		Block of 4	1.25	.30 ☐☐☐☐☐
1768	A1157	15¢ blue & multicolored	.30	.03 ☐☐☐☐☐
1769	A1158	15¢ red & multicolored	.30	.03 ☐☐☐☐☐
1770	A1159	15¢ blue	.30	.06 ☐☐☐☐☐
1771	A1160	15¢ multicolored	.30	.06 ☐☐☐☐☐
1772	A1161	15¢ orange red	.30	.06 ☐☐☐☐☐
1773	A1162	15¢ dark blue	.30	.06 ☐☐☐☐☐
1774	A1163	15¢ chocolate	.30	.06 ☐☐☐☐☐
1775	A1164	15¢ multicolored	.30	.06 ☐☐☐☐☐
1776	A1165	15¢ multicolored	.30	.06 ☐☐☐☐☐
1777	A1166	15¢ multicolored	.30	.06 ☐☐☐☐☐
1778	A1167	15¢ multicolored	.30	.06 ☐☐☐☐☐
1778a		Block of 4, #1775-1778	1.20	— ☐☐☐☐☐
1779	A1168	15c blk. & brick red	.30	.06 ☐☐☐☐☐
1780	A1169	15c blk. & brick red	.30	.06 ☐☐☐☐☐
1781	A1170	15c blk. & brick red	.30	.06 ☐☐☐☐☐
1782	A1171	15c blk. & brick red	.30	.06 ☐☐☐☐☐
1782a		Block of 4, 1779-1782	1.20	— ☐☐☐☐☐
1783	A1172	15c multi	.30	.06 ☐☐☐☐☐
1784	A1173	15c multi	.30	.06 ☐☐☐☐☐
1785	A1174	15c multi	.30	.06 ☐☐☐☐☐
1786	A1175	15c multi	.30	.06 ☐☐☐☐☐
1786a		Block of 4, 1783-1786	1.20	— ☐☐☐☐☐
1787	A1176	15c multi	.30	.06 ☐☐☐☐☐

Scott® No.	Illus No.	Description	Unused Price	Used Price	//////
....	....				☐☐☐☐☐
....	....				☐☐☐☐☐
....	....				☐☐☐☐☐
....	....				☐☐☐☐☐
....	....				☐☐☐☐☐
....	....				☐☐☐☐☐
....	....				☐☐☐☐☐
....	....				☐☐☐☐☐
....	....				☐☐☐☐☐
....	....				☐☐☐☐☐
....	....				☐☐☐☐☐
....	....				☐☐☐☐☐
....	....				☐☐☐☐☐
....	....				☐☐☐☐☐
....	....				☐☐☐☐☐
....	....				☐☐☐☐☐
....	....				☐☐☐☐☐
....	....				☐☐☐☐☐
....	....				☐☐☐☐☐
....	....				☐☐☐☐☐
....	....				☐☐☐☐☐
....	....				☐☐☐☐☐
....	....				☐☐☐☐☐
....	....				☐☐☐☐☐
....	....				☐☐☐☐☐
....	....				☐☐☐☐☐
....	....				☐☐☐☐☐
....	....				☐☐☐☐☐
....	....				☐☐☐☐☐
....	....				☐☐☐☐☐
....	....				☐☐☐☐☐
....	....				☐☐☐☐☐
....	....				☐☐☐☐☐
....	....				☐☐☐☐☐
....	....				☐☐☐☐☐
....	....				☐☐☐☐☐
....	....				☐☐☐☐☐
....	....				☐☐☐☐☐
....	....				☐☐☐☐☐
....	....				☐☐☐☐☐
....	....				☐☐☐☐☐
....	....				☐☐☐☐☐
....	....				☐☐☐☐☐
....	....				☐☐☐☐☐
....	....				☐☐☐☐☐
....	....				☐☐☐☐☐
....	....				☐☐☐☐☐
....	....				☐☐☐☐☐
....	....				☐☐☐☐☐

Scott® No.	Illus No.	Description	Unused Price	Used Price	/////
....	....	....		....	☐☐☐☐☐
....	....	....		....	☐☐☐☐☐
....	....	....		....	☐☐☐☐☐
.....-	....	....		....	☐☐☐☐☐
....	....	....		....	☐☐☐☐☐
....	....	....		....	☐☐☐☐☐
....	....	....		....	☐☐☐☐☐
....	....	....		....	☐☐☐☐☐
....	....	....		....	☐☐☐☐☐
....	....	....		....	☐☐☐☐☐
....	....	....		....	☐☐☐☐☐
....	....	....		....	☐☐☐☐☐
....	....	....		....	☐☐☐☐☐
....	....	....		....	☐☐☐☐☐
....	....	....		....	☐☐☐☐☐
....	....	....		....	☐☐☐☐☐
....	....	....		....	☐☐☐☐☐
....	....	....		....	☐☐☐☐☐
....	....	....		....	☐☐☐☐☐
....	....	....		....	☐☐☐☐☐
....	....	....		....	☐☐☐☐☐
....	....	....		....	☐☐☐☐☐
....	....	....		....	☐☐☐☐☐
....	....	....		....	☐☐☐☐☐
....	....	....		....	☐☐☐☐☐
....	....	....		....	☐☐☐☐☐
....	....	....		....	☐☐☐☐☐
....	....	....		....	☐☐☐☐☐
....	....	....		....	☐☐☐☐☐
....	....	....		....	☐☐☐☐☐
....	....	....		....	☐☐☐☐☐
....	....	....		....	☐☐☐☐☐
....	....	....		....	☐☐☐☐☐
....	....	....		....	☐☐☐☐☐
....	....	....		....	☐☐☐☐☐
....	....	....		....	☐☐☐☐☐
....	....	....		....	☐☐☐☐☐
....	....	....		....	☐☐☐☐☐
....	....	....		....	☐☐☐☐☐
....	....	....		....	☐☐☐☐☐
....	....	....		....	☐☐☐☐☐
....	....	....		....	☐☐☐☐☐
....	....	....		....	☐☐☐☐☐
....	....	....		....	☐☐☐☐☐
....	....	....		....	☐☐☐☐☐
....	....	....		....	☐☐☐☐☐
....	....	....		....	☐☐☐☐☐

AP1

AP2

AP3

AP5

AP6

AP7

AP8

AP9

AP10

AP11

AP12

AP13

AP14

AP15

AIR POST STAMPS

For prepayment of postage on all mailable matter sent by airmail.

Scott® No.	Illus No.	Description	Unused Price	Used Price	/ / / / / /
1918					
C1	AP1	6¢ orange	125.00	25.00 □□□□□
C2	AP1	16¢ green	175.00	35.00 □□□□□
C3	AP1	24¢ carmine rose & blue	160.00	35.00 □□□□□
C3a	AP1	Center inverted	100000.00	□□□□□
1923					
C4	AP2	8¢ dark green	50.00	15.00 □□□□□
C5	AP3	16¢ dark blue	175.00	32.50 □□□□□
C6	AP4	24¢ carmine	200.00	25.00 □□□□□
1926-28		*Perf.11*			
C7	AP5	10¢ dark blue	4.50	.50 □□□□□
C8	AP5	15¢ olive brown	5.00	2.75 □□□□□
C9	AP5	20¢ yellow green ('27)	15.00	2.25 □□□□□
C10	AP6	10¢ dark blue	12.50	3.50 □□□□□
C10a	AP6	Booklet pane of 3	100.00	50.00 □□□□□
C11	AP7	5¢ carmine & blue	5.25	.65 □□□□□
C12	AP8	5¢ violet	16.50	.65 □□□□□
1930					
C13	AP9	65¢ green	700.00	250.00 □□□□□
C14	AP10	1.30 brown	1400.00	450.00 □□□□□
C15	AP11	2.60 blue	2100.00	650.00 □□□□□
1931-32		*Perf. 10½x11*			
C16	AP8	5¢ violet	6.50	.50 □□□□□
C17	AP8	8¢ olive bistre ('32)	2.00	.30 □□□□□
1933					
C18	AP12	50¢ green	165.00	65.00 □□□□□
1934					
C19	AP8	6¢ dull orange	1.65	.10 □□□□□
1935					
C20	AP13	25¢ blue	3.00	1.75 □□□□□
1937					
C21	AP14	20¢ green	20.00	2.50 □□□□□
C22	AP14	50¢ carmine	20.00	5.75 □□□□□
1938					
C23	AP15	6¢ dark blue & carmine	.50	.06 □□□□□
1939					
C24	AP16	30¢ dull blue	11.00	1.50 □□□□□
1941-1944					
C25	AP17	6¢ carmine	.18	.03 □□□□□
C25a	AP17	Booklet pane of 3 ('43)	6.50	1.00 □□□□□
C26	AP17	8¢ olive green ('44)	.25	.05 □□□□□
C27	AP17	10¢ violet	1.25	.20 □□□□□
C28	AP17	15¢ brown car.	2.75	.35 □□□□□
C29	AP17	20¢ bright green	2.25	.30 □□□□□

AP16

AP17

AP19

AP18

AP20

AP21

AP22

AP24

AP23

AP25

AP26

AP27

AP28

AP29

AP30

150

Scott® No.	Illus No.	Description	Unused Price	Used Price	/ / / / / /
C30	AP17	30¢ blue	3.00	.30 □□□□□
C31	AP17	50¢ orange	21.00	4.00 □□□□□

1946 — *Perf. 10½x11.*

C32	AP18	5¢ carmine	.15	.04 □□□□□

1947

C33	AP19	5¢ carmine	.15	.04 □□□□□
C34	AP20	10¢ black	.40	.06 □□□□□
C35	AP21	15¢ bright blue green	.55	.05 □□□□□
C36	AP22	25¢ blue	1.25	.12 □□□□□

1948 — Coil Stamp. *Perf. 10 Horizontally*

C37	AP19	5¢ carmine	1.75	.50 □□□□□

1948

C38	AP23	5¢ bright carmine	.22	.20 □□□□□

1949 — *Perf. 10½x11.*

C39	AP19	6¢ carmine	.18	.03 □□□□□
C39a	AP19	Bklt. pane of 6	13.50	5.00 □□□□□

1949

C40	AP24	6¢ carmine	.18	.10 □□□□□

Coil Stamp. *Perf. 10 Horizontally.*

C41	AP19	6¢ carmine	4.25	.05 □□□□□

1949

C42	AP25	10¢ violet	.55	.30 □□□□□
C43	AP26	15¢ ultramarine	.70	.40 □□□□□
C44	AP27	25¢ rose carmine	1.10	.75 □□□□□
C45	AP28	6¢ magenta	.16	.10 □□□□□

1952-58

C46	AP29	80¢ bright red violet	8.50	1.20 □□□□□
C47	AP30	6¢ carmine	.16	.10 □□□□□
C48	AP31	4¢ bright blue	.12	.08 □□□□□
C49	AP32	6¢ blue	.20	.10 □□□□□
C50	AP31	5¢ rose red	.22	.08 □□□□□

Perf. 10½x11

C51	AP33	7¢ blue	.22	.03 □□□□□
C51a	AP33	Bklt. pane of 6	16.50	6.50 □□□□□

Coil Stamp *Perf. 10 Horizontally*

C52	AP33	7¢ blue	5.75	.18 □□□□□
C53	AP34	7¢ dark blue	.25	.12 □□□□□
C54	AP35	7¢ dark blue & red	.25	.12 □□□□□
C55	AP36	7¢ rose red	.25	.12 □□□□□
C56	AP37	10¢ violet blue & bright red	.40	.25 □□□□□
C57	AP38	10¢ black & green ('60)	3.00	.50 □□□□□
C58	AP39	15¢ black & orange	.75	.06 □□□□□

1959-66

C59	AP40	25¢ black & maroon ('60)	.65	.06 □□□□□
C59a	AP40	Tagged ('66)	.65	.15 □□□□□

AP31

AP32

AP33

AP34

AP35

AP36

AP38

AP37

AP39

AP40

AP42

AP41-Redrawn

AP43

AP45

AP44

AP46

AP47

152

Scott® No.	Illus No.	Description	Unused Price	Used Price	/ / / / / /
		Perf. 10½x11			
C60	AP33	7¢ carmine	.28	.05 ☐☐☐☐☐
C60a	AP33	Booklet pane of 6	22.50	7.00 ☐☐☐☐☐
		Coil Stamp *Perf. 10 Horizontally*			
C61	AP33	7¢ carmine	7.00	.25 ☐☐☐☐☐

1961-67

C62	AP38	13¢ black & red	.50	.10 ☐☐☐☐☐
C62a	AP38	Tagged ('67)	.70	.25 ☐☐☐☐☐
C63	AP41	15¢ black & orange	.40	.08 ☐☐☐☐☐
C63a	AP41	Tagged ('67)	.50	.12 ☐☐☐☐☐
		Perf. 10½x11			
C64	AP42	8¢ carmine	.18	.03 ☐☐☐☐☐
C64a	AP42	Tagged ('63)	.18	.03 ☐☐☐☐☐
C64b	AP42	Bklt. pane 5 + label	7.50	1.25 ☐☐☐☐☐
C64c	AP42	As 'b,' tagged ('64)	2.25	.50 ☐☐☐☐☐
		Coil Stamp *Perf. 10 Horizontally*			
C65	AP42	8¢ carmine	.45	.08 ☐☐☐☐☐
C65a	AP42	Tagged ('65)	.60	.10 ☐☐☐☐☐
C66	AP43	15¢ carmine, deep claret & blue	1.50	.50 ☐☐☐☐☐
C67	AP44	6¢ red	.15	.08 ☐☐☐☐☐
C67a	AP44	Tagged ('67)	4.00	.50 ☐☐☐☐☐
C68	AP45	8¢ car. & maroon	.35	.10 ☐☐☐☐☐
C69	AP46	8¢ blue, red & bis.	1.00	.15 ☐☐☐☐☐
C70	AP47	8¢ brown	.75	.12 ☐☐☐☐☐
C71	AP48	20¢ multicolored	1.10	.15 ☐☐☐☐☐

1968

		Perf. 11x10½			
C72	AP49	10¢ carmine	.25	.03 ☐☐☐☐☐
C72b	AP49	Booklet pane of 8	2.25	.75 ☐☐☐☐☐
C72c	AP49	Booklet pane of 5 + label	2.50	.75 ☐☐☐☐☐
		Coil Stamp *Perf. 10 Vertically*			
C73	AP49	10¢ carmine	.50	.04 ☐☐☐☐☐
C74	AP50	10¢ bl., blk. & red	.75	.10 ☐☐☐☐☐
C75	AP51	20¢ red, bl. & black	.85	.06 ☐☐☐☐☐

1969

C76	AP52	10¢ multicolored	.25	.10 ☐☐☐☐☐

1971-73

C77	AP53	9¢ red	.18	.06 ☐☐☐☐☐
C78	AP54	11¢ carmine	.22	.03 ☐☐☐☐☐
C78a	AP54	Booklet pane of 4 + 2 labels	1.50	.40 ☐☐☐☐☐
C78b	AP54	Untagged (Bureau precanceled)		.25 ☐☐☐☐☐
C79	AP55	13¢ carmine ('73)	.26	.10 ☐☐☐☐☐
C79a	AP55	Booklet pane of 5 + label ('73)	1.35	.70 ☐☐☐☐☐
C79b	AP55	Untagged (Bureau precanceled)		.30 ☐☐☐☐☐

AP50

AP48

AP51

AP49

AP52

AP53

AP54

AP55

AP56

AP57

AP58

AP59

AP60

AP61

AP62

AP63

Scott® No.	Illus No.	Description	Unused Price	Used Price	/ / / / / /
1971-73					
C80	AP56	17¢ bluish blk., red & dk. green	.40	.15 ☐☐☐☐☐	
C81	AP51	21¢ red, bl. & blk.	.42	.21 ☐☐☐☐☐	
		Rotary Press Printing	Perf. 10 Vertically		
C82	AP54	11¢ carmine	.27	.06 ☐☐☐☐☐	
C83	AP55	13¢ carmine ('73)	.30	.10 ☐☐☐☐☐	
1972-74					
C84	AP57	11¢ org. & multi.	.30	.11 ☐☐☐☐☐	
C85	AP58	11¢ multicolored	.25	.11 ☐☐☐☐☐	
C86	AP59	11¢ rose lilac & multicolored	.30	.11 ☐☐☐☐☐	
C87	AP60	18¢ carmine, black & ultra.	.45	.18 ☐☐☐☐☐	
C88	AP61	26¢ ultra., black & carmine	.60	.26 ☐☐☐☐☐	
1976					
C89	AP62	25¢ ultra., red & black	.50	.25 ☐☐☐☐☐	
C90	AP63	31¢ ultra., red & black	.62	.30 ☐☐☐☐☐	
1978					
C91	AP64	31¢ ultra & multi	.62	.30 ☐☐☐☐☐	
C92	AP65	31¢ ultra & multi	.62	.30 ☐☐☐☐☐	
C92a		Pair, #C91-C92	1.25	.65 ☐☐☐☐☐	
1979					
C93	AP66	21¢ multicolored	.42	.20 ☐☐☐☐☐	
C94	AP67	21¢ multicolored	.42	.20 ☐☐☐☐☐	
C94a		Pair,#C93-#C94	.85	— ☐☐☐☐☐	
......				☐☐☐☐☐	
......				☐☐☐☐☐	
......				☐☐☐☐☐	
......				☐☐☐☐☐	
......				☐☐☐☐☐	
......				☐☐☐☐☐	
......				☐☐☐☐☐	
......				☐☐☐☐☐	
......				☐☐☐☐☐	
......				☐☐☐☐☐	
......				☐☐☐☐☐	
......				☐☐☐☐☐	
......				☐☐☐☐☐	
......				☐☐☐☐☐	
......				☐☐☐☐☐	
......				☐☐☐☐☐	
......				☐☐☐☐☐	
......				☐☐☐☐☐	
......				☐☐☐☐☐	
......				☐☐☐☐☐	
......				☐☐☐☐☐	
......				☐☐☐☐☐	

AP64

AP66

AP65

AP67

APSD1

SD1

SD2

SD3

SD5

SD4

SD6

SD7

SD8

SD9

AIR POST SPECIAL DELIVERY STAMPS

1934

CE1	APSD1 16¢ dark blue		.80	.70 ☐☐☐☐☐
CE2	APSD1 16¢ red & blue		.50	.18 ☐☐☐☐☐

SPECIAL DELIVERY STAMPS

1885-93

E1	SD1	10¢ blue	175.00	22.50 ☐☐☐☐☐
E2	SD2	10¢ blue	175.00	6.50 ☐☐☐☐☐
E3	SD2	10¢ orange	100.00	10.00 ☐☐☐☐☐

1894　　Line under "Ten Cents".

E4	SD3	10¢ blue	400.00	15.00 ☐☐☐☐☐

1895　　Wmkd. USPS (191)

E5	SD3	10¢ blue	75.00	2.50 ☐☐☐☐☐

1902

E6	SD4	10¢ ultramarine	45.00	2.50 ☐☐☐☐☐

1908

E7	SD5	10¢ green	50.00	20.00 ☐☐☐☐☐

1911　　Wmkd. USPS (190)　　*Perf. 12*

E8	SD4	10¢ ultramarine	55.00	3.00 ☐☐☐☐☐

1914　　*Perf. 10*

E9	SD4	10¢ ultramarine	150.00	4.00 ☐☐☐☐☐

1916　　*Perf. 10.*　　Unwmkd.

E10	SD4	10¢ pale ultra.	250.00	15.00 ☐☐☐☐☐

1917-25　　*Perf. 11*

E11	SD4	10¢ ultramarine	12.00	.18 ☐☐☐☐☐
E12	SD6	10¢ gray violet	25.00	.10 ☐☐☐☐☐
E13	SD6	15¢ deep orange	15.00	.30 ☐☐☐☐☐
E14	SD7	20¢ black	3.00	1.00 ☐☐☐☐☐

1927-51　　*Perf. 11x10½*

E15	SD6	10¢ gray violet	.60	.04 ☐☐☐☐☐
E16	SD6	15¢ orange	.65	.08 ☐☐☐☐☐
E17	SD6	13¢ blue	.50	.06 ☐☐☐☐☐
E18	SD6	17¢ orange yellow	5.00	1.35 ☐☐☐☐☐
E19	SD7	20¢ black	1.50	.12 ☐☐☐☐☐

1954-57

E20	SD8	20¢ deep blue	.70	.08 ☐☐☐☐☐
E21	SD8	30¢ lake ('57)	1.00	.04 ☐☐☐☐☐

1969-71

E22	SD9	45¢ car. & vio. bl.	2.25	.12 ☐☐☐☐☐
E23	SD9	60¢ violet blue & carmine ('71)	1.20	.12 ☐☐☐☐☐

REGISTRATION STAMP
CERTIFIED MAIL STAMP

RS1

CM1

Scott® No.	Illus No.	Description	Unused Price	Used Price	/ / / / / /
	Wmkd. USPS (190) Engraved.				
F1	RS1	10¢ ultramarine	85.00	4.00 ☐☐☐☐☐
FA1	CM1	15¢ red	.50	.30 ☐☐☐☐☐

POSTAGE DUE STAMPS

D1

D2

D3

D4

D5

Scott® No.	Illus No.	Description	Unused Price	Used Price	/ / / / / /
1879		*Perf. 12.*			
J1	D1	1¢ brown	10.00	2.25 ☐☐☐☐☐
J2	D1	2¢ brown	80.00	3.25 ☐☐☐☐☐
J3	D1	3¢ brown	5.00	1.50 ☐☐☐☐☐
J4	D1	5¢ brown	90.00	11.50 ☐☐☐☐☐
J5	D1	10¢ brown	160.00	5.00 ☐☐☐☐☐
J6	D1	30¢ brown	55.00	10.00 ☐☐☐☐☐
J7	D1	50¢ brown	90.00	20.00 ☐☐☐☐☐

Scott® No.	Illus No.	Description	Unused Price	Used Price	/ / / / / /
1879		*Special Printing.*			
J8	D1	1¢ deep brown	2500.00		☐☐☐☐☐
J9	D1	2¢ deep brown	1350.00		☐☐☐☐☐
J10	D1	3¢ deep brown	1250.00		☐☐☐☐☐
J11	D1	5¢ deep brown	900.00		☐☐☐☐☐
J12	D1	10¢ deep brown	850.00		☐☐☐☐☐
J13	D1	30¢ deep brown	750.00		☐☐☐☐☐
J14	D1	50¢ deep brown	750.00		☐☐☐☐☐
1884-89					
J15	D1	1¢ red brown	11.00	1.75	☐☐☐☐☐
J16	D1	2¢ red brown	10.00	1.50	☐☐☐☐☐
J17	D1	3¢ red brown	150.00	40.00	☐☐☐☐☐
J18	D1	5¢ red brown	60.00	4.25	☐☐☐☐☐
J19	D1	10¢ red brown ('87)	50.00	2.50	☐☐☐☐☐
J20	D1	30¢ red brown	45.00	12.00	☐☐☐☐☐
J21	D1	50¢ red brown	450.00	70.00	☐☐☐☐☐
1891-93					
J22	D1	1¢ bright claret	2.50	.50	☐☐☐☐☐
J23	D1	2¢ bright claret	3.00	.45	☐☐☐☐☐
J24	D1	3¢ bright claret	4.00	2.25	☐☐☐☐☐
J25	D1	5¢ bright claret	7.50	2.25	☐☐☐☐☐
J26	D1	10¢ bright claret	15.00	4.00	☐☐☐☐☐
J27	D1	30¢ bright claret	100.00	40.00	☐☐☐☐☐
J28	D1	50¢ bright claret	110.00	47.50	☐☐☐☐☐
1894					
J29	D2	1¢ vermilion	175.00	30.00	☐☐☐☐☐
J30	D2	2¢ vermilion	55.00	15.00	☐☐☐☐☐
J31	D2	1¢ deep claret	5.50	2.00	☐☐☐☐☐
J32	D2	2¢ deep claret	4.50	1.00	☐☐☐☐☐
J33	D2	3¢ deep claret	17.50	10.00	☐☐☐☐☐
J34	D2	5¢ deep claret	25.00	11.00	☐☐☐☐☐
J35	D2	10¢ deep rose	15.00	6.00	☐☐☐☐☐
J36	D2	30¢ deep claret	60.00	22.50	☐☐☐☐☐
J36a	D2	30c carmine	50.00	21.00	☐☐☐☐☐
J36b	D2	30c pale rose	50.00	21.00	☐☐☐☐☐
J37	D2	50¢ deep claret	150.00	55.00	☐☐☐☐☐
J37a	D2	50c pale rose	140.00	50.00	☐☐☐☐☐

Wmkd. USPS (191)

Scott® No.	Illus No.	Description	Unused Price	Used Price	/ / / / / /
1895					
J38	D2	1¢ deep claret	1.50	.20	☐☐☐☐☐
J39	D2	2¢ deep claret	1.25	.12	☐☐☐☐☐
J40	D2	3¢ deep claret	6.00	1.00	☐☐☐☐☐
J41	D2	5¢ deep claret	6.00	.50	☐☐☐☐☐
J42	D2	10¢ deep claret	7.00	1.00	☐☐☐☐☐
J43	D2	30¢ deep claret	100.00	12.00	☐☐☐☐☐
J44	D2	50¢ deep claret	35.00	12.00	☐☐☐☐☐

Scott® No.	Illus No.	Description	Unused Price	Used Price	/ / / / / /
1910-12		Wmkd. USPS (190)			
J45	D2	1¢ deep claret	5.50	2.00 ☐☐☐☐☐
J45a	D2	1c rose carmine	5.00	1.75 ☐☐☐☐☐
J46	D2	2¢ deep claret	4.50	.15 ☐☐☐☐☐
J46a	D2	2c rose carmine	4.00	.15 ☐☐☐☐☐
J47	D2	3¢ deep claret	110.00	10.00 ☐☐☐☐☐
J48	D2	5¢ deep claret	15.00	2.00 ☐☐☐☐☐
J49	D2	10¢ deep claret	17.50	4.50 ☐☐☐☐☐
J50	D2	50¢ dp. claret ('12)	250.00	42.50 ☐☐☐☐☐
1914-15		*Perf. 10.*			
J52	D2	1¢ carmine lake	15.00	6.00 ☐☐☐☐☐
J53	D2	2¢ carmine lake	5.00	.15 ☐☐☐☐☐
J53a	D2	2c dull rose	5.00	.10 ☐☐☐☐☐
J53b	D2	2c vermilion	5.00	.10 ☐☐☐☐☐
J54	D2	3¢ carmine lake	125.00	8.50 ☐☐☐☐☐
J55	D2	5¢ carmine lake	5.00	1.00 ☐☐☐☐☐
J56	D2	10¢ carmine lake	10.00	.60 ☐☐☐☐☐
J56a	D2	10c dull rose	10.00	.40 ☐☐☐☐☐
J57	D2	30¢ carmine lake	45.00	12.00 ☐☐☐☐☐
J58	D2	50¢ carmine lake	1750.00	200.00 ☐☐☐☐☐
1916		*Perf. 10* Unwmkd.			
J59	D2	1¢ rose	400.00	100.00 ☐☐☐☐☐
J60	D2	2¢ rose	20.00	1.25 ☐☐☐☐☐
1917		*Perf. 11*			
J61	D2	1¢ carmine rose	.50	.05 ☐☐☐☐☐
J62	D2	2¢ carmine rose	.50	.04 ☐☐☐☐☐
J63	D2	3¢ carmine rose	2.00	.08 ☐☐☐☐☐
J63a	D2	3c rose red	2.00	.07 ☐☐☐☐☐
J63b	D2	3c deep claret	3.00	.25 ☐☐☐☐☐
J64	D2	5¢ carmine	2.00	.08 ☐☐☐☐☐
J64a	D2	5c rose red	1.75	.08 ☐☐☐☐☐
J64b	D2	5c deep claret	1.75	.05 ☐☐☐☐☐
J65	D2	10¢ carmine rose	2.50	.20 ☐☐☐☐☐
J65a	D2	10c rose red	2.25	.06 ☐☐☐☐☐
J65b	D2	10c deep claret	2.25	.06 ☐☐☐☐☐
J66	D2	30¢ carmine rose	10.00	.20 ☐☐☐☐☐
J66a	D2	30c deep claret	9.00	.20 ☐☐☐☐☐
J67	D2	50¢ carmine rose	12.50	.08 ☐☐☐☐☐
J68	D2	½ dull red	.25	.06 ☐☐☐☐☐
1930-31		*Perf. 11*			
J69	D3	½ carmine	1.50	.18 ☐☐☐☐☐
J70	D3	1¢ carmine	1.00	.18 ☐☐☐☐☐
J71	D3	2¢ carmine	2.00	.10 ☐☐☐☐☐
J72	D3	3¢ carmine	7.50	.40 ☐☐☐☐☐
J73	D3	5¢ carmine	6.00	.50 ☐☐☐☐☐
J74	D3	10¢ carmine	7.50	.30 ☐☐☐☐☐
J75	D3	30¢ carmine	30.00	.50 ☐☐☐☐☐

Scott® No.	Illus No.	Description	Unused Price	Used Price	/ / / / / /

1930-31

Scott® No.	Illus No.	Description	Unused Price	Used Price	
J76	D3	50¢ carmine	35.00	.12	☐☐☐☐☐
J77	D4	$1 carmine	12.00	.12	☐☐☐☐☐
J77a	D4	$1 scarlet	10.00	.06	☐☐☐☐☐
J78	D4	$5 carmine	20.00	.18	☐☐☐☐☐
J78a	D4	$5 scarlet	17.50	.18	☐☐☐☐☐

1931-56   *Perf. 11x10½.*   *Perf. 10½x11*

Scott® No.	Illus No.	Description	Unused Price	Used Price	
J79	D3	½ dull carmine	.50	.08	☐☐☐☐☐
J80	D3	1¢ dull carmine	.08	.03	☐☐☐☐☐
J81	D3	2¢ dull carmine	.10	.03	☐☐☐☐☐
J82	D3	3¢ dull carmine	.15	.03	☐☐☐☐☐
J83	D3	5¢ dull carmine	.20	.03	☐☐☐☐☐
J84	D3	10¢ dull carmine	.60	.03	☐☐☐☐☐
J85	D3	30¢ dull carmine	3.25	.08	☐☐☐☐☐
J86	D3	50¢ dull carmine	4.25	.06	☐☐☐☐☐
J87	D4	$1 scarlet ('56)	15.00	.20	☐☐☐☐☐

1959

Scott® No.	Illus No.	Description	Unused Price	Used Price	
J88	D5	½ carmine rose	.60	.30	☐☐☐☐☐
J89	D5	1¢ carmine rose	.04	.04	☐☐☐☐☐
J90	D5	2¢ carmine rose	.06	.05	☐☐☐☐☐
J91	D5	3¢ carmine rose	.07	.04	☐☐☐☐☐
J92	D5	4¢ carmine rose	.08	.04	☐☐☐☐☐
J93	D5	5¢ carmine rose	.10	.04	☐☐☐☐☐
J94	D5	6¢ carmine rose	.12	.05	☐☐☐☐☐
J95	D5	7¢ carmine rose	.14	.05	☐☐☐☐☐
J96	D5	8¢ carmine rose	.16	.05	☐☐☐☐☐
J97	D5	10¢ carmine rose	.20	.04	☐☐☐☐☐
J98	D5	30¢ carmine rose	.70	.05	☐☐☐☐☐
J99	D5	50¢ carmine rose	1.10	.06	☐☐☐☐☐
J100	D5	$1 carmine rose	2.00	.06	☐☐☐☐☐
J101	D5	$5 carmine rose	8.00	.15	☐☐☐☐☐

1978

Scott® No.	Illus No.	Description	Unused Price	Used Price	
J102	D5	11¢ carmine rose	.22	.04	☐☐☐☐☐
J103	D5	13¢ carmine rose	.26	.04	☐☐☐☐☐

......	....				☐☐☐☐☐
......	....				☐☐☐☐☐
......	....				☐☐☐☐☐
......	....				☐☐☐☐☐
......	....				☐☐☐☐☐
......	....				☐☐☐☐☐
......	....				☐☐☐☐☐
......	....				☐☐☐☐☐
......	....				☐☐☐☐☐
......	....				☐☐☐☐☐
......	....				☐☐☐☐☐
......	....				☐☐☐☐☐

Scott® No.	Illus No.	Description	Unused Price	Used Price	/ / / / / /

SHANGHAI

United States Stamps
of 1917-19
Surcharged

2¢

CHINA

1919

K1	A140	2¢ on 1c green	9.00	10.00 ☐☐☐☐☐
K2	A140	4¢ on 2c rose	9.00	10.00 ☐☐☐☐☐
K3	A140	6¢ on 3c violet	20.00	22.50 ☐☐☐☐☐
K4	A140	8¢ on 4c brown	25.00	30.00 ☐☐☐☐☐
K5	A140	10¢ on 5c blue	27.50	32.50 ☐☐☐☐☐
K6	A140	12¢ on 6c red org.	32.50	40.00 ☐☐☐☐☐
K7	A140	14¢ on 7c black	35.00	45.00 ☐☐☐☐☐
K8	A148	16¢ on 8c ol. bis.	26.00	30.00 ☐☐☐☐☐
K8a	A148	16c on 8c olive green	22.50	25.00 ☐☐☐☐☐
K9	A148	18¢ on 9c sal. red	27.50	35.00 ☐☐☐☐☐
K10	A148	20¢ on 10c orange yellow	25.00	30.00 ☐☐☐☐☐
K11	A148	24¢ on 12c brown carmine	30.00	35.00 ☐☐☐☐☐
K12	A148	30¢ on 15c gray	32.50	37.50 ☐☐☐☐☐
K13	A148	40¢ on 20c deep ultramarine	40.00	45.00 ☐☐☐☐☐
K14	A148	60¢ on 30c orange red	40.00	45.00 ☐☐☐☐☐
K15	A148	$1 on 50c lt. vio.	325.00	250.00 ☐☐☐☐☐
K16	A148	$2 on $1 violet brown	185.00	200.00 ☐☐☐☐☐

SHANGHAI

Nos. 498 and 528B
Surcharged

2 Cts.

1922

CHINA

K17	A140	2¢ on 1c green	50.00	40.00 ☐☐☐☐☐
K18	A140	4¢ on 2c carmine, Type VII	50.00	45.00 ☐☐☐☐☐
....				☐☐☐☐☐
....				☐☐☐☐☐
....				☐☐☐☐☐
....				☐☐☐☐☐
....				☐☐☐☐☐
....				☐☐☐☐☐
....				☐☐☐☐☐
....				☐☐☐☐☐
....				☐☐☐☐☐
....				☐☐☐☐☐
....				☐☐☐☐☐
....				☐☐☐☐☐
....				☐☐☐☐☐
....				☐☐☐☐☐
....				☐☐☐☐☐

O1 O2 O3 O4 O5

O6 O7 O8 O9 O10

O11

OFFICIAL STAMPS

1873		**Dept. of Agriculture.**				
O1	O1	1¢ yèllow	25.00	15.00	☐☐☐☐☐
O2	O1	2¢ yellow	12.50	6.00	☐☐☐☐☐
O3	O1	3¢ yellow	10.00	1.65	☐☐☐☐☐
O4	O1	6¢ yellow	15.00	7.00	☐☐☐☐☐
O5	O1	10¢ yellow	35.00	25.00	☐☐☐☐☐
O6	O1	12¢ yellow	60.00	45.00	☐☐☐☐☐
O7	O1	15¢ yellow	35.00	27.50	☐☐☐☐☐
O8	O1	24¢ yellow	45.00	32.50	☐☐☐☐☐
O9	O1	30¢ yellow	60.00	40.00	☐☐☐☐☐
		Executive Dept.				
O10	O2	1¢ carmine	110.00	55.00	☐☐☐☐☐
O11	O2	2¢ carmine	65.00	40.00	☐☐☐☐☐
O12	O2	3¢ carmine	75.00	32.50	☐☐☐☐☐
O12a	O2	3c violet rose	65.00	32.50	☐☐☐☐☐

Scott® No.	Illus No.	Description	Unused Price	Used Price	/ / / / / /
1873					
O13	O2	6¢ carmine	125.00	80.00 ☐☐☐☐☐
O14	O2	10¢ carmine	115.00	75.00 ☐☐☐☐☐
		Dept. of the Interior.			
O15	O3	1¢ vermilion	4.25	1.50 ☐☐☐☐☐
O16	O3	2¢ vermilion	3.00	1.00 ☐☐☐☐☐
O17	O3	3¢ vermilion	9.50	1.00 ☐☐☐☐☐
O18	O3	6¢ vermilion	7.00	1.00 ☐☐☐☐☐
O19	O3	10¢ vermilion	5.00	2.25 ☐☐☐☐☐
O20	O3	12¢ vermilion	8.50	1.75 ☐☐☐☐☐
O21	O3	15¢ vermilion	17.50	5.00 ☐☐☐☐☐
O22	O3	24¢ vermilion	12.50	3.50 ☐☐☐☐☐
O23	O3	30¢ vermilion	13.50	4.00 ☐☐☐☐☐
O24	O3	90¢ vermilion	35.00	6.00 ☐☐☐☐☐
		Dept. of Justice.			
O25	O4	1¢ purple	11.00	10.00 ☐☐☐☐☐
O26	O4	2¢ purple	22.50	13.00 ☐☐☐☐☐
O27	O4	3¢ purple	30.00	5.00 ☐☐☐☐☐
O28	O4	6¢ purple	20.00	6.00 ☐☐☐☐☐
O29	O4	10¢ purple	22.50	15.00 ☐☐☐☐☐
O30	O4	12¢ purple	12.00	6.00 ☐☐☐☐☐
O31	O4	15¢ purple	40.00	27.50 ☐☐☐☐☐
O32	O4	24¢ purple	130.00	70.00 ☐☐☐☐☐
O33	O4	30¢ purple	120.00	50.00 ☐☐☐☐☐
O34	O4	90¢ purple	200.00	100.00 ☐☐☐☐☐
		Navy Dept.			
O35	O5	1¢ ultramarine	12.50	6.00 ☐☐☐☐☐
O36	O5	2¢ ultramarine	9.00	5.00 ☐☐☐☐☐
O37	O5	3¢ ultramarine	10.00	2.25 ☐☐☐☐☐
O38	O5	6¢ ultramarine	6.50	3.25 ☐☐☐☐☐
O39	O5	7¢ ultramarine	70.00	30.00 ☐☐☐☐☐
O40	O5	10¢ ultramarine	11.50	6.50 ☐☐☐☐☐
O41	O5	12¢ ultramarine	16.50	5.00 ☐☐☐☐☐
O42	O5	15¢ ultramarine	32.50	13.00 ☐☐☐☐☐
O43	O5	24¢ ultramarine	32.50	20.00 ☐☐☐☐☐
O44	O5	30¢ ultramarine	25.00	9.00 ☐☐☐☐☐
O45	O5	90¢ ultramarine	120.00	50.00 ☐☐☐☐☐
		Post Office Dept.			
O47	O6	1¢ black	3.75	2.00 ☐☐☐☐☐
O48	O6	2¢ black	3.25	1.65 ☐☐☐☐☐
O49	O6	3¢ black	1.00	.50 ☐☐☐☐☐
O50	O6	6¢ black	3.00	1.20 ☐☐☐☐☐
O51	O6	10¢ black	15.00	10.00 ☐☐☐☐☐
O52	O6	12¢ black	7.00	2.00 ☐☐☐☐☐
O53	O6	15¢ black	8.00	4.25 ☐☐☐☐☐
O54	O6	24¢ black	11.50	4.00 ☐☐☐☐☐

Scott® No.	Illus No.	Description	Unused Price	Used Price	/ / / / / /
1873					
O55	O6	30¢ black	11.00	4.00 ☐☐☐☐☐
O56	O6	90¢ black	15.00	5.00 ☐☐☐☐☐
		Dept. of State.			
O57	O7	1¢ dark green	12.50	6.50 ☐☐☐☐☐
O58	O7	2¢ dark green	32.50	15.00 ☐☐☐☐☐
O59	O7	3¢ bright green	9.00	5.00 ☐☐☐☐☐
O60	O7	6¢ bright green	7.00	5.00 ☐☐☐☐☐
O61	O7	7¢ dark green	21.00	10.00 ☐☐☐☐☐
O62	O7	10¢ dark green	12.50	8.50 ☐☐☐☐☐
O63	O7	12¢ dark green	27.50	20.00 ☐☐☐☐☐
O64	O7	15¢ dark green	16.00	10.00 ☐☐☐☐☐
O65	O7	24¢ dark green	67.50	50.00 ☐☐☐☐☐
O66	O7	30¢ dark green	52.50	30.00 ☐☐☐☐☐
O67	O7	90¢ dark green	135.00	70.00 ☐☐☐☐☐
O68	O8	$2 green & black	250.00	135.00 ☐☐☐☐☐
O69	O8	$5 green & black	2000.00	1200.00 ☐☐☐☐☐
O70	O8	$10 green & black	1150.00	800.00 ☐☐☐☐☐
O71	O8	$20 green & black	1000.00	650.00 ☐☐☐☐☐
		Treasury Dept.			
O72	O9	1¢ brown	5.00	1.10 ☐☐☐☐☐
O73	O9	2¢ brown	7.50	1.10 ☐☐☐☐☐
O74	O9	3¢ brown	3.25	.50 ☐☐☐☐☐
O75	O9	6¢ brown	7.00	.50 ☐☐☐☐☐
O76	O9	7¢ brown	11.00	7.00 ☐☐☐☐☐
O77	O9	10¢ brown	11.00	1.50 ☐☐☐☐☐
O78	O9	12¢ brown	11.00	.75 ☐☐☐☐☐
O79	O9	15¢ brown	12.50	1.50 ☐☐☐☐☐
O80	O9	24¢ brown	65.00	25.00 ☐☐☐☐☐
O81	O9	30¢ brown	20.00	1.50 ☐☐☐☐☐
O82	O9	90¢ brown	20.00	1.25 ☐☐☐☐☐
		War Dept.			
O83	O10	1¢ rose	22.50	1.25 ☐☐☐☐☐
O84	O10	2¢ rose	22.50	2.50 ☐☐☐☐☐
O85	O10	3¢ rose	20.00	.65 ☐☐☐☐☐
O86	O10	6¢ rose	75.00	1.10 ☐☐☐☐☐
O87	O10	7¢ rose	16.50	11.00 ☐☐☐☐☐
O88	O10	10¢ rose	5.00	1.50 ☐☐☐☐☐
O89	O10	12¢ rose	18.50	1.00 ☐☐☐☐☐
O90	O10	15¢ rose	2.25	.65 ☐☐☐☐☐
O91	O10	24¢ rose	3.25	1.10 ☐☐☐☐☐
O92	O10	30¢ rose	3.00	.90 ☐☐☐☐☐
O93	O10	90¢ rose	10.00	6.00 ☐☐☐☐☐
1879		**Dept. of Agriculture.**			
O94	O1	1¢ yellow	750.00	☐☐☐☐☐
O95	O1	3¢ yellow	75.00	12.50 ☐☐☐☐☐

Scott® No.	Illus No.	Description	Unused Price	Used Price	/ / / / / /
1879		**Dept. of the Interior.**			
O96	O3	1¢ vermilion	45.00	30.00 ☐☐☐☐☐	
O97	O3	2¢ vermilion	.75	.55 ☐☐☐☐☐	
O98	O3	3¢ vermilion	.60	.35 ☐☐☐☐☐	
O99	O3	6¢ vermilion	.75	.55 ☐☐☐☐☐	
O100	O3	10¢ vermilion	11.00	10.00 ☐☐☐☐☐	
O101	O3	12¢ vermilion	20.00	15.00 ☐☐☐☐☐	
O102	O3	15¢ vermilion	47.50	35.00 ☐☐☐☐☐	
O103	O3	24¢ vermilion	700.00	☐☐☐☐☐	
		Dept. of Justice.			
O106	O4	3¢ bluish purple	15.00	10.00 ☐☐☐☐☐	
O107	O4	6¢ bluish purple	45.00	35.00 ☐☐☐☐☐	
		Post Office Dept.			
O108	O6	3¢ black	2.00	.90 ☐☐☐☐☐	
		Treasury Dept.			
O109	O9	3¢ brown	6.50	2.00 ☐☐☐☐☐	
O110	O9	6¢ brown	15.00	10.00 ☐☐☐☐☐	
O111	O9	10¢ brown	25.00	6.00 ☐☐☐☐☐	
O112	O9	30¢ brown	400.00	100.00 ☐☐☐☐☐	
O113	O9	90¢ brown	400.00	100.00 ☐☐☐☐☐	
		War Dept.			
O114	O10	1¢ rose red	.45	.45 ☐☐☐☐☐	
O115	O10	2¢ rose red	.70	.65 ☐☐☐☐☐	
O116	O10	3¢ rose red	.55	.35 ☐☐☐☐☐	
O117	O10	6¢ rose red	.45	.40 ☐☐☐☐☐	
O118	O10	10¢ rose red	5.00	5.00 ☐☐☐☐☐	
O119	O10	12¢ rose red	3.50	1.00 ☐☐☐☐☐	
O120	O10	30¢ rose red	15.00	15.00 ☐☐☐☐☐	
		Official Postal Savings Mail.			
1911		Wmkd. USPS (191)			
O121	O11	2¢ black	5.00	.60 ☐☐☐☐☐	
O122	O11	50¢ dark green	55.00	20.00 ☐☐☐☐☐	
O123	O11	$1 ultramarine	35.00	6.50 ☐☐☐☐☐	
		Wmkd. USPS (190)			
O124	O11	1¢ dark violet	2.00	.50 ☐☐☐☐☐	
O125	O11	2¢ black	12.50	2.25 ☐☐☐☐☐	
O126	O11	10¢ carmine	5.00	.60 ☐☐☐☐☐	
......	....	....	....	☐☐☐☐☐	
......	....	....	....	☐☐☐☐☐	
......	....	....	....	☐☐☐☐☐	
......	....	....	....	☐☐☐☐☐	
......	....	....	....	☐☐☐☐☐	
......	....	....	....	☐☐☐☐☐	
......	....	....	....	☐☐☐☐☐	
......	....	....	....	☐☐☐☐☐	

Scott® No.	Illus No.	Description	Unused Price	Used Price	/ / / / / /
....	....				☐☐☐☐☐
....	....				☐☐☐☐☐
....	....				☐☐☐☐☐
....	....				☐☐☐☐☐
....	....				☐☐☐☐☐
....	....				☐☐☐☐☐
....	....				☐☐☐☐☐
....	....				☐☐☐☐☐
....	....				☐☐☐☐☐
....	....				☐☐☐☐☐
....	....				☐☐☐☐☐
....	....				☐☐☐☐☐
....	....				☐☐☐☐☐
....	....				☐☐☐☐☐
....	....				☐☐☐☐☐
....	....				☐☐☐☐☐
....	....				☐☐☐☐☐
....	....				☐☐☐☐☐
....	....				☐☐☐☐☐
....	....				☐☐☐☐☐
....	....				☐☐☐☐☐
....	....				☐☐☐☐☐
....	....				☐☐☐☐☐
....	....				☐☐☐☐☐
....	....				☐☐☐☐☐
....	....				☐☐☐☐☐
....	....				☐☐☐☐☐
....	....				☐☐☐☐☐
....	....				☐☐☐☐☐
....	....				☐☐☐☐☐
....	....				☐☐☐☐☐
....	....				☐☐☐☐☐
....	....				☐☐☐☐☐
....	....				☐☐☐☐☐
....	....				☐☐☐☐☐
....	....				☐☐☐☐☐
....	....				☐☐☐☐☐
....	....				☐☐☐☐☐
....	....				☐☐☐☐☐
....	....				☐☐☐☐☐
....	....				☐☐☐☐☐
....	....				☐☐☐☐☐

N1   N2   N3

N4   N5   N6   N7

N8   N9   N10   N11

N12   N13   N14

NEWSPAPER STAMPS

Scott® No.	Illus No.	Description	Unused Price	Used Price	/ / / / / /
1865		Thin Hard Paper, No Gum.			
PR1	N1	5¢ dark blue	80.00		☐☐☐☐☐
PR2	N2	10¢ blue green	35.00		☐☐☐☐☐
PR3	N3	25¢ orange red	25.00		☐☐☐☐☐
		White Border. Yellowish Paper.			
PR4	N1	5¢ light blue	16.50	15.00	☐☐☐☐☐
1875		Hard White Paper, No Gum.			
PR5	N1	5¢ dull blue	30.00		☐☐☐☐☐
PR6	N2	10¢ dark bluish green	20.00		☐☐☐☐☐
PR7	N3	25¢ dark carmine	35.00		☐☐☐☐☐
1880		Soft Porous Paper. White Border.			
PR8	N1	5¢ dark blue	60.00		☐☐☐☐☐
1875		Thin Hard Paper			
PR9	N4	2¢ black	3.00	2.50	☐☐☐☐☐
PR10	N4	3¢ black	5.00	3.50	☐☐☐☐☐
PR11	N4	4¢ black	4.00	3.25	☐☐☐☐☐
PR12	N4	6¢ black	5.50	5.00	☐☐☐☐☐
PR13	N4	8¢ black	8.50	5.50	☐☐☐☐☐
PR14	N4	9¢ black	15.00	10.00	☐☐☐☐☐
PR15	N4	10¢ black	8.00	4.00	☐☐☐☐☐
PR16	N5	12¢ rose	15.00	6.00	☐☐☐☐☐
PR17	N5	24¢ rose	22.50	12.50	☐☐☐☐☐
PR18	N5	36¢ rose	25.00	15.00	☐☐☐☐☐
PR19	N5	48¢ rose	52.50	20.00	☐☐☐☐☐
PR20	N5	60¢ rose	22.50	15.00	☐☐☐☐☐
PR21	N5	72¢ rose	55.00	35.00	☐☐☐☐☐
PR22	N5	84¢ rose	70.00	40.00	☐☐☐☐☐
PR23	N5	96¢ rose	50.00	30.00	☐☐☐☐☐
PR24	N6	1.92 dark brown	55.00	25.00	☐☐☐☐☐
PR25	N7	$3 vermilion	70.00	35.00	☐☐☐☐☐
PR26	N8	$6 ultramarine	140.00	65.00	☐☐☐☐☐
PR27	N9	$9 yellow	175.00	70.00	☐☐☐☐☐
PR28	N10	$12 blue green	185.00	75.00	☐☐☐☐☐
PR29	N11	$24 dk. gray vio.	185.00	85.00	☐☐☐☐☐
PR30	N12	$36 brown rose	250.00	125.00	☐☐☐☐☐
PR31	N13	$48 red brown	325.00	200.00	☐☐☐☐☐
PR32	N14	$60 violet	325.00	150.00	☐☐☐☐☐
		Special Printing. Hard White Paper. Without Gum.			
PR33	N4	2¢ gray black	35.00		☐☐☐☐☐
PR34	N4	3¢ gray black	35.00		☐☐☐☐☐
PR35	N4	4¢ gray black	35.00		☐☐☐☐☐
PR36	N4	6¢ gray black	45.00		☐☐☐☐☐
PR37	N4	8¢ gray black	50.00		☐☐☐☐☐
PR38	N4	9¢ gray black	55.00		☐☐☐☐☐
PR39	N4	10¢ gray black	60.00		☐☐☐☐☐

N15

N16

N17

N18

N19

N20

N21

N22

Scott® No.	Illus No.	Description	Unused Price	Used Price	/ / / / / /
1875					
PR40	N5	12¢ pale rose	80.00		☐☐☐☐☐
PR41	N5	24¢ pale rose	125.00		☐☐☐☐☐
PR42	N5	36¢ pale rose	150.00		☐☐☐☐☐
PR43	N5	48¢ pale rose	200.00		☐☐☐☐☐
PR44	N5	60¢ pale rose	275.00		☐☐☐☐☐
PR45	N5	72¢ pale rose	350.00		☐☐☐☐☐
PR46	N5	84¢ pale rose	375.00		☐☐☐☐☐
PR47	N5	96¢ pale rose	450.00		☐☐☐☐☐
PR48	N6	1.92 dk. brown	1250.00		☐☐☐☐☐
PR49	N7	$3 vermilion	2000.00		☐☐☐☐☐
PR50	N8	$6 ultramarine	2750.00		☐☐☐☐☐
PR51	N9	$9 yellow			☐☐☐☐☐
PR52	N10	$12 blue green			☐☐☐☐☐
PR53	N11	$24 dk. gray vio.			☐☐☐☐☐
PR54	N12	$36 brown rose			☐☐☐☐☐
PR55	N13	$48 red brown			☐☐☐☐☐
PR56	N14	$60 violet			☐☐☐☐☐
1879		Soft Porous Paper			
PR57	N4	2¢ black	1.75	1.50	☐☐☐☐☐
PR58	N4	3¢ black	2.25	1.75	☐☐☐☐☐
PR59	N4	4¢ black	2.25	2.00	☐☐☐☐☐
PR60	N4	6¢ black	5.25	5.00	☐☐☐☐☐
PR61	N4	8¢ black	5.25	5.00	☐☐☐☐☐
PR62	N4	10¢ black	5.00	3.75	☐☐☐☐☐
PR63	N5	12¢ red	16.00	10.00	☐☐☐☐☐
PR64	N5	24¢ red	16.00	8.50	☐☐☐☐☐
PR65	N5	36¢ red	65.00	37.50	☐☐☐☐☐
PR66	N5	48¢ red	45.00	25.00	☐☐☐☐☐
PR67	N5	60¢ red	35.00	25.00	☐☐☐☐☐
PR68	N5	72¢ red	85.00	50.00	☐☐☐☐☐
PR69	N5	84¢ red	62.50	42.50	☐☐☐☐☐
PR70	N5	96¢ red	45.00	30.00	☐☐☐☐☐
PR71	N6	1.92 pale brown	35.00	25.00	☐☐☐☐☐
PR72	N7	$3 red verm.	35.00	25.00	☐☐☐☐☐
PR73	N8	$6 blue	60.00	35.00	☐☐☐☐☐
PR74	N9	$9 orange	37.50	20.00	☐☐☐☐☐
PR75	N10	$12 yellow green	55.00	30.00	☐☐☐☐☐
PR76	N11	$24 dark violet	77.50	40.00	☐☐☐☐☐
PR77	N12	$36 Indian red	100.00	50.00	☐☐☐☐☐
PR78	N13	$48 yel. brown	125.00	60.00	☐☐☐☐☐
PR79	N14	$60 purple	140.00	60.00	☐☐☐☐☐
1883		Special Printing.			
PR80	N4	2¢ intense black	85.00		☐☐☐☐☐
1885					
PR81	N4	1¢ black	1.50	1.10	☐☐☐☐☐
PR82	N5	12¢ carmine	6.00	3.50	☐☐☐☐☐

PP1

PP2

PP3

PP4

PP5

PP6

PP7

PP8

PP9

PP10

PP11

PP12

Scott® No.	Illus No.	Description	Unused Price	Used Price	//////
1885					
PR83	N5	24¢ carmine	7.00	5.00 □□□□□
PR84	N5	36¢ carmine	10.00	6.00 □□□□□
PR85	N5	48¢ carmine	15.00	10.00 □□□□□
PR86	N5	60¢ carmine	22.00	14.00 □□□□□
PR87	N5	72¢ carmine	30.00	17.50 □□□□□
PR88	N5	84¢ carmine	55.00	32.50 □□□□□
PR89	N5	96¢ carmine	37.50	25.00 □□□□□
1894					
PR90	N4	1¢ intense black	8.50	□□□□□
PR91	N4	2¢ intense black	8.50	□□□□□
PR92	N4	4¢ intense black	10.00	□□□□□
PR93	N4	6¢ intense black	400.00	□□□□□
PR94	N4	10¢ intense black	16.00	□□□□□
PR95	N5	12¢ pink	100.00	□□□□□
PR96	N5	24¢ pink	85.00	□□□□□
PR97	N5	36¢ pink	600.00	□□□□□
PR98	N5	60¢ pink	600.00	□□□□□
PR99	N5	96¢ pink	1000.00	□□□□□
PR100	N7	$3 scarlet	1750.00	□□□□□
PR101	N8	$6 pale blue	2500.00	□□□□□
1895					
PR102	N15	1¢ black	6.00	1.35 □□□□□
PR103	N15	2¢ black	7.00	1.75 □□□□□
PR104	N15	5¢ black	8.50	2.25 □□□□□
PR105	N15	10¢ black	20.00	7.50 □□□□□
PR106	N16	25¢ carmine	25.00	8.50 □□□□□
PR107	N16	50¢ carmine	60.00	25.00 □□□□□
PR108	N17	$2 scarlet	70.00	10.00 □□□□□
PR109	N18	$5 ultramarine	100.00	40.00 □□□□□
PR110	N19	$10 green	90.00	40.00 □□□□□
PR111	N20	$20 slate	175.00	85.00 □□□□□
PR112	N21	$50 dull rose	175.00	75.00 □□□□□
PR113	N22	$100 purple	200.00	100.00 □□□□□
1895-97		Wmkd. USPS (191)			
PR114	N15	1¢ black ('96)	.80	.70 □□□□□
PR115	N15	2¢ black	.75	.60 □□□□□
PR116	N15	5¢ black ('96)	1.60	1.40 □□□□□
PR117	N15	10¢ black	.85	.65 □□□□□
PR118	N16	25¢ carmine	1.50	1.20 □□□□□
PR119	N16	50¢ carmine	1.75	1.10 □□□□□
PR120	N17	$2 scarlet ('97)	3.50	3.00 □□□□□
1912-13		**PARCEL POST STAMPS**			
Q1	PP1	1¢ carmine rose	2.50	.55 □□□□□
Q2	PP2	2¢ carmine rose	3.00	.40 □□□□□
Q3	PP3	3¢ carmine ('13)	6.00	3.00 □□□□□

PP13

PPD1

OC1

OC2

Scott® No.	Illus No.	Description	Unused Price	Used Price	/ / / / / /
1912-13					
Q4	PP4	4¢ carmine rose	15.00	1.10 ☐☐☐☐☐
Q5	PP5	5¢ carmine rose	12.50	.60 ☐☐☐☐☐
Q6	PP6	10¢ carmine rose	27.50	1.25 ☐☐☐☐☐
Q7	PP7	15¢ carmine rose	35.00	6.50 ☐☐☐☐☐
Q8	PP8	20¢ carmine rose	85.00	10.00 ☐☐☐☐☐
Q9	PP9	25¢ carmine rose	30.00	3.50 ☐☐☐☐☐
Q10	PP10	50¢ carmine rose ('13)	120.00	25.00 ☐☐☐☐☐
Q11	PP11	75¢ carmine rose	35.00	20.00 ☐☐☐☐☐
Q12	PP12	$1 carmine rose ('13)	250.00	12.00 ☐☐☐☐☐

SPECIAL HANDLING STAMPS

Scott® No.	Illus No.	Description	Unused Price	Used Price	/ / / / / /
1925-29					
QE1	PP13	10¢ yel. grn. ('28)	1.25	.75 ☐☐☐☐☐
QE2	PP13	15¢ yel. grn. ('28)	1.50	.75 ☐☐☐☐☐
QE3	PP13	20¢ yel. grn. ('28)	1.75	1.25 ☐☐☐☐☐
QE4	PP13	25¢ yel. grn. ('29)	22.50	5.75 ☐☐☐☐☐
QE4a	PP13	25c deep green ('25)	25.00	3.50 ☐☐☐☐☐

PARCEL POST POSTAGE DUE STAMPS

Scott® No.	Illus No.	Description	Unused Price	Used Price	/ / / / / /
1912					
JQ1	PPD1	1¢ dark green	6.00	2.00 ☐☐☐☐☐
JQ2	PPD1	2¢ dark green	60.00	15.00 ☐☐☐☐☐
JQ3	PPD1	5¢ dark green	6.50	2.50 ☐☐☐☐☐
JQ4	PPD1	10¢ dark green	100.00	32.50 ☐☐☐☐☐
JQ5	PPD1	25¢ dark green	40.00	2.00 ☐☐☐☐☐

CARRIER'S STAMPS

Scott® No.	Illus No.	Description	Unused Price	Used Price	/ / / / / /
1851					
LO1	OC1	1¢ dull blue (shades), *rose*	1200.00	1750.00 ☐☐☐☐☐
LO2	OC2	1¢ blue	15.00	20.00 ☐☐☐☐☐

GOVERNMENT REPRINTS

Scott® No.	Illus No.	Description	Unused Price	Used Price	/ / / / / /
1875					
LO3	OC1	1¢ blue, *rose* imperf.	25.00	☐☐☐☐☐
LO4	OC1	1¢ blue perf. 12	1200.00	☐☐☐☐☐
LO5	OC2	1¢ blue imperf.	17.50	☐☐☐☐☐
LO6	OC2	1¢ blue perf. 12	50.00	☐☐☐☐☐

Scott® No.	Illus No.	Description	Unused Price	Used Price	/ / / / / /
......	......				☐☐☐☐☐
......	......				☐☐☐☐☐
......	......				☐☐☐☐☐
......	......				☐☐☐☐☐
......	......				☐☐☐☐☐
......	......				☐☐☐☐☐
......	......				☐☐☐☐☐
......	......				☐☐☐☐☐
......	......				☐☐☐☐☐
......	......				☐☐☐☐☐
......	......				☐☐☐☐☐
......	......				☐☐☐☐☐
......	......				☐☐☐☐☐
......	......				☐☐☐☐☐
......	......				☐☐☐☐☐
......	......				☐☐☐☐☐
......	......				☐☐☐☐☐
......	......				☐☐☐☐☐
......	......				☐☐☐☐☐
......	......				☐☐☐☐☐
......	......				☐☐☐☐☐
......	......				☐☐☐☐☐
......	......				☐☐☐☐☐
......	......				☐☐☐☐☐
......	......				☐☐☐☐☐
......	......				☐☐☐☐☐
......	......				☐☐☐☐☐
......	......				☐☐☐☐☐
......	......				☐☐☐☐☐
......	......				☐☐☐☐☐
......	......				☐☐☐☐☐
......	......				☐☐☐☐☐
......	......				☐☐☐☐☐
......	......				☐☐☐☐☐
......	......				☐☐☐☐☐
......	......				☐☐☐☐☐
......	......				☐☐☐☐☐
......	......				☐☐☐☐☐
......	......				☐☐☐☐☐
......	......				☐☐☐☐☐
......	......				☐☐☐☐☐
......	......				☐☐☐☐☐
......	......				☐☐☐☐☐
......	......				☐☐☐☐☐
......	......				☐☐☐☐☐
......	......				☐☐☐☐☐

PLATE NUMBER BLOCKS, SHEET AND FIRST DAY COVER PRICES

The Plate Block and First Day Cover prices have been derived from the 1979 edition of Scott's Specialized Catalogue of United States Stamps. The sheet prices were developed by the Editiorial Staff of Scott Publishing Co. exclusively for this edition. Sheet prices start with the 1957 Flag Issue (Scott 1094), the beginning of contemporary multicolor and multiple plate number printing.
All plate blocks are blocks of four, unless otherwise indicated in parenthesis.

Scott No.		Pl. Blk.	Sheet	FDC	Scott No.		Pl. Blk.	Sheet	FDC
		1893			281	(6)	275.00		
230	(6)	400.00		1,200.00	282	(6)	375.00		
231	(6)	375.00		850.00	282C	(6)	1,100.00		
232	(6)	675.00		3,000.00	283	(6)	800.00		
233	(6)	850.00		3,000.00	284	(6)	1,000.00		
234	(6)	1,000.00		3,250.00			**1898**		
235	(6)	900.00		4,000.00	285		200.00		2,500.00
236	(6)	675.00			286		200.00		2,300.00
237	(6)	1,500.00		4,000.00	287		1,100.00		
238	(6)	2,500.00			288		900.00		3,250.00
239	(6)	3,500.00			289		1,300.00		5,000.00
240	(6)	5,000.00			290		1,500.00		
241	(6)	11,500.00			291		7,250.00		6,000.00
242	(6)	12,500.00		7,500.00	292		19,000.00		
243	(6)	20,000.00			293		37,500.00		
244	(6)	35,000.00					**1901**		
245	(6)	38,500.00			294		75.00		1,650.00
		1894			295		75.00		1,500.00
		With Triangles			296		450.00		2,500.00
		Unwatermarked			297		450.00		2,600.00
246	(6)	165.00			298		575.00		
247	(6)	300.00			299		775.00		
248	(6)	95.00					**1902-03**		
249	(6)	525.00			300	(6)	100.00		2,000.00
250	(6)	150.00			301	(6)	115.00		2,000.00
251	(6)	1,150.00			302	(6)	425.00		2,000.00
252	(6)	500.00			303	(6)	425.00		2,000.00
253	(6)	450.00			304	(6)	425.00		2,200.00
254	(6)	450.00			305	(6)	550.00		2,200.00
255	(6)	325.00			306	(6)	350.00		2,400.00
256	(6)	575.00			307	(6)	600.00		2,400.00
257	(6)	425.00			308	(6)	325.00		
258	(6)	1,000.00			309	(6)	2,000.00		
259	(6)	1,750.00			310	(6)	4,250.00		
260	(6)	2,350.00			311	(6)	8,000.00		
261	(6)	6,000.00			312	(6)	12,000.00		
261A	(6)	9,500.00			313	(6)	35,000.00		
262	(6)	12,000.00					**1906-08**		
263	(6)	—					**Imperforate**		
		1895			314	(6)	185.00		
		With Triangles			315	(6)	4,250.00		
		Watermarked					**1903**		
264	(6)	75.00			319	(6)	75.00		
265	(6)	200.00					**1906**		
266	(6)	250.00					**Imperforate**		
267	(6)	55.00			320	(6)	165.00		
268	(6)	300.00					**1904**		
269	(6)	300.00			323		165.00		1,750.00
270	(6)	275.00			324		185.00		1,750.00
271	(6)	475.00			325		500.00		2,100.00
272	(6)	225.00			326		650.00		2,250.00
273	(6)	400.00			327		1,850.00		4,500.00
274	(6)	1,400.00					**1907**		
275	(6)	2,100.00			328	(6)	225.00		—
276	(6)	5,000.00			329	(6)	300.00		
276A	(6)	8,000.00			330	(6)	2,000.00		
277	(6)	7,500.00					**1908-09**		
278	(6)	20,000.00			331	(6)	50.00		750.00
		1898			332	(6)	35.00		750.00
279	(6)	90.00			333	(6)	160.00		1,200.00
279B	(6)	80.00			334	(6)	185.00		
280	(6)	250.00							

Scott No.	Pl. Blk.	Sheet	FDC	Scott No.	Pl. Blk.	Sheet	FDC
335	(6) 275.00		*1,000.00*		**1912-14**		
336	(6) 400.00		*1,000.00*		**Perforated 12**		
337	(6) 250.00		*1,000.00*	414	(6) 250.00		*1,110.00*
338	(6) 450.00		*1,200.00*	415	(6) 325.00		*800.00*
339	(6) 300.00		*1,200.00*	416	(6) 250.00		*1,100.00*
340	(6) 400.00		*1,200.00*	417	(6) 185.00		*1,000.00*
341	(6) *3,000.00*			418	(6) 400.00		*1,200.00*
342	(6) *4,500.00*			419	(6) 900.00		*1,000.00*
	1908-09			420	(6) 825.00		*1,100.00*
	Imperforate			421	(6) 3,750.00		
343	(6) 55.00		*750.00*		**1914**		
344	(6) 95.00				**Watermarked**		
345	(6) 150.00				**Double-Line USPS**		
346	(6) 400.00			422	(6) 2,100.00		
347	(6) 700.00			423	(6) 5,000.00		
	1909				**1914-15**		
	Bluish Paper				**Perforated 10**		
357	(6) 700.00			424	(6) 35.00		
358	(6) 675.00			425	(6) 21.00		
359	(6) 8,500.00			426	(6) 70.00		
361	(6) ———			427	(6) 275.00		
362	(6) 6,500.00			428	(6) 185.00		
363	(6) ———			429	(6) 250.00		
364	(6) 7,000.00			430	(6) 450.00		
365	(6) 12,500.00			431	(6) 225.00		
366	(6) 5,750.00			432	(6) 275.00		
	1909			433	(6) 210.00		
367	(6) 160.00		*325.00*	434	(6) 110.00		
368	(6) 325.00		*1,450.00*	435	(6) 120.00		
369	(6) 2,750.00			437	(6) 500.00		
370	(6) 275.00		*1,450.00*	438	(6) 1,300.00		
371	(6) 500.00		*1,750.00*	439	(6) 2,250.00		
372	(6) 265.00		*700.00*	440	(6) 4,500.00		
373	(6) 575.00		*1,500.00*		**1915**		
	1910-11			460	(6) 5,500.00		
	Watermarked				**1915**		
	Single-Line USPS				**Perforated 11**		
374	(6) 52.50			461	(6) 550.00		
375	(6) 45.00				**1916-17**		
376	(6) 100.00				**Perforated 10**		
377	(6) 140.00				**Unwatermarked**		
378	(6) 165.00			462	(6) 65.00		
379	(6) 325.00			463	(6) 45.00		
380	(6) 575.00			464	(6) 625.00		
381	(6) 525.00			465	(6) 400.00		
382	(6) 950.00			466	(6) 525.00		
	1911			468	(6) 525.00		
	Imperforate			469	(6) 900.00		
383	(6) 50.00			470	(6) 350.00		
384	(6) 135.00			471	(6) 300.00		
	1913			472	(6) 750.00		
397	(6) 165.00		*2,150.00*	473	(6) 140.00		
398	(6) 285.00		*2,350.00*	474	(6) 250.00		
399	(6) 2,000.00		*2,850.00*	475	(6) 1,100.00		
400	(6) 2,500.00		*4,250.00*	476	(6) 1,600.00		
400A	(6) 8,000.00			476A	(6) ———		
	1914-15			477	(6) 9,500.00		
	Perforated 10			478	(6) 5,500.00		
401	(6) 285.00		*1,000.00*	479	(6) 4,750.00		
402	(6) 1,200.00			480	(6) 3,250.00		
403	(6) 3,500.00		*2,400.00*		**1916-17**		
404	(6) 10,000.00				**Imperforate**		
	1912-14			481	(6) 10.00		*700.00*
	Perforated 12			482	(6) 22.50		
405	(6) 40.00		*1,000.00*	483	(6) 120.00		
406	(6) 50.00		*750.00*	484	(6) 85.00		
407	(6) 600.00		*900.00*		**1917-19**		
	1914				**Perforated 11**		
	Imperforate			498	(6) 10.00		*750.00*
408	(6) 15.00		*650.00*	499	(6) 9.00		*750.00*
409	(6) 30.00		*650.00*	500	(6) 1,750.00		
				501	(6) 85.00		*750.00*

Scott No.		Pl. Blk.	Sheet	FDC	Scott No.		Pl. Blk.	Sheet	FDC
502	(6)	110.00			554	(6)	21.00		30.00
503	(6)	100.00		800.00	555	(6)	175.00		25.00
504	(6)	80.00		800.00	556	(6)	170.00		30.00
506	(6)	95.00		800.00	557	(6)	200.00		65.00
507	(6)	275.00		850.00	558	(6)	325.00		125.00
508	(6)	120.00		850.00	559	(6)	50.00		65.00
509	(6)	160.00		900.00	560	(6)	600.00		60.00
510	(6)	140.00		900.00	561	(6)	125.00		60.00
511	(6)	80.00		900.00	562	(6)	225.00		70.00
512	(6)	67.50		900.00	563	(6)	32.50		350.00
513	(6)	100.00			564	(6)	55.00		85.00
514	(6)	350.00		900.00	565	(6)	45.00		200.00
515	(6)	350.00		1,000.00	566	(6)	175.00		200.00
516	(6)	375.00		1,100.00	567	(6)	210.00		200.00
517	(6)	675.00		1,300.00	568	(6)	185.00		400.00
518	(6)	900.00		2,500.00	569	(6)	300.00		500.00
		1917			570	(6)	700.00		550.00
		Type of 1908-09			571	(6)	550.00		2,000.00
		Perforated 11			572	(6)	1,750.00		6,000.00
519	(6)	1,400.00			573	(8)	8,750.00		9,500.00
		1918					**1923-25**		
523	(8)	20,000.00					**Imperforate**		
524	(8)	6,500.00		4,500.00	575	(6)	80.00		
		1918-20			576	(6)	30.00		25.00
		Offset Printing			577	(6)	35.00		
525	(6)	22.50		500.00			**1923-26**		
526	(6)	150.00		450.00			**Perforated 11X10**		
527	(6)	125.00			578		475.00		
528	(6)	37.50			579		275.00		
528A	(6)	300.00					**Perforated 10**		
528B	(6)	110.00			581		50.00		1,500.00
529	(6)	30.00		350.00	582		30.00		35.00
530	(6)	10.00		350.00	583		20.00		
		1918-20			584		185.00		35.00
		Offset, Imperforate			585		125.00		35.00
531	(6)	75.00		450.00	586		120.00		35.00
532	(6)	250.00		550.00	587		45.00		45.00
533	(6)	1,300.00			588		70.00		40.00
534	(6)	75.00			589		210.00		45.00
534A	(6)	275.00			590		35.00		55.00
534B	(6)	9,500.00			591		450.00		60.00
535	(6)	60.00		500.00			**Perforated 11**		
		1919					**Rotary**		
		Offset, Perf. 12½			595		900.00		
536	(6)	115.00		400.00			**1923**		
		1919			610	(6)	27.50		40.00
537	(6)	160.00		475.00	611	(6)	130.00		65.00
		1919			612	(6)	350.00		80.00
		Perforated 11X10					**1924**		
538		65.00		450.00	614	(6)	55.00		30.00
539		8,500.00			615	(6)	90.00		45.00
540		70.00			616	(6)	425.00		70.00
541		350.00		550.00			**1925**		
		1920			617	(6)	50.00		25.00
		Perforated 10X11			618	(6)	110.00		35.00
542	(6)	75.00		300.00	619	(6)	350.00		55.00
		1921			620	(8)	325.00		25.00
		Rotary			621	(8)	1,000.00		55.00
543		12.00					**1925-26**		
545		625.00			622	(6)	165.00		22.50
546		400.00			623	(6)	175.00		22.50
		1920					**1926**		
547	(8)	6,750.00			627	(6)	65.00		15.00
548	(6)	75.00		425.00	628	(6)	110.00		22.50
549	(6)	100.00		350.00	629	(6)	65.00		5.00
550	(6)	750.00			631		65.00		10.00
		1922-25					**1926-34**		
		Perforated 11					**Perforated 11X10½**		
551	(6)	4.00		10.00	632		2.00		35.00
552	(6)	20.00		22.50	633		65.00		35.00
553	(6)	32.50		25.00	634		.75		37.50

179

Scott No.		Pl. Blk.	Sheet	FDC	Scott No.		Pl. Blk.	Sheet	FDC
634A		1,500.00			**1931**				
635		3.00			702		2.50		1.50
636		80.00		35.00	703		4.00		1.75
637		17.50		35.00	**1932**				
638		17.50		40.00	704		4.50		2.25
639		20.00		45.00	705		5.50		3.00
640		21.00		40.00	706		25.00		3.00
641		21.00		55.00	707		1.75		3.00
642		32.50		55.00	708		22.50		3.50
1927					709		7.00		3.50
643	(6)	55.00		4.50	710		25.00		4.00
644	(6)	65.00		15.00	711		90.00		4.50
1928					712		8.50		4.50
645	(6)	42.50		5.00	713		115.00		4.50
646		50.00		10.00	714		75.00		5.00
647		185.00		12.00	715		190.00		6.50
648		400.00		25.00	**1932**				
649		17.50		6.50	716	(6)	18.50		2.50
650	(6)	77.50		9.00	717		11.50		1.75
1929					718		27.50		2.50
651	(6)	13.50		4.00	719		37.50		5.00
653		1.00		13.00	720		1.50		4.50
654	(6)	45.00		6.00	724	(6)	20.00		2.00
655		75.00		45.00	725	(6)	35.00		2.00
657	(6)	40.00		2.50	**1933**				
"Kansas"					726	(6)	22.50		2.00
658		21.00		15.00	727		7.00		1.00
659		32.50		15.00	728		3.00		1.00
660		35.00		15.00	729		4.00		1.00
661		135.00		20.00	732		2.00		1.75
662		130.00		20.00	733	(6)	27.50		2.50
663		110.00		22.50	734	(6)	55.00		3.75
664		225.00		27.50	**1934**				
665		267.50		30.00	736	(6)	13.50		.70
666		525.00		55.00	737	(6)	1.50		1.00
667		115.00		45.00	738	(6)	6.75		1.25
668		235.00		45.00	739	(6)	6.50		.75
"Nebraska"					740	(6)	1.50		1.00
669		21.00		15.00	741	(6)	2.00		1.00
670		30.00		15.00	742	(6)	3.50		1.00
671		22.50		15.00	743	(6)	10.00		1.20
672		120.00		20.00	744	(6)	12.00		1.35
673		135.00		22.50	745	(6)	24.00		1.75
674		125.00		22.50	746	(6)	14.50		1.75
675		250.00		35.00	747	(6)	28.50		1.75
676		150.00		35.00	748	(6)	22.50		2.00
677		225.00		35.00	749	(6)	47.50		3.50
678		260.00		40.00	**1935**				
679		575.00		45.00	752	(6)	16.50		6.00
1929					753	(6)	22.50		7.00
680	(6)	42.50		2.25	754	(6)	35.00		7.00
681	(6)	35.00		2.25	755	(6)	35.00		7.00
1930					756	(6)	6.00		7.00
682	(6)	42.50		2.25	757	(6)	8.00		7.00
683	(6)	70.00		2.75	758	(6)	20.00		7.00
684	(6)	1.50		2.25	759	(6)	27.50		7.50
685	(6)	6.50		3.50	760	(6)	32.50		7.50
688	(6)	55.00		3.50	761	(6)	40.00		7.50
689	(6)	35.00		3.50	762	(6)	40.00		8.00
1931					763	(6)	50.00		8.00
690	(6)	23.50		2.25	764	(6)	50.00		9.00
Regular Issue					765	(6)	65.00		10.00
692		16.50		55.00	771	(6)	125.00		17.50
693		32.50		55.00	772		2.00		2.50
694		15.00		55.00	773		2.00		2.50
695		20.00		55.00	774	(6)	2.25		3.00
696		42.50		55.00	775		2.00		2.50
697		23.50		200.00	**1936**				
698		57.50		75.00	776		1.75		2.50
699		40.00		210.00	777		2.00		2.50
700		120.00		150.00	782		1.85		2.50
701		400.00		200.00	783		1.75		2.50
					784		.75		2.00

Scott No.		Pl. Blk.	Sheet	FDC
		1936-37		
785		1.00		2.00
786		1.10		2.00
787		1.50		2.00
788		12.00		2.00
789		12.50		2.50
790		1.00		2.00
791		1.10		2.00
792		1.50		2.00
793		12.00		2.00
794		12.50		2.50
		1937		
795		1.75		2.00
796	(6)	10.00		2.25
798		1.65		2.00
799		1.75		2.00
800		1.75		2.25
801		1.75		2.25
802		1.75		2.25
		1938		
803		.50		.80
804		.30		1.10
805		.35		1.00
806		.35		1.00
807		.50		1.00
808		1.75		1.00
809		2.00		1.60
810		1.50		1.60
811		1.85		1.60
812		2.00		1.60
813		2.25		1.60
814		2.25		1.60
815		2.25		1.70
816		3.50		1.70
817		4.25		1.70
818		4.75		1.70
819		5.00		2.25
820		3.25		2.25
821		6.50		2.50
822		6.00		2.50
823		8.75		2.75
824		8.00		2.75
825		5.00		2.75
826		8.50		3.00
827		10.00		3.75
828		12.50		3.75
829		7.50		3.75
830		35.00		4.00
831		52.50		7.50
832		80.00		32.50
833		225.00		45.00
834		1100.00		80.00
		1938		
835		6.00		2.75
836	(6)	6.00		2.75
837		16.50		2.75
838		8.00		2.75
		1939		
852		1.65		2.50
853		2.00		2.50
854	(6)	4.25		3.00
855		3.50		4.00
856	(6)	6.00		2.50
857		1.65		2.50
858		1.65		2.50
		1940		
859		1.25		1.10
860		1.50		1.10
861		2.00		1.25
862		14.00		2.00
863		60.00		4.50
864		1.85		1.10

Scott No.	Pl. Blk.	Sheet	FDC
865	2.25		1.10
866	4.00		1.10
867	14.00		2.00
868	60.00		5.50
869	1.85		1.10
870	1.65		1.10
871	3.75		1.10
872	15.00		2.00
873	40.00		4.50
874	1.50		1.10
875	1.30		1.10
876	1.75		1.10
877	11.00		2.00
878	37.50		4.50
879	1.50		1.10
880	1.50		1.10
881	2.00		1.25
882	15.00		2.00
883	57.50		4.50
884	1.10		1.10
885	1.10		1.10
886	1.25		1.10
887	12.50		2.00
888	47.50		4.50
889	3.00		1.10
890	1.75		1.10
891	2.75		1.10
892	25.00		2.00
893	120.00		9.00
	1940		
894	7.50		2.00
895	7.00		2.00
896	3.25		2.00
897	3.25		2.00
898	3.25		2.00
899	.60		1.50
900	.70		1.50
901	1.40		1.50
902	7.75		2.00
	1941-43		
903	2.75		1.75
904	1.75		1.75
905	.60		1.50
906	18.50		3.00
907	.50		1.25
908	1.00		1.10
909	13.50		4.00
910	4.75		3.00
911	3.50		2.75
912	3.50		2.75
913	3.50		2.75
914	3.50		2.00
915	3.50		2.00
916	20.00		2.00
917	9.00		2.00
918	7.50		2.00
919	7.50		2.00
920	8.00		2.00
921	12.50		3.25
	1944		
922	1.75		1.25
923	2.00		1.25
924	1.60		1.25
925	2.75		1.25
926	1.50		1.25
	1945		
927	.80		1.25
928	.70		1.00
929	.60		1.00
	1945-46		
930	.30		.90
931	.50		.90

Scott No.	Pl. Blk.	Sheet	FDC	Scott No.	Pl. Blk.	Sheet	FDC
932	.55		.90	**1951**			
933	.65		.90	998	.50		.60
				999	.50		.60
1945				1000	.50		.60
934	.50		.70	1001	.50		.60
935	.50		.70	1002	.50		.60
936	.50		.70	1003	.50		.60
937	.55		.70	**1952**			
938	.50		.70	1004	.50		.60
				1005	.50		.60
1946				1006	.50		.60
939	.50		.70	1007	.50		.60
940	.55		.70	1008	.50		.60
941	.50		.70	1009	.50		.60
942	.50		.70	1010	.50		.60
943	.50		.70	1011	.50		.60
944	.50		.70	1012	.50		.60
				1013	.50		.60
1947				1014	.50		.60
945	.50		.70	1015	.50		.60
946	.50		.70	1016	.50		.60
947	.50		.70				
949	.50		.70	**1953-54**			
950	.50		.70	1017	.50		.60
951	.50		.70	1018	1.00		.60
952	.50		.70	1019	.55		.60
				1020	.50		.60
1948				1021	2.00		.60
953	.50		.60	1022	.50		.60
954	.50		.60	1023	.50		.60
955	.50		.60	1024	.50		.60
956	.50		.60	1025	.50		.60
957	.50		.60	1026	.50		.60
958	.85		.70	1027	.50		.60
959	.50		.60	1028	.50		.60
960	.60		.60	1029	.50		.60
961	.50		.60				
962	.50		.60	**1954-68**			
963	.50		.60	1030	.30		.60
964	1.00		.60	1031	.25		.60
965	2.50		.60	1031A	1.75		.60
966	4.25		1.00	1032	7.50		.60
967	.60		.60	1033	.25		.60
968	.80		.60	1034	2.00		.60
969	.65		.60	1035	.40		.60
970	.65		.60	1036	.50		.60
971	.75		.60	1037	1.50		.60
972	.75		.60	1038	.65		.65.
973	1.00		.60	1039	1.00		.65
974	.65		.60	1040	1.00		.70
975	1.00		.60	1041	5.75		.80
976	5.25		.60	1042	1.25		.60
977	.65		.60	1042A	1.25		.60
978	.70		.60	1043	1.25		.90
979	.65		.60	1044	1.35		.90
980	.75		.60	1044A	1.50		.90
				1045	2.50		.90
1949				1046	2.75		1.00
981	.50		.60	1047	3.25		1.20
982	.50		.60	1048	7.50		1.30
983	.50		.60	1049	8.50		1.50
984	.50		.60	1050	13.50		1.75
985	.50		.60	1051	16.00		4.50
986	.60		.60	1052	42.50		8.50
				1053	625.00		55.00
1950				**1954**			
987	.50		.60	1060	.50		.60
988	.55		.60	1061	.50		.60
989	.50		.60	1062	.60		.60
990	.50		.60	1063	.50		.60
991	.50		.60				
992	.50		.60	**1955**			
993	.50		.60	1064	.50		.60
994	.50		.60	1065	.50		.60
995	.55		.60	1066	1.75		.60
996	.50		.60	1067	.50		.60
997	.50		.60				

Scott No.	Pl. Blk.	Sheet	FDC	Scott No.	Pl. Blk.	Sheet	FDC
1068	.50		.60		**1960-61**		
1069	.50		.60	1138	.50	7.00	.60
1070	1.50		.60	1139	1.00	9.25	.75
1071	.50		.60	1140	1.00	9.25	.75
1072	.60		.60	1141	1.00	9.25	.75
	1956			1142	1.00	9.25	.75
1073	.50		.60	1143	1.00	9.25	.75
1074	.50		.60	1144	1.00	9.25	.75
1076	.50		.60		**1960**		
1077	.65		.60	1145	.50	5.00	.60
1078	.65		.60	1146	.50	5.00	.60
1079	.65		.60	1147	.60	7.25	.60
1080	.50		.60	1148	2.50	15.50	.65
1081	.50		.60	1149	.50	5.00	.60
1082	.50		.60	1150	.65	5.25	.60
1083	.50		.60	1151	.50	7.00	.60
1084	.50		.60	1152	.50	5.00	.60
1085	.50		.60	1153	.50	5.00	.60
	1957			1154	.50	5.00	.60
1086	.50		.60	1155	.50	5.00	.60
1087	.50		.60	1156	.50	5.00	.60
1088	.50		.60	1157	.50	5.00	.60
1089	.50		.60	1158	.50	5.00	.60
1090	.50		.60	1159	.55	7.25	.60
1091	.50		.60	1160	2.00	15.25	.65
1092	.90		.60	1161	.50	7.00	.60
1093	.50		.60	1162	.50	5.00	.60
1094	.70	5.50	.60	1163	.50	5.00	.60
1095	.70	7.25	.60	1164	.50	5.00	.60
1096	1.90	11.50	.65	1165	.55	7.25	.60
1097	.50	5.00	.60	1166	2.25	15.25	.65
1098	.65	5.25	.60	1167	.50	5.00	.60
1099	.50	5.00	.60	1168	.55	7.25	.60
	1958			1169	2.25	15.25	.65
1100	.50	5.00	.60	1170	.50	7.00	.60
1104	.50	5.00	.60	1171	.50	7.00	.60
1105	.60	7.25	.60	1172	.55	7.25	.60
1106	.50	5.00	.60	1173	4.00	30.00	.75
1107	1.50	8.50	.60		**1961**		
1108	.50	5.00	.60	1174	.55	7.25	.60
1109	.50	5.00	.60	1175	2.25	16.00	.65
1110	.60	7.25	.60	1176	.65	5.25	.60
1111	6.00	23.00	.65	1177	.55	7.25	.60
1112	.50	5.00	.60		**1961-65**		
	1958-59			1178	1.25	9.50	.60
1113	.40	2.75	.60	1179	1.00	8.00	.60
1114	.60	5.25	.60	1180	1.00	8.00	.60
1115	.55	5.25	.60	1181	1.00	8.00	.60
1116	.65	5.25	.60	1182	1.10	9.50	.60
	1958				**1961**		
1117	.60	7.25	.60	1183	.60	5.25	.60
1118	4.25	18.50	.65	1184	.55	5.25	.60
1119	.50	5.00	.60	1185	.55	5.25	.60
1120	.50	5.00	.60	1186	.55	5.25	.60
1121	.50	7.00	.60	1187	1.20	8.00	.60
1122	.60	5.25	.60	1188	.55	5.25	.60
1123	.50	5.00	.60	1189	.55	5.25	.60
	1959			1190	.70	5.25	.60
1124	.50	5.00	.60		**1962**		
1125	.55	7.25	.60	1191	.55	5.25	.60
1126	2.25	15.00	.65	1192	1.00	8.25	.60
1127	.50	7.00	.60	1193	1.50	11.00	.60
1128	.85	6.75	.60	1194	.55	5.25	.60
1129	1.50	10.75	.60	1195	.55	5.25	.60
1130	.50	5.00	.60	1196	.70	5.25	.60
1131	.50	5.00	.60	1197	.55	5.25	.60
1132	.50	5.00	.60	1198	.55	5.25	.60
1133	.65	5.25	.60	1199	.55	5.25	.60
1134	.50	5.00	.60	1200	1.00	8.00	.60
1135	.50	5.00	.60	1201	.55	5.25	.60
1136	.60	7.25	.60	1202	.55	5.25	.60
1137	2.25	15.00	.65	1203	.70	6.25	.60

Scott No.	Pl. Blk.	Sheet	FDC	Scott No.		Pl. Blk.	Sheet	FDC
1204	5.00	13.00	6.00	1291		3.00	60.00	1.20
1205	.50	10.00	.60	1292		4.00	80.00	1.60
1206	.55	5.25	.60	1293		5.00	100.00	2.50
1207	1.50	8.50	.60	1294		10.00	200.00	5.00
	1962-63			1295		50.00	1,000.00	45.00
1208	.55	12.00	.60		**1966**			
1209	.25	5.00	.60	1306		1.00	8.00	.60
1213	.65	12.00	.60	1307		.90	7.75	.60
	1963			1308		.75	6.50	.60
1230	.60	6.00	.60	1309		.90	6.50	.60
1231	.60	6.00	.60	1310		.90	6.50	.60
1232	.60	6.00	.60	1312		.75	6.50	.60
1233	.60	6.00	.60	1313		.90	8.00	.60
1234	.60	6.00	.60	1314		.75	6.50	.60
1235	.60	6.00	.60	1315		1.00	6.75	.60
1236	.60	6.00	.60	1316		1.00	6.75	.60
1237	1.35	10.50	.60	1317		1.00	6.75	.60
1238	.60	6.00	.60	1318		1.75	8.75	.60
1239	.60	6.00	.60	1319		1.00	6.75	.60
1240	.60	12.00	.60	1320		1.00	6.75	.60
1241	1.25	8.25	.60	1321		.75	12.50	.60
	1964			1322		2.75	12.50	.60
1242	.60	6.00	.60		**1967**			
1243	1.20	8.25	.60	1323		.90	6.50	.60
1244	1.65	9.00	.60	1324		.90	6.50	.60
1245	.60	6.00	.60	1325		.90	6.50	.60
1246	.60	6.00	.60	1326		.90	6.50	.60
1247	.60	6.00	.60	1327		.90	6.50	.60
1248	.60	6.00	.60	1328		.90	6.50	.60
1249	.60	6.00	.60	1329		1.20	6.75	.60
1250	.60	6.00	.60	1330		1.00	6.75	.60
1251	.60	6.00	.60	1331a		17.50	125.00	5.50
1252	.60	6.00	.60	1333		3.00	10.50	.60
1253	.60	6.00	.60	1334		3.50	11.00	.60
1254-1257	5.00	112.50	.60	1335		3.00	11.50	.60
1258	.60	6.00	.60	1336		.60	6.25	.60
1259	.75	6.25	.60	1337		2.50	10.00	.60
1260	.75	6.25	.60		**1968-71**			
	1965			1338		.60	13.00	.60
1261	.75	6.25	.60	1338D	(20)	3.25	13.00	.60
1262	.75	6.25	.60	1338F	(20)	3.50	16.50	.60
1263	.75	6.25	.60		**1968**			
1264	.75	6.25	.60	1339		1.00	9.50	.60
1265	.75	6.25	.60	1340		1.00	9.50	.60
1266	.75	6.25	.60	1341		19.00	192.50	5.00
1267	.75	6.25	.60	1342		1.00	9.50	.60
1268	.75	6.25	.60	1343		1.00	9.50	.60
1269	.75	6.25	.60	1344		1.00	9.50	.60
1270	.75	6.25	.60	1345-1354	(20)	22.50	52.50	2.00ea.
1271	1.00	6.50	.60	1355		1.75	11.50	.60
1272	1.00	6.50	.60	1356		1.10	10.50	.60
1273	1.25	9.50	.60	1357		1.10	10.50	.60
1274	13.50	37.50	.75	1358		1.10	10.50	.60
1275	.75	6.25	.60	1359		1.20	10.50	.60
1276	.60	12.00	.60	1360		1.65	11.00	.60
	1965-73			1361		2.75	14.00	.60
1278	.20	3.00	.35	1362		3.50	17.50	.60
1279	20.00	40.00	.35	1363	(10)	2.75	10.75	.60
1280	.30	4.25	.35	1364		3.50	18.00	.60
1281	.50	6.75	.35		**1969**			
1282	.40	8.00	.35	1365-1368		13.50	110.00	1.50ea.
1283	.50	10.00	.45	1369		1.10	10.50	.60
1283B	1.00	12.00	.45	1370		1.35	13.00	.60
1284	.65	12.50	.45	1371		3.50	17.00	.60
1285	1.25	17.00	.50	1372		1.00	10.50	.60
1286	1.00	20.00	.60	1373		1.00	10.50	.60
1286A	1.50	25.00	.50	1374		1.00	10.50	.60
1287	1.50	26.50	.65	1375		1.00	10.50	.60
1288	1.50	31.00	.60	1376-1379		15.00	152.50	1.75ea.
1289	2.00	40.00	.80	1380		1.35	10.50	.60
1290	2.50	50.00	1.00	1381		1.75	13.25	.60

Scott No.		Pl. Blk.	Sheet	FDC
1382		1.85	13.25	.60
1383		1.00	6.75	.60
1384	(10)	2.25	9.50	.60
1385		1.00	9.50	.60
1386		1.20	6.25	.60
1970				
1387-1390		3.75	13.50	1.25
1391		1.10	9.50	.60
1392		1.10	9.50	.60
1970-74				
1393		.60	12.00	.60
1393D		1.35	15.00	.60
1394		1.00	16.50	.60
1396	(12)	7.50	30.00	.60
1397		2.35	30.00	.85
1398		2.35	33.50	.65
1399		1.80	36.50	1.00
1400		2.10	42.50	1.00
1970				
1405		1.00	9.50	.60
1406		1.00	9.50	.60
1407		1.00	9.50	.60
1408		1.00	9.50	.60
1409		1.00	9.50	.60
1410-1413	(10)	9.00	47.50	1.25ea.
1414	(8)	3.00	12.00	1.20
1415-1418	(8)	12.00	60.00	1.20
1419		1.25	9.75	.60
1420		1.25	9.75	.60
1421-1422		7.00	25.00	.60ea.
1971				
1423		1.00	9.50	.60
1424		1.00	9.50	.60
1425		1.00	9.50	.60
1426	(12)	3.50	11.50	.60
1427-1430		2.25	11.00	1.25ea.
1431		1.65	13.25	.60
1432		7.50	46.50	.75
1433		1.65	12.00	.60
1434a		2.25	16.50	1.00
1436		1.25	9.75	.60
1437		1.25	9.75	.60
1438	(6)	1.85	10.00	.60
1439	(8)	2.10	10.00	.60
1440-1443		2.25	11.50	1.00ea.
1444	(12)	2.50	9.50	.60
1445	(12)	2.50	9.50	.60
1972				
1446		1.00	9.50	.60
1447		1.50	9.75	.60
1451a		2.50	9.00	.60
1452		1.25	8.75	.60
1453		1.00	6.25	.60
1454		2.50	19.00	.60
1455		1.00	8.50	.60
1456-1459		3.00	17.50	.85ea.
1460	(10)	2.00	7.00	.75
1461	(10)	2.25	8.75	.85
1462	(10)	4.00	16.00	1.00
1463		1.00	9.25	.60
1464-1467		1.25	8.00	1.25ea.
1468	(12)	2.75	9.25	.60
1469	(6)	1.35	9.25	.60
1470		1.00	8.50	.60
1471	(12)	2.75	9.00	.60
1472	(12)	2.75	9.00	.60
1473		1.00	8.50	.60
1474		1.00	6.75	.60
1973				
1475		1.35	8.50	.60
1476		1.35	10.75	.60
1477		1.35	10.75	.60
1478		1.35	10.75	.60
1479		1.35	10.75	.60
1480-1483		1.35	11.50	1.50ea.
1484	(12)	2.75	6.25	.60
1485	(12)	2.75	6.25	.60
1486	(12)	2.75	6.25	.60
1487	(12)	2.75	6.25	.60
1488		.80	8.25	.60
1489-1498	(10)	2.25	12.00	.90ea.
1499		1.00	5.50	.60
1500		1.25	6.75	.65
1501		1.00	8.50	.65
1502		2.25	16.00	.75
1503	(12)	2.50	5.75	.60
1973-74				
1504		1.00	8.50	.60
1505		1.00	10.50	.60
1506		1.00	10.50	.60
1507	(12)	2.10	8.25	.60
1508	(12)	2.10	8.25	.60
1509	(20)	4.50	20.00	.60
1510		1.00	20.00	.60
1511	(8)	1.80	20.00	.60
1974				
1525		1.25	10.50	.60
1526		1.00	10.50	.60
1527	(12)	2.60	8.25	.60
1528	(12)	2.60	10.50	.60
1529		1.00	10.50	.60
1530-1537	(10)	2.60	6.75	.90ea.
1538-1541		1.25	9.75	1.25ea.
1542		1.00	10.50	.60
1543-1546		1.20	10.75	.90ea.
1547		1.00	10.50	.60
1548		1.00	10.50	.60
1549		1.00	10.50	.60
1550	(10)	2.20	10.50	.60
1551	(12)	2.60	10.50	.60
1552	(20)	5.50	12.50	.60
1975				
1553	(10)	2.20	10.50	.60
1554	(10)	2.20	10.50	.60
1555		1.00	10.50	.60
1556		1.00	10.50	.75
1557		1.00	10.50	.75
1558	(8)	1.80	10.50	.60
1559	(10)	1.75	8.25	.60
1560	(10)	2.20	10.50	.60
1561	(10)	2.20	10.50	.60
1562	(10)	4.00	19.00	.70
1563	(12)	2.60	8.25	.60
1564	(12)	2.60	8.25	.60
1565-1568	(12)	2.60	10.50	.75ea.
1569-1570	(12)	2.60	5.00	.85ea.
1571	(6)	1.40	10.75	.60
1572-1575	(12)	2.60	10.50	.60ea.
1576		1.00	10.50	.60
1577-1578		1.00	8.50	.60ea.
1579	(12)	2.60	10.50	.60
1580	(12)	2.60	10.50	.60
1975-79				
1581		.15	3.00	.40
1582		.20	4.00	.40
1584		.30	6.00	.40
1585		.40	8.00	.40
1591		.90	18.50	.60
1592		1.00	20.50	.60
1593		1.10	19.50	.60
1596	(12)	3.38	26.50	.60
1597	(6)	2.10	30.50	.65

Scott No.		Pl. Blk.	Sheet	FDC
1599		1.60	32.50	.65
1603		2.40	50.00	.75
1604		2.80	56.50	1.20
1605		2.90	59.00	1.10
1606		3.00	61.00	
1608		5.00	101.00	
1610		10.00	202.50	
1611		20.00	405.00	
1612		50.00	1,010.00	
1622	(20)	5.50	26.50	.65
1976				
1629-1631	(12)	3.40	13.50	.65ea.
1632		1.30	13.50	.65
1633-1682	(50)	25.00	25.00	1.50ea.
1683		1.30	13.50	.65
1684	(10)	2.90	13.50	.65
1685	(12)	3.40	13.50	.65
1690		1.30	13.50	.65
1691-1694	(20)	5.50	14.00	.65ea.
1695-1698	(12)	3.40	14.00	.65ea.
1699	(12)	3.40	11.00	.65
1700		1.30	9.00	.65
1701	(12)	3.40	13.50	.65
1702	(10)	2.86	13.50	.65
1703	(20)	5.70	13.50	.65
1977				
1704	(10)	2.90	10.75	.65
1705		1.30	13.50	.65
1706-1709	(10)	3.00	11.00	.65ea.
1710	(12)	3.65	13.50	.65
1711	(12)	3.65	13.50	.65
1712-1715	(12)	3.65	13.50	.65ea.
1716		1.30	11.00	.65
1717-1720	(12)	3.65	13.50	.65ea.
1721		1.30	13.50	.65
1722	(10)	3.10	11.00	.65ea.
1723-1724	(12)	3.65	11.00	.65ea.
1725		1.30	13.50	.65
1726		1.30	13.50	.65
1727		1.30	13.50	.65
1728	(10)	3.10	11.00	.65
1729	(20)	5.70	26.50	.65
1730	(10)	3.10	26.50	.65
1978				
1731		1.30	13.50	.65
1732		1.30		.65
1733		1.30		.65
1732-1733	(20)	5.75	13.50	
1734		1.30	39.00	.65
1735		1.50	30.00	.65
1744	(12)	3.65	13.50	.65
1745-1748	(12)	3.65	13.00	.65ea.
1749-1752	(12)	3.65	13.00	.65ea.
1753		1.30	13.50	.65
1754		1.30	13.50	.65
1755	(12)	3.65	13.00	.65
1756	(12)	4.20	15.50	.65
1758	(12)	4.20	12.50	.65
1759		1.50	15.50	.65
1760-1763		1.50	15.50	.65ea.
1764-1767	(12)	4.20	12.50	.65ea.
1768	(12)	4.20	30.50	.65
1769	(12)	4.20	30.50	.65
1979				
1770		1.50	15.00	.65
1771	(12)	4.20	15.50	.65
1772		1.50	15.50	.65
1773		1.50	15.50	.65
1774		1.50	15.50	.65
1775-1778	(10)	3.50	12.50	.65ea.
1779-1782		1.50	15.00	.65ea.
1783-1786	(12)	4.20	15.50	.65ea.
1787		1.50	15.50	.65

Scott No.		Pl. Blk.	Sheet	FDC
Air Post				
1918				
C1	(6)	1,250.00		9,000.00
C2	(6)	2,750.00		9,000.00
C3		925.00		10,000.00
1923				
C4	(6)	750.00		250.00
C5	(6)	3,500.00		525.00
C6	(6)	4,250.00		625.00
1926-28				
C7	(6)	87.50		50.00
C8	(6)	90.00		55.00
C9	(6)	210.00		60.00
C10	(6)	250.00		30.00
C11	(6)	75.00		40.00
C12	(6)	300.00		12.50
C13	(6)	6,750.00		650.00
C14	(6)	15,000.00		700.00
C15	(6)	23,500.00		1,000.00
1931-34				
C16		190.00		225.00
C17		67.50		17.50
C18	(6)	1,850.00		110.00
C19		35.00		175.00
1935-39				
C20	(6)	65.00		12.00
C21	(6)	275.00		15.00
C22	(6)	275.00		17.50
C23		12.50		3.50
C24	(6)	275.00		15.00
1941-44				
C25		1.00		1.50
C26		1.50		1.50
C27		14.50		2.00
C28		18.50		2.50
C29		17.50		3.25
C30		20.00		4.50
C31		160.00		11.50
1946-47				
C32		.75		1.00
C33		.75		.75
C34		2.50		1.00
C35		2.85		1.10
C36		6.75		1.50
1948-49				
C38		20.00		1.10
C39		.85		.75
C40		.95		.75
C42		4.75		.85
C43		3.75		.95
C44		15.00		1.35
C45		.85		.55
1952-54				
C46		75.00		8.00
C47		.85		.55
C48		6.00		.50
1957-59				
C49		1.50	10.75	.55
C50		4.00	24.00	.65
C51		1.30	22.50	.65
C53		1.75	13.25	.50
C54		1.75	13.25	.50
C55		1.75	13.25	.50
C56		8.00	26.50	.75
1959-62				
C57		13.50	152.50	.75
C58		4.75	39.50	.90
C59		4.00	34.00	1.25
C60		1.35	28.00	.55
C62		6.00	29.00	.65
C63		2.25	20.50	.90
C64		1.10	18.50	.65

Scott No.		Pl. Blk.	Sheet	FDC
		1963-64		
C66		14.00	83.00	1.15
C67		4.50	19.00	.50
C68		5.25	21.50	1.10
C69		7.50	54.00	1.20
		1967-69		
C70		10.00	46.00	.55
C71		9.00	60.00	1.25
C72		2.00	26.00	.50
C74		13.50	52.50	.60
C75		6.00	45.00	.90
C76		2.50	10.00	.65
		1971-73		
C77		2.00	19.75	.50
C78		1.35	22.50	.50
C79		1.50	26.50	.55
C80		2.75	21.50	.60
C81		2.50	22.25	.75
C84		2.75	17.00	.50
C85	(10)	3.50	13.75	.50
C86		1.75	16.00	.50
		1974-76		
C87		2.25	23.50	.65
C88		2.85	31.50	.85
C89		2.50	26.00	.85
C90		3.10	32.00	1.10
		1978-79		
C91-C92		3.10	62.50	1.15ea.
C93-C94		2.10	42.50	1.00ea.

Air Post
Special Delivery
1934-36

Scott No.		Pl. Blk.	Sheet	FDC
CE1	(6)	45.00		10.00
CE2		12.50		8.00

Special Delivery
1885-95

Scott No.		Pl. Blk.	Sheet	FDC
E1	(8)	6,500.00		6,000.00
E2	(8)	6,500.00		
E3	(8)	3,750.00		
E4	(7)	7,500.00		
E5	(6)	2,000.00		
		1902-17		
E6	(6)	1,350.00		
E7	(6)	700.00		
E8	(6)	1,650.00		
E9	(6)	3,250.00		
E10	(6)	4,500.00		
E11	(6)	225.00		
		1922-25		
E12	(6)	400.00		375.00
E13	(6)	135.00		150.00
E14	(6)	47.50		90.00
		1927-51		
E15		5.00		75.00
E16		5.00		85.00
E17		4.25		7.50
E18		25.00		7.50
E19		6.75		5.00
		1954-57		
E20		4.50		2.50
E21		5.00		2.25
		1969-71		
E22		14.50		4.00
E23		6.00		4.00

Registration

Scott No.		Pl. Blk.	Sheet	FDC
F1	(6)	1,100.00		3,250.00

Certified Mail

Scott No.		Pl. Blk.	Sheet	FDC
FA1		6.25		2.50

Scott No.		Pl. Blk.	Sheet	FDC
		Postage Due		
		1910-12		
J45	(6)	125.00		
J46	(6)	100.00		
J47	(6)	1,000.00		
J48	(6)	225.00		
J49	(6)	250.00		
J50	(6)	2,750.00		
		1914-15		
J52	(6)	250.00		
J53	(6)	100.00		
J54	(6)	1,150.00		
J55	(6)	110.00		
J56	(6)	150.00		
J57	(6)	650.00		
J58	(6)	18,500.00		
		1916		
J59	(6)	3,500.00		
J60	(6)	175.00		
		1917-25		
J61	(6)	4.75		
J62	(6)	6.50		
J63	(6)	16.00		
J64	(6)	15.00		
J65	(6)	17.50		
J66	(6)	70.00		
J67	(6)	90.00		
J68	(6)	2.50		
		1930-31		
		Perforated 11		
J69	(6)	12.50		
J70	(6)	7.00		
J71	(6)	14.00		
J72	(6)	60.00		
J73	(6)	42.50		
J74	(6)	50.00		
J75	(6)	210.00		
J76	(6)	250.00		
J77	(6)	85.00		
J78	(6)	185.00		
		1931-56		
		Perforated 11X10½		
J79		6.00		
J80		1.50		
J81		1.50		
J82		2.00		
J83		2.50		
J84		4.00		
J85		15.00		
J86		20.00		
J87		75.00		
		1959		
J88		65.00		
J89		.50		
J90		.60		
J91		.70		
J92		1.25		
J93		.75		
J94		1.40		
J95		1.60		
J96		1.75		
J97		1.25		
J98		5.50		
J99		6.50		
J100		10.00		
J101		40.00		
		1978		
J102		1.10		
J103		1.30		

A1   A2   A3   A4

A5   A6   A7   A8

A9   A10   A11   A12

A13   A14   A15   A16

A17   A18   A19   A20

CANADA AND PROVINCES

Scott® No.	Illus No.	Description	Unused Price	Used Price	/ / / / / /

1851 — *Imperf.* Laid Paper.

1	A1	3p red	7500.00	500.00	☐☐☐☐☐☐
2	A2	6p grayish purple	7500.00	550.00	☐☐☐☐☐☐
3	A3	12p black	40000.00	25000.00	☐☐☐☐☐☐

1852-55 Wove Paper

| 4 | A1 | 3p red | 1000.00 | 150.00 | ☐☐☐☐☐☒ 4 |
| 5 | A2 | 6p slate gray ('55) | 5000.00 | 500.00 | ☐☐☐☐☐☐ |

1855

| 7 | A4 | 10p blue | 3500.00 | 600.00 | ☐☐☐☐☐☒ |

1857

8	A5	½p rose	500.00	300.00	☐☐☐☐☒ 2
9	A6	7½p green	3500.00	1250.00	☐☐☐☐☐☐
10	A2	6p reddish purple	6000.00	1500.00	☐☐☐☐☐☐

1858-59 Wove Paper. *Perf. 12.*

11	A5	½p rose	1000.00	500.00	☐☐☐☐☐☒
12	A1	3p red	1500.00	275.00	☐☐☐☐☐☐
13	A2	6p brown violet ('59)	4000.00	2250.00	☐☐☐☐☐☐

1859

14	A7	1c rose	125.00	22.50	☐☐☐☐☒ 2
15	A8	5c vermilion	150.00	12.00	☐☐☐☐☒ 30
16	A9	10c blk. brown	4000.00	1000.00	☐☐☐☐☒
17	A9	10c red lilac *SHADES*	375.00	45.00	☐☐☐☐☒ 6
18	A10	12½c yellow green	250.00	37.50	☐☐☐☐☒ 2
19	A11	17c blue	325.00	60.00	☐☐☐☐☒ 7

1864

| 20 | A12 | 2c rose | 200.00 | 125.00 | ☐☐☐☐☒ |

Dominion of Canada.

1868-76

21	A13	½c black	35.00	30.00	☐☐☐☐☒
22	A14	1c brown red	200.00	40.00	☐☐☐☐☒ 3
23	A14	1c yel. orange	450.00	50.00	☐☐☐☐☒ 4
24	A15	2c green	200.00	30.00	☐☐☐☐☒ 2
25	A16	3c red	400.00	12.00	☐☐☐☐☒ 4
26	A17	5c olive green,	400.00	60.00	☐☐☐☐☒ 3
27	A18	6c dark brown	450.00	35.00	☐☐☐☐☒ 3
28	A19	12½c blue	250.00	35.00	☐☐☐☐☐☐
29	A20	15c gray violet *†11½x12*	30.00	20.00	☐☐☐☐☒ 3
30	A20	15c gray	30.00	20.00	☐☐☐☐☒ 5

1868 Laid Paper.

31	A14	1c brown red	5000.00	1200.00	☐☐☐☐☐☐
32	A15	2c green		45000.00	☐☐☐☐☐☐
33	A16	3c bright red	5000.00	250.00	☐☐☐☐☐☐

1870-89 Wove Paper.

| 34 | A21 | ½c black ('82) | 6.00 | 6.00 | ☒☐☐☐☐☒ 2 |

KISS ☐ IS MINT 5800

A21

A22   A23   A24   A25

A26   A27   A28   A29

A31   A30   A32

A32a   A32b   A33   A34

Scott® No.	Illus No.	Description	Unused Price	Used Price	M BLOX U

1870-89

35	A22	1c yellow	17.50	*5* .50 ☒☐☐☐☐☒ 7
36	A23	2c green ('72)	25.00	.90 ☒☐☐☐☐☒ 4
37	A24	3c dull red ('72)	50.00	2.00 ☐☐☐☐☐☒
37c	A24	3c org. red ('73)	40.00	1.35 ☒☐☐☐☐☒
38	A25	5c slate green ('76)	125.00	12.00 ☐☐☐☐☐☒
39	A26	6c yellow brown ('72)	125.00	12.00 ☒☐☐☐☐☒
40	A27	10c dull rose lilac ('77)	175.00	35.00 ☐☐☐☐☐☒ 4

1888-93

41	A24	3c bright verm.	15.00	.30 ☐☐☐☐☐☒
42	A25	5c gray	30.00	3.50 ☐☐☐☐☐☒
43	A26	6c red brown	35.00	8.00 ☒☐☐☐☐☒
44	A28	8c gray ('93)	35.00	3.50 ☐☐☐☐☐☒ 5
45	A27	10c brown red *M-STRIP 4*	90.00	22.50 ☐☒☐☐☐☐
46	A29	20c vermilion ('93)	150.00	40.00 ☐☐☐☐☐☒
47	A29	50c dp. blue ('93)	225.00	25.00 ☐☐☐☐☐☒ 3

1897

50	A30	½c black	75.00	75.00 ☒☐☐☐☐
51	A30	1c orange	*2* 7.50	6.50 ☒☒☐☐☐
52	A30	2c green	10.00	10.00 ☒☐☐☐☐
53	A30	3c bright rose	7.50	1.75 ☒☒☐☐☐
54	A30	5c deep blue	25.00	20.00 ☒☐☐☐☒
55	A30	6c yellow brown	125.00	125.00 ☐☐☐☐☐
56	A30	8c dark violet	27.50	27.50 ☒☐☐☐☐
57	A30	10c brown violet	65.00	65.00 ☒☐☐☐☐
58	A30	15c steel blue	110.00	110.00 ☐☐☐☐☐
59	A30	20c vermilion	125.00	125.00 ☐☐☐☐☐
60	A30	50c ultramarine	150.00	125.00 ☐☐☐☐☒
61	A30	$1 lake	550.00	500.00 ☐☐☐☐☐
62	A30	$2 dark purple	1250.00	325.00 ☐☐☐☐☐
63	A30	$3 yellow bistre	1350.00	800.00 ☐☐☐☐☐
64	A30	$4 purple	1350.00	800.00 ☐☐☐☐☐
65	A30	$5 olive green	1350.00	800.00 ☐☐☐☐☐

1897-98

66	A31	½c black	5.00	5.00 ☒☒☐☐☐
67	A31	1c blue green	8.00	.75 ☒☐☐☐☒
68	A31	2c purple	10.00	1.25 ☒☐☐☐☐
69	A31	3c carmine ('98)	12.50	.30 ☒☐☐☐☒
70	A31	5c dark bl., *bluish*	40.00	4.00 ☒☐☐☐☐
71	A31	6c brown	40.00	20.00 ☒☐☐☐☐
72	A31	8c orange	65.00	7.00 ☒☐☐☐☐
73	A31	10c brn. vio. ('98)	100.00	52.50 ☒☐☐☐☐

TWO CENTS:

Type I. Frame of four very thin lines.
Type II. Frame of a thick line between
two thin ones.

1898-1902

| 74 | A32 | ½c black | 1.50 | 1.25 ☒☒☐☐☐ |

3 2

1874•8

A35

A36

A37

A38

A39

A40

A41

A42

A43

A44

Scott® No.	Illus No.	Description	Unused Price	Used Price	/ / / / / /
1898-1902					M BLOX S
75	A32	1c gray green	12.00	.10	☒☐☐☐☐☒ 3
76	A32	2c purple (I)	2.10.00	.10	☒☐☐☐☐☒ 2
77	A32	2c car. (I) ('99)	15.00	.08	☒☐☐☐☐☒ 3
78	A32	3c carmine	17.50	.35	☒☐☐☐☐
79	A32	5c blue, *bluish*	65.00	.90	☐☐☐☐☐
80	A32	6c brown	65.00	25.00	☒☐☐☐☐
81	A32	7c olive yellow ('02)	35.00	11.00	☒☐☐☐☐
82	A32	8c orange	85.00	15.00	☒☐☐☐☐
83	A32	10c brown violet	125.00	12.00	☒☐☐☐☐
84	A32	20c olive green ('00)	250.00	60.00	☒☐☐☐☐
85	A33	2c black, lavender & carmine	18.00	6.00	☐☐☐☐☐
86	A33	2c black, blue & carmine	3 18.00	6.00	☒☐☐☐☐
87	A31	2c on 3c carmine	2 6.00	5.00	☒☐☐☐☐
88	A32	2c on 3c carmine	6.00	2.50	☒☒☐☐☐
88B	A32a	1c on one-third of 3c carmine (Bl)			☐☐☐☐☐
88C	A32b	2c on two-thirds of 3c carmine (V)			☐☐☐☐☐
1903-08					
89	A34	1c green	10.00	.10	☐☐☐☐☒☒
90	A34	2c carmine	10.00	.05	☐☐☐☐☒
90b	A34	Booklet pane of 6	900.00	900.00	☐☐☐☐☐
91	A34	5c blue, *blue*	55.00	2.00	☐☐☐☐☒
92	A34	7c olive bistre	55.00	2.50	☐☐☐☐☒
93	A34	10c brown lilac	125.00	5.00	☐☐☐☐☒
94	A34	20c olive green	250.00	20.00	☐☐☐☐☒
95	A34	50c purple ('08)	400.00	42.50	☐☐☐☐☒ 2
1908 9°		*IMPERF* ☐ ☐ ⊞	15°²	3 ☒ ☒	
96	A35	½c black brown	5.00	5.00	☒☒☐☐☐
97	A36	1c blue green	310.00	5.25	☒☒☐☒☐
98	A37	2c carmine	2 15.00	1.10	☒☒☐☐☐
99	A38	5c dark blue	60.00	35.00	☐☒☐☐☐
100	A39	7c olive green	65.00	37.50	☐☐☐☐☒
101	A40	10c dark violet	125.00	85.00	☒☐☐☐☐
102	A41	15c red orange	150.00	110.00	☒☐☐☐☐
103	A42	20c yellow brown	175.00	140.00	☐☐☐☐☒
1912-25		*Perf. 12*			
104	A43	1c green	5.00	.05	☒☐☐☐☐☒ 7
104a	A43	Booklet pane of 6	20.00	20.00	☒☐☐☐☐
105	A43	1c yellow ('22)	4.50	.10	☒☐☐☐☐☒
105a	A43	Booklet pane of 4 + 2 labels	45.00	45.00	☒☒☐☐☐
105b	A43	Booklet pane of 6	35.00	35.00	☒☐☐☐☒
106	A43	2c carmine	5.00	.05	☐☐☐☐☒ 10
106a	A43	Booklet pane of 6	30.00	30.00	☒☐☐☐☐
107	A43	2c yel. green ('22)	2 4.50	.05	☒☐☐☐☒ 8
107b	A43	Booklet pane of 4 + 2 labels	45.00	45.00	☒☐☐☐☐

2091.64

A45

A46

A47

A48

A49

A51

A50

A52

No. 109 Surcharged:

2 CENTS
a

2 CENTS
b

Scott® No.	Illus No.	Description	Unused Price	Used Price	/ / / / / /

1912-25

M BLOX U (handwritten)

Scott® No.	Illus No.	Description	Unused Price	Used Price	
107c	A43	Booklet pane of 6	275.00	275.00	☐☐☐☐☐
108	A43	3c brown ('18)	6.00	.05	☐☐☐☐☒ 4
108a	A43	Booklet pane of 4 + 2 labels	65.00	65.00	☐☐☐☐☐
109	A43	3c carmine ('23)	4 4.50	.05	☒☐☐☐☐☒
109a	A43	Booklet pane of 4 + 2 labels	30.00	30.00	☒☐☐☐☐
110	A43	4c olive bistre ('22)	15.00	2.25	☒☐☐☐☐
111	A43	5c dark blue	55.00	.25	☒☐☐☐☐
112	A43	5c violet ('22)	2 10.00	.35	☒☒☐☐☐
113	A43	7c yellow ochre	15.00	1.50	☒☐☐☐☐
114	A43	7c red brown ('24)	15.00	6.00	☐☒☐☐☐
115	A43	8c blue ('25)	20.00	6.00	☒☐☐☐☒
116	A43	10c plum	90.00	1.00	☐☐☐☐☒
117	A43	10c blue ('22)	27.50	1.00	☒☐☐☐☒
118	A43	10c bis. brown ('25)	27.50	.85	☒☐☐☐☒
119	A43	20c olive green	40.00	.65	☒☐☐☐☒
120	A43	50c blk. brown ('25)	42.50	2.00	☒☐☐☐☐
122	A43	$1 orange ('23)	110.00	6.00	☒☐☐☒☒ 3

1912   Coil Stamps.   *Perf. 8 Horizontally.*

123	A43	1c dark green	65.00	25.00	☐☐☐☐☐
124	A43	2c carmine	65.00	25.00	☐☐☐☐☐

1912-24   *Perf. 8 Vertically*

125	A43	1c green	9.00	.50	☐☐☐☐☒
126	A43	1c yellow ('23)	6.00	6.00	☒☐☒☐☒ 2
127	A43	2c carmine	12.00	.30	☐☐☐☐☐
128	A43	2c green ('22)	7.00	.50	☐☒☐☐☐
129	A43	3c brown ('18)	6.00	.50	☐☐☐☐☐
130	A43	3c carmine ('24)	45.00	6.00	☐☐☐☐☐

1915-24   *Perf. 12 Horizontally*

131	A43	1c dark green	5.00	5.00	☐☐☐☐☐
132	A43	2c carmine	15.00	15.00	☐☐☐☐☐
133	A43	2c yel. grn. ('24)	75.00	75.00	☐☐☐☐☐
134	A43	3c brown ('21)	5.50	5.50	☐☐☐☐☐

1917

135	A44	3c brown	20.00	.40	☒☒☐☐☐

1924   *Imperf.*

136	A43	1c yellow	52.50	52.50	☐☐☐☐☒
137	A43	2c green	52.50	52.50	☐☐☐☐☐
138	A43	3c carmine	20.00	20.00	☐☒☐☐☐ 10

1926

139	A43(a)	2c on 3c carmine	50.00	50.00	☐☒☐☐☐
140	A43(b)	2c on 3c carmine	21.00	21.00	☐☒☐☐☒

1927

141	A45	1c orange	2 3.00	.50	☒☐☐☐☒

1303.75 (handwritten)

A53

A54

A55

A56

A57

A58

A59

Die I. The top of the letter "P" encloses a tiny dot of color.
Die II. The top of the "P" encloses a
larger spot of color than in die I. The "P"
appears almost like a "D."

A60

A61

A62

A63

A64

Scott® No.	Illus No.	Description	Unused Price	Used Price	/ / / / / /

Scott® No.	Illus No.	Description	Unused Price	Used Price	/ / / / / /
142	A46	2c green	2 1.50	.10 ☒☐☒☐☐☒ ²
143	A47	3c brown carmine	2 7.50	5.00 ☒☒☐☒☐☐
144	A48	5c violet	3.50	2.25 ☒☒☐☐☐☐
145	A49	12c dark blue	3 10.00	4.25 ☒☒☐☐☐☐
146	A50	5c violet	5 3.00	2.25 ☒☒☐☐☐☐
147	A51	12c green	2 7.50	4.25 ☒☐☐☐☐☐
148	A52	20c brown carmine	12.50	4.25 ☒☐☐☐☒☐

1928-29

Scott® No.	Illus No.	Description	Unused Price	Used Price	/ / / / / /
149	A53	1c orange	2.50	.15 ☒☐☐☐☐
149a	A53	Booklet pane of 6	17.50	17.50 ☒☐☐☐☐
150	A53	2c green	2 .90	.04 ☒☐☐☐☒ ¹¹
150a	A53	Booklet pane of 6	17.50	17.50 ☒☐☐☐☐
151	A53	3c dark carmine	15.00	9.00 ☐☐☐☒☐
152	A53	4c bistre ('29)	12.50	4.50 ☒☒☐☐☐
153	A53	5c deep violet	5.00	2.00 ☒☒☐☐☐
153a	A53	Booklet pane of 6	85.00	85.00 ☐☐☐☐☐
154	A53	8c blue	2 8.00	4.00 ☒☐☐☒☐
155	A54	10c green	7.50	.90 ☐☐☐☐☐
156	A55	12c gray ('29)	12.50	6.00 ☒☐☐☒☐
157	A56	20c dk. carmine('29)	22.50	7.00 ☒☐☐☒☒
158	A57	50c dark blue ('29)	300.00	45.00 ☒☐☐☒☒ ²
159	A58	$1 olive green ('29)	375.00	50.00 ☐☐☐☐☐

1929

Coil Stamps.   *Perf. 8 Vertically*

Scott® No.	Illus No.	Description	Unused Price	Used Price	/ / / / / /
160	A53	1c orange	15.00	15.00 ☒☒☐☐☐
161	A53	2c green	10.00	1.25 ☐☒☐☐☐ ᴾᵁ

1930-31

Perf. 11

Scott® No.	Illus No.	Description	Unused Price	Used Price	/ / / / / /
162	A59	1c orange	.75	.40 ☐☐☐☐☐
163	A59	1c deep green	1.00	.05 ☐☐☐☐☒
163a	A59	Booklet pane of 4 + 2 labels	115.00	115.00 ☐☐☐☐☐
163c	A59	Booklet pane of 6	30.00	30.00 ☒☐☐☐☐
164	A59	2c dull green (I)	1.00	.08 ☐☐☐☐☒
164a	A59	Booklet pane of 6	35.00	35.00 ☐☐☐☐☐
165	A59	2c deep red (II)	1.00	.05 ☐☐☐☐☐☒ ³
165a	A59	Die I	1.00	.10 ☐☐☐☐☒
165b	A59	Booklet pane of 6(I)	16.00	16.00 ☒☐☐☐☐
166	A59	2c dark brown (II) ('31)	1.00	.05 ☐☐☐☐☐
166a	A59	Booklet pane of 4 + 2 labels (II)	115.00	115.00 ☐☐☐☐☐
166b	A59	Die I	4.00	4.00 ☐☐☐☐☐
166c	A59	Booklet pane of 6 (I)	30.00	30.00 ☒☐☐☐☐
167	A59	3c deep red ('31)	1.25	.05 ☒☐☐☐☒ ¹⁴
167a	A59	Booklet pane of 4 + 2 labels	30.00	30.00 ☐☐☐☐☐

13 55.77

A65

A66

A68

A67

A69

A70

A71

A72

A73

A74

Scott® No.	Illus No.	Description	Unused Price	Used Price	/ / / / / /
1930-31					
168	A59	4c yellow bistre	8.00	4.50 ☐☐☐☐☐
169	A59	5c dull violet	5.00	4.50 ☒☒☐☐☐
170	A59	5c dull blue	2.50	.10 ☐☐☐☐☐
171	A59	8c dark blue	12.50	9.00 ☒☐☐☐☐
172	A59	8c red orange	4.50	4.00 ☒☐☐☒☐
173	A60	10c olive green	6.00	1.00 ☒☐☐☐☐
174	A61	12c gray black	11.00	5.00 ☐☐☐☐☐
175	A62	20c brown red	22.50	.35 ☐☐☐☐☐
✗ 176	A63	50c dull blue	225.00	10.00 ☐☐☐☐☐
177	A64	$1 dk. olive grn.	225.00	22.50 ☐☐☐☐☐
1930-31		Coil Stamps. *Perf. 8½ Vertically.*			
178	A59	1c orange	10.00	8.00 ☐☐☐☐☐
179	A59	1c deep green	4.50	3.25 ☐☐☐☐☒
180	A59	2c dull green *LINE*	5.00	2.25 ☐☒☐☐☐
181	A59	2c deep red *LINE*	6.00	2.00 ☐☒☐☐☐
182	A59	2c dk. brown ('31) *LINE* *CK*	5.50	.50 ☐☐☒☐☐
183	A59	3c deep red ('31) *LINE*	10.00	.25 ☐☐☒☐☐
1931					
184	A43	3c carmine	2.50	2.00 ☐☒☐☐☐
1931					
190	A65	10c dark green	7.50	.10 ☒☐☐☒☐
1932					
191	A59	3c on 2c deep red(II)	.75	.10 ☐☒☐☐☐
191a	A59	Die I	2.00	1.25 ☐☒☐☐☐
192	A66	3c deep red	.65	.10 ☒☐☐☐☐ 2
193	A67	5c dull blue	6.00	2.00 ☒☐☐☐☐
194	A68	13c deep green	2 7.00	5.00 ☒☐☐☐☐
195	A69	1c dark green	.50	.05 ☒☐☐☐☒ 6
195a	A69	Booklet pane of 4 + 2 labels	85.00	85.00 ☐☐☐☐☐
195b	A69	Booklet pane of 6	20.00	20.00 ☒☐☐☐☐
196	A69	2c black brown	.80	.05 ☒☐☐☐☒ 20
196a	A69	Booklet pane of 4 + 2 labels	85.00	85.00 ☐☐☐☐☐
196b	A69	Booklet pane of 6	21.00	21.00 ☐☐☐☐☐
197	A69	3c deep red *DIE 1+11*	1.10	.04 ☒☐☐☒☒ 44
197a	A69	Booklet pane of 4 + 2 labels	30.00	30.00 ☐☐☐☐☐
198	A69	4c ochre	35.00	4.50 ☐☐☐☐☐
199	A69	5c dark blue	4.00	.10 ☐☐☐☐☐
200	A69	8c red orange	12.50	3.00 ☐☐☐☒☐
201	A61	13c dull violet	25.00	2.50 ☐☐☐☒☐
1933					
202	A70	5c dark blue	9.00	3.00 ☒☐☐☐☐

199

274.5

A75

A77

A76

A79

A78

A80

A82

A81

A83

A84

A85

A86

A87

A88

Scott® No.	Illus No.	Description	Unused Price	Used Price	/ / / / / /
1933					M BLOXU
203	A62	20c brown red	40.00	13.50	☐ ☐ ☐ ☒ ☐
204	A71	5c dark blue	2 9.00	3.00	☒ ☐ ☐ ☐ ☐
1933		Coil Stamps. *Perf. 8½ Vertically*			
205	A69	1c dark green *LINE*	15.00	2.00	☐ ☒ ☐ ☐ ☒
206	A69	2c black brown *LINE*	12.50	.75	☐ ☒ ☒ ☐ ☐
207	A69	3c deep red	7.50	.20	☐ ☒ ☐ ☐ ☒
1934					
208	A72	3c blue	2 4.50	1.25	☒ ☐ ☐ ☐ ☐
209	A73	10c olive green	25.00	7.00	☒ ☐ ☐ ☐ ☐
210	A74	2c red brown	2 2.25	2.25	☒ ☒ ☐ ☒ ☐
1935					
211	A75	1c green	.50	.30	☒ ☒ ☐ ☐ ☐
212	A76	2c brown	1.00	.20	☒ ☒ ☐ ☐ ☐
213	A77	3c carmine	2 2.25	.10	☒ ☐ ☐ ☐ ☒ 3
214	A78	5c blue	6.00	3.50	☒☒ ☐ ☐ ☐
215	A79	10c green	7.00	3.00	☒ ☐ ☐ ☐ ☐
216	A80	13c dark blue	10.00	6.50	☒ ☐ ☐ ☒ ☐
217	A81	1c green	.40	.10	☐ ☐ ☐ ☐ ☒ 9
217a	A81	Booklet pane of 4 + 2 labels	70.00	70.00	☐ ☐ ☐ ☐ ☐
217b	A81	Booklet pane of 6	22.50	22.50	☒ ☐ ☐ ☐ ☐
218	A81	2c brown	.60	.05	☐ ☐ ☐ ☐ ☒ 7
218a	A81	Booklet pane of 4 + 2 labels	70.00	70.00	☐ ☐ ☐ ☐ ☐
218b	A81	Booklet pane of 6	22.50	22.50	☒ ☐ ☐ ☐ ☐
219	A81	3c dark carmine	2 1.00	.05	☒ ☒ ☐ ☐ ☒ 14
219a	A81	Booklet pane of 4 + 2 labels	22.50	22.50	☐ ☐ ☐ ☐ ☐
220	A81	4c yellow	3.00	.40	☐ ☒ ☐ ☐ ☐
221	A81	5c blue	3.00	.10	☐ ☐ ☐ ☐ ☐
222	A81	8c deep orange	3.00	2.00	☐ ☐ ☐ ☐ ☐
223	A82	10c carmine rose	9.00	.15	☐ ☐ ☐ ☐ ☒
224	A83	13c violet	10.00	.80	☐ ☐ ☐ ☐ ☒ 2
225	A84	20c olive green	32.50	.50	☒ ☐ ☐ ☒ ☒
226	A85	50c dull violet	50.00	5.50	☐ ☐ ☐ ☒ ☒
227	A86	$1 deep blue	110.00	12.50	☐ ☐ ☐ ☐ ☒
1935		Coil Stamps. *Perf. 8 Vertically.*			
228	A81	1c green	10.00	2.00	☐ ☐ ☐ ☐ ☐
229	A81	2c brown	9.00	.60	☐ ☐ ☐ ☐ ☒
230	A81	3c dark carmine	8.00	.30	☐ ☐ ☐ ☐ ☒
1937					
231	A87	1c green	.45	.03	☒ ☒ ☒ ☐ ☒ 35
231a	A87	Booklet pane of 4 + 2 labels	12.50	12.50	☐ ☐ ☐ ☐ ☐
231b	A87	Booklet pane of 6	2.50	2.50	☒ ☐ ☐ ☐ ☒

449.7

A90

A89

A91

A92

A93

A94

A95

A96

A97

A98

A99

A100

A102

A101

A103

A104

A105

A106

Scott® No.	Illus No.	Description	Unused Price	Used Price	/ / / / / /

(handwritten above checkboxes: M BLOX U)

1937

Scott® No.	Illus No.	Description	Unused Price	Used Price	
232	A87	2c brown	.60	.03	☒☒☐☐☒ 26
232a	A87	Booklet pane of 4 + 2 labels	12.50	12.50	☒☐☐☐☐
232b	A87	Booklet pane of 6	7.50	7.50	☐☐☐☐☐
233	A87	3c carmine	.75	.03	☒☒☐☐☒ 38
233a	A87	Booklet pane of 4 + 2 labels	3.00	3.00	☐☐☐☐☐
234	A87	4c yellow	2 3.00	.15	☒☒☐☐☒
235	A87	5c blue	2.50	.04	☒☐☐☐☒ 5
236	A87	8c orange	3 2.75	.30	☒☐☐☐☒
237	A88	3c carmine	.25	.08	☐☐☐☐☐

1937

Coil Stamps. *Perf. 8 Vertically.*

Scott® No.	Illus No.	Description	Unused Price	Used Price	
238	A87	1c green	1.50	1.00	☐☐☐☐☒
239	A87	2c brown	2.25	.30	☐☐☐☐☐
240	A87	3c carmine	3.00	.10	☐☒☐☒☐

1938

Scott® No.	Illus No.	Description	Unused Price	Used Price	
241	A89	10c dark carmine	3 10.00	.10	☒☒☐☐☒ 27
242	A90	13c deep blue	2 15.00	.50	☒☐☐☐☐
243	A91	20c red brown	30.00	.35	☐☐☐☐☒
244	A92	50c green	60.00	5.25	☒☐☐☐☒
245	A93	$1 dull violet POST CARD	150.00	8.50	☒☐☐☒☒

1939

Scott® No.	Illus No.	Description	Unused Price	Used Price	
246	A94	1c green & black	6 .30	.12	☒☒☐☐☒
247	A95	2c brown & black	6 .30	.08	☒☒☐☐☒
248	A96	3c dark carmine & black	6 .35	.05	☒☒☐☐☒

1942-43

Perf. 12.

Scott® No.	Illus No.	Description	Unused Price	Used Price	
249	A97	1c green	.25	.03	☒☒☐☐☒ 8
249a	A97	Booklet pane of 4 + 2 labels	6.00	6.00	☐☐☐☐☐
249b	A97	Booklet pane of 6	2.25	2.25	☒☐☐☐☐
249c	A97	Booklet pane of 3	1.25	1.25	☒☐☐☐☐
250	A98	2c brown	.50	.03	☒☐☐☐☒ 5
250a	A98	Booklet pane of 4 + 2 labels	6.00	6.00	☒☐☐☐☐
250b	A98	Booklet pane of 6	5.00	5.00	☐☐☐☐☐
251	A99	3c dark carmine	.50	.03	☒☐☐☐☒
251a	A99	Booklet pane of 4 + 2 labels	2.50	2.50	☒☐☐☐☐
252	A99	3c rose violet ('43)	2 .45	.03	☒☐☐☐☒ 26
252a	A99	Booklet pane of 4 + 2 labels	2.50	2.50	☒☐☐☐☐
252b	A99	Booklet pane of 3	2.00	2.00	☒☐☐☐☐
252c	A99	Booklet pane of 6	6.00	6.00	☒☐☐☐☐
253	A100	4c greenish black	1.75	.60	☒☒☐☐☐
254	A98	4c dk. carmine('43)	2 .45	.03	☒☒☐☐☒ 24

(handwritten at bottom: 5 14.09)

A107   A108   A109

A110   A111   A112

A113   A115   A114

A116   A117   A118

A119   A120   A121

A122   A123

Scott® No.	Illus No.	Description	Unused Price	Used Price	/ / / / / /

1942-43   *M BLOX U* (handwritten)

254a	A98	Booklet pane of 6	2.50	2.50	☒☐☐☐☐☐
254b	A98	Booklet pane of 3	2.00	2.00	☒☐☐☐☐☐
255	A97	5c deep blue	1.25	.05	☐☐☐☐☐☐
256	A101	8c red brown	2.50	.50	☒☐☐☐☐☒ 3
257	A102	10c brown	4.50	.10	☐☐☐☐☐☐
258	A103	13c dull green	6.00	4.00	☐☒☒☐☐☒ 2
259	A103	14c dull green ('43)	9.00	.25	☐☐☐☐☐☒ 10
260	A104	20c chocolate	7.50	.25	☐☐☐☐☐☒ 3
261	A105	50c violet	45.00	2.25	☒☐☐☐☒☒
262	A106	$1 deep blue	140.00	8.00	☐☐☐☐☐☐

1942-43   Coil Stamps.   *Perf. 8 Vertically*

(handwritten margin: 05 / 108 / 1875)

263	A97	1c green *Pu*	1.00	.60	☒☒☒☐☐☐
264	A98	2c brown	1.25	1.25	☐☒☐☒☒☐
265	A99	3c dark carmine *158⁰*	1.25	1.00	☒☒☒☐☐☐
266	A99	3c rose violet ('43) *2*	2.50	.35	☒☒☐☐☐☐
267	A98	4c dk. car. ('43) *8 2*	3.50	.20	☒☒☒☒☐☐

1946

(handwritten: 486.8 / 26.50)

268	A107	8c red brown	1.75	.85	☒☒☐☐☐☒
269	A108	10c olive	2.25	.10	☒☐☐☐☐☒ 2
270	A109	14c black brown	3.75	.20	☒☐☐☐☐☒
271	A110	20c slate black	4.25	.15	☒☐☐☐☐☒ 2
272	A111	50c dk. bl. green	30.00	2.25	☒☒☐☐☐☒ 34
273	A112	$1 red violet	75.00	3.50	☐☐☐☐☐☒ 3+1

1947

| 274 | A113 | 4c deep blue *1½ SHEET* | .20 | .12 | ☒☒☒☐☐☒ 2 |
| 275 | A114 | 4c deep blue | .20 | .12 | ☒☒☒☐☐☒ |

1948

| 276 | A115 | 4c deep blue | .20 | .06 | ☒☒☐☐☐☐ |
| 277 | A116 | 4c gray | .20 | .05 | ☒☒☐☐☐☐ |

1948   Coil Stamps.   *Perf. 9½ Vertically*

278	A97	1c green *Pu. 2+⁰⁰*	3.50	2.50	☒☒☒☒☐☐
279	A98	2c brown	12.00	11.00	☒☒☐☐☐☐
280	A99	3c rose violet	7.00	2.25	☒☐☐☐☐☐
281	A98	4c dark carmine	8.00	2.50	☒☒☒☐☐☐

1949

282	A117	4c deep green	.20	.05	☒☒☐☐☐☐
283	A118	4c purple	.20	.10	☐☒☐☐☐☐
284	A119	1c green *WITH P-P*	.12	.03	☒☒☐☐☐☒ 5
284a	A119	Bklt.pane of 3 ('51)	.50	.50	☒☐☐☐☐☐
285	A120	2c sepia *BROWN*	.30	.04	☒☐☐☐☐☒ 2
286	A121	3c rose violet	.35	.03	☒☒☐☐☐☒ 7
286a	A121	Bklt. pane of 3 ('50)	1.25	1.25	☒☐☐☐☐☐
286b	A121	Booklet pane of 4 + 2 labels	1.50	1.50	☒☐☐☐☐☐
287	A122	4c dark carmine	.50	.03	☒☒☐☐☐☒ 7

(handwritten at bottom: 670-)

A124

A125

A126

A127

A128

A129

A130

A131

A132

A133

A134

A135

A136

A137

Scott® No.	Illus No.	Description	Unused Price	Used Price	//////
1949					M BLOX u
287a	A122	Bklt. pane of 3 ('51)	8.50	8.50	☒☐☐☐☐
287b	A122	Bklt. pane of 6 ('51)	10.00	10.00	☐☐☐☐☐
288	A123	5c deep blue	1.25	.10 ₃	☒☐☐☐☒
1950		"POSTES POSTAGE" Omitted			
289	A119	1c green	.12	.05 ₃	☒☒☐☐☐
290	A120	2c sepia	.35	.15	☒☒☐☐☐
291	A121	3c rose violet	.25	.04	☒◪☐☐☐
292	A122	4c dark carmine	₂ .35	.04	☒☒☐☐☐
293	A123	5c deep blue	1.50	1.25	☒☐☐☐☐
1950					
294	A124	50c dull green	20.00	1.50	☐☐☐☐☐☒ +18
1950		"POSTES POSTAGE" Omitted. *Perf. 9½ Vertically.*			
295	A119	1c green	.40	.40	☒☒☐☐☐
296	A121	3c rose violet	.75	.75	☒☒☐☐☐
		With "POSTES POSTAGE" *Perf. 9½ Vertically.*			
297	A119	1c green	.30	.30 ₂	☒☒P☐☐
298	A120	2c sepia BROWN	1.75	1.75	☒☒I☐☐
299	A121	3c rose violet	1.25	.25	☒☒☐☐☐
300	A122	4c dark carmine	6.50	1.00	☒☒☒☐☐
1950					₂ ₂
301	A125	10c black brown	₃ 1.10	.07	☒☒☐☐☐
1951					
302	A126	$1 bright ultra.	110.00	15.00	☐☐☐☒☒5
303	A127	3c turquoise green	.30	.10	☐☐☐☐☐
304	A128	4c rose pink	.35	.10	☐☒☐☐☐
305	A120	2c olive green	₃ .20	.03	☒☐☐☐☒
306	A122	4c orange vermilion	.30	.03	☒☐☐☐☐
306a	A122	Booklet pane of 3	1.75	1.75	☒☐☐☐☐
306b	A122	Booklet pane of 6	2.00	2.00	☒☐☐☐☐
		Coil Stamps. *Perf. 9½ Vertically*			
309	A120	2c olive green	.60	.60	☒☐I☐☐
310	A122	4c orange vermilion	.90	.75	☒☐I☐☐
1951					
311	A129	4c dark gray	.65	.15	☒☒☐☐☐
312	A129	5c purple 50 ▨	2.50	2.00	☒☒☐☐☐
313	A129	7c deep blue	1.50	.45	☒☐☐☐☐
314	A130	15c bright red	1.50	.40	☒☒☐☐☐
315	A131	4c violet	.25	.06 ₂	☒☐☐☐☐
1952					
316	A132	20c gray	2.00	.05	☒☐☐☐☐
317	A133	4c blue & red	.25	.05	☒☐☐☐☐
318	A134	3c rose lilac	₁₂.25	.04	☒☒☐☐☐
319	A135	4c orange vermilion	.30	.04	☒☒☒☐☐
320	A136	7c blue	₃ .50	.05	☒☒☐☐☐

-4751.32

4/7.07

A138

A140

A139

A142

A141

A143

A144

A145

A146

A147

A148

A149

A150

A152

A151

A153

A154

A156

A155

Scott® No.	Illus No.	Description	Unused Price	Used Price	/ / / / / /

1953

Scott No.	Illus No.	Description	Unused Price	Used Price	
321	A137	$1 gray	25.00	1.00	☒☐☐☒☒
322	A138	2c deep blue	₂ .18	.08	☒☒☐☐☐
323	A138	3c black brown	.25	.05	☒☐☐☐☐
324	A138	4c slate	.30	.05	☒☐☐☐☐
325	A139	1c violet brown	.10	.03	☒☐☐☐☐
325a	A139	Booklet pane of 3	.50	.50	☒☐☐☐☐
326	A139	2c green	.15	.03	☒☐☐☐☐
327	A139	3c carmine rose	.20	.03	☒☒☐☐☒
327a	A139	Booklet pane of 3	1.00	1.00	☒☐☐☐☐
327b	A139	Booklet pane of 4+2 labels	1.50	1.50	☒☐☐☐☐
328	A139	4c violet	.30	.03	☒☐☐☐☐
328a	A139	Booklet pane of 3	1.25	1.25	☒☐☐☐☐
328b	A139	Booklet pane of 6	2.00	2.00	☒☐☐☐☐
329	A139	5c ultramarine	.40	.05	☒☐☐☐☐
330	A140	4c violet	₃ .25	.05	☒☒☐☐☐

Coil Stamps. *Perf. 9½ Vertically*

Scott No.	Illus No.	Description	Unused Price	Used Price	
331	A139	2c green	1.25	1.25	☐☒☐☐☐
332	A139	3c carmine rose	1.25	1.25	☒☒☐☐☐
333	A139	4c violet	2.25	1.75	☐☐☐☐☐

1953-54

Scott No.	Illus No.	Description	Unused Price	Used Price	
334	A141	50c light green	5.00	.30	☐☐☐☐☒
335	A142	4c gray	₂ .40	.05	☒☐☐☐☐
336	A143	5c ultramarine	.45	.05	☒☐☐☐☐
336a	A143	Bklt. pane of 5+label	2.50	2.50	☒☐☐☐☐

1954-61

Scott No.	Illus No.	Description	Unused Price	Used Price	
337	A144	1c violet brown	.10	.03	☒☒☐☐☒ 7
337a	A144	Bklt. pane of 5 + label	.75	.75	☒☐☐☐☐
338	A144	2c green	.15	.03	☒☒☐☐☒ 11
338a	A144	Pane of 25 ('61)	5.00	5.00	☒☐☐☐☐
339	A144	3c carmine rose	.20	.05	☒☒☐☐☒ 3
340	A144	4c violet	.25	.03	☒☒☒☐☒ 21
340a	A144	Bklt. pane of 5+label	1.75	1.75	☒☐☐☐☐
340b	A144	Booklet pane of 6	3.25	3.25	☒☐☐☐☐
341	A144	5c bright blue	.35	.03	☒☒☐☐☒ 11
341a	A144	Bklt. pane of 5+label	2.25	2.25	☐☐☐☐☐
341b	A144	Pane of 20 (5×4) ('61)	9.00	9.00	☒☐☐☐☐
342	A144	6c orange	.40	.10	☒☒☐☐☐
343	A145	15c gray	₂ 1.25	.10	☒☐☐☐☐

1962

Tagged

Scott No.	Illus No.	Description	Unused Price	Used Price	
337p	A144	1c violet brown	1.25	1.25	☐☐☐☐☐
338p	A144	2c green	1.25	1.25	☐☐☐☐☐
339p	A144	3c carmine rose	1.25	1.25	☐☐☐☐☐
340p	A144	4c violet	4.00	4.00	☐☒☐☐☐
341p	A144	5c bright blue	3.75	3.75	☐☐☐☐☐

A157

A159

A158

A161

A160

A162

A163

A164

A165

A166

A167

A168

A169

A170

A171

A172

A173

Scott® No.	Illus No.	Description	Unused Price	Used Price	/ / / / / /

1954 Coil Stamps. *Perf. 9½ Vertically* M BLOX U

Scott® No.	Illus No.	Description	Unused Price	Used Price	M	BLOX	U		
345	A144	2c green	.50	.25	☒	☒	☒	☐	☐
347	A144	4c violet	1.00	.30	☐	☒	☒	☐	☐
348	A144	5c bright blue	1.25	.25	☐	☐	☒	☐	☐

1954

349	A146	4c violet	.35	.05	☒	☒	☐	☐	☐
350	A147	5c bright blue	.35	.05	☒	☐	☐	☐	☐

1955

351	A148	10c violet brown	.50	.04	☒	☒	☐	☐	☐
352	A149	4c purple	2 .40	.05	☒	☐	☐	☐	☐
353	A150	5c blue	.40	.05	☒	☐	☐	☐	☐
354	A151	5c light blue	.50	.15	☒	☐	☐	☐	☐
355	A152	5c ultramarine	4 .45	.15	☒	☒	☐	☐	☐
356	A153	5c green & orange brown	.45	.12	☒	☒	☐	☐	☐
357	A154	4c violet	.40	.05	☒	☒	☐	☐	☐
358	A155	5c ultramarine	.45	.05	☒	☒	☐	☐	☐

1956

359	A156	5c ultramarine	3 .40	.10	☒	☐	☐	☐	☐
360	A157	4c deep violet	.45	.05	☒	☒	☐	☐	☐
361	A158	5c ultramarine	.45	.05	☒	☒	☐	☐	☐
362	A159	20c green	1.75	.08	☐	☒	☐	☐	☐
363	A160	25c red	2.25	.10	☒	☒	☐	☐	☐
364	A161	5c gray & red	.40	.04	☐	☒	☐	☐	☐

1957

365	A162	5c ultramarine	.50	.30	☒	☒	☐	☐	☐
366	A162	5c ultramarine	.50	.30	☒	☒	☐	☐	☐
367	A162	5c ultramarine	2 SHEETS .50	.30	☒	☒	☐	☐	☐
368	A162	5c ultramarine	.50	.30	☒	☒	☐	☐	☐
369	A163	5c black	2 .40	.05	☒	☒	☐	☐	☐
370	A164	5c ultramarine	.40	.10	☒	☒	☐	☐	☐
371	A165	5c dark blue	½ SHT 65 .40	.05	☒	☒	☐	☐	☐
372	A166	15c dark blue	26 2.75	2.50	☒	☒	☐	☐	☐
373	A167	5c black	2 .35	.10	☒	☒	☐	☐	☐
374	A168	5c black	.35	.10	☒	☒	☐	☐	☐

1958

375	A169	5c black	.40	.15	☒	☒	☐	☐	☐
376	A170	5c blue	.40	.10	☒	☒	☐	☐	☐
377	A171	5c bluish green	.40	.10	☒	☒	☐	☐	☐
378	A172	5c bright ultramarine	.40	.10	☒	☒	☐	☐	☐
379	A173	5c dark green & bistre brown	.40	.10	☒	☒	☐	☐	☐
380	A174	5c rose lilac	.40	.07	☒	☒	☐	☐	☐
381	A175	5c olive & red	.40	.07	☒	☒	☐	☐	☐
382	A176	5c slate blue	.40	.10	☒	☒	☐	☐	☐

1959

383	A177	5c blue & black	.40	.08	☒	☒	☐	☐	☐
384	A178	5c violet blue	.40	.08	☒	☒	☐	☐	☐

238.2

A174

A176

A175

A178

A177

A179

A181

A180

A182

A183

A184

A185

A186

A187

A188

A189

A190

Scott® No.	Illus No.	Description	Unused Price	Used Price	/ / / / / /

M BLOX U

1959

385	A179	5c apple green & black	.40	.08	☒☒☐☐☐
386	A180	5c dark carmine	3 .40	.05	☒☒☐☐☐
387	A181	5c red & blue	.40	.08	☒☒☐☐☐
388	A182	5c crimson rose & dark green	.40	.07	☒☒☐☐☐

1960

| 389 | A183 | 5c brown orange & ultramarine | .40 | .07 | ☒☒☐☐☐ |
| 390 | A184 | 5c ultramarine & bistre brown | .40 | .07 | ☒☒☐☐☐ |

1961

391	A185	5c green & vermilion	.40	.07	☒☒☐☐☐
392	A186	5c green & red	.40	.07	☒☒☐☐☐
393	A187	5c ultramarine	.40	.07	☒☒☐☐☐
394	A188	5c lt. red brown & blue	.40	.07	☒☒☐☐☐
395	A189	5c brown & blue green	.40	.07	☒☒☐☐☐

1962

396	A190	5c black & light red brown	.40	.07	☒☒☐☐☐
397	A191	5c lt. green & violet brown	.40	.08	☒☒☐☐☐
398	A192	5c dark blue	.40	.07	☒☒☐☐☐
399	A193	5c black & rose	.40	.08	☒☒☐☐☐
400	A194	5c brn. org. & blk.	.40	.10	☒☒☐☐☐

1962-63

401	A195	1c dp. brown ('63)	.10	.03	☐☒☐☐☐☒ ᴸ
401a	A195	Bklt. pane 5 + label ('63)	4.00	4.00	☒☐☐☐☐
402	A195	2c green ('63)	.15	.03	☒☐☐☐☐☒ ᴸ
402a	A195	Pane of 25 ('63)	4.50	4.50	☒☐☐☐☐
403	A195	3c purple ('63)	.20	.03	☒☐☐☐☐
404	A195	4c carmine ('63)	.25	.03	☐☐☐☐☒ ᴮ
404a	A195	Bklt. pane 5 + label ('63)	3.75	3.75	☒☐☐☐☐
404b	A195	Pane of 25 ('63)	6.00	6.00	☒☐☐☐☐
405	A195	5c violet blue	.30	.03	☒☐☐☐☒ 3
405a	A195	Bklt. pane of 5 + label ('63)	3.75	3.75	☒☐☐☐☐
405b	A195	Pane of 20 ('63)	8.00	8.00	☒☐☐☐☐

1963 Tagged

401p	A195	1c deep brown	.10	.08	☒☒☐☐☐
402p	A195	2c green	.15	.12	☒☒☐☐☐
403p	A195	3c purple	.20	.09	☒☒☐☐☐
404p	A195	4c carmine	.45	.15	☒☒☐☐☐
405p	A195	5c violet blue	.35	.20	☒☒☐☐☐
405q	A195	Pane of 20	17.50		☐☐☐☐☐

1963-64 Coil Stamps Perf. 9½ Horiz.

406	A195	2c green	1.50	1.25	☒☒☒☐☐
407	A195	3c purple ('64)	1.00	.90	☒☒☐☐☐
408	A195	4c carmine	1.25	.90	☒☒☒☐☐
409	A195	5c violet blue	1.00	.35	☒☐☒☐☐

92-

A191

A193

A192

A195

A194

A196

A197

A198

A199

A200

A201

A202

A203

A204

A205

A206

A207

A208

Scott® No.	Illus No.	Description	Unused Price	Used Price	/ / / / / /

M BLU✓ U

1963

410	A196	5c rose lilac	.40	.07 ☒☒☐☐☐
411	A197	$1 rose carmine	40.00	3.50 ☒☐☐☐☐☒	1
412	A198	5c ultramarine	.40	.07 ☒☒☐☐☐
413	A199	5c grn. & red brn.	.40	.07 ☒☒☐☐☐

1963-64

| 414 | A200 | 7c blue ('64) | .60 | .60 ☐☐☐☐☐ |
| 415 | A201 | 15c deep ultra. | 4.50 | .25 ☐☐☐☐☐ |

1964

| 416 | A202 | 5c greenish blue, Pruss. blue & ocher | .40 | .07 ☒☒☐☐☐ |

1964-66

417	A203	5c light blue & dark carmine	.35	.10 ☒☒☐☐☐
418	A204	5c red brown, buff & green	.35	.20 ☐☒☐☐☒
419	A204	5c grn., yel. & org.	.35	.15 ☒☒☐☐☐
420	A204	5c bl., pink & grn. ('65)	.35	.15 ☒☒☐☐☐
421	A204	5c carm., grn. & vio. ('65)	.35	.15 ☒☒☐☐☐
422	A204	5c red brn., lilac & dull grn. ('65)	.35	.15 ☒☒☐☐☐
423	A204	5c lilac, grn. & bister ('65)	.35	.15 ☒☒☐☐☐
424	A204	5c violet, green & deep rose ('65)	.35	.15 ☒☒☐☐☐
425	A204	5c sepia, orange & green ('66)	.35	.20 ☒☒☐☐☐
426	A204	5c dull green, yel. & carmine ('66)	.35	.15 ☒☒☐☐☐
427	A204	5c black, green & carmine ('66)	.35	.15 ☒☒☐☐☐
428	A204	5c dk. blue, rose & green ('66)	.35	.20 ☒☒☐☐☒
429	A204	5c olive, yellow & green ('66)	.35	.20 ☒☒☐☐☐
429A	A204	5c dark blue & dp. red ('66)	.35	.15 ☐☒☐☐☐

1964

430	A200	8c on 7c blue	.50	.50 ☐☒☐☐☐
431	A205	5c black	2.40	.07 ☒☒☐☐☐
432	A206	5c dk. brown & rose	.35	.05 ☒☒☐☐☐
433	A207	5c claret	.35	.08 ☒☒☐☐☐
434	A208	3c red	.25	.03 ☒☒☐☐☐
434a	A208	Pane of 25	10.00	10.00 ☒☐☐☐☐
434p	A208	Tagged	.75	.65 ☒☒☐☐☐
434q	A208	As "a," tagged	15.00	15.00 ☐☐☐☐☐
435	A208	5c blue	.35	.04 ☒☒☐☐☐
435p	A208	Tagged	2.25	2.00 ☒☒☐☐☐
436	A200	8c blue	.55	.30 ☐☐☐☐☐

1965

| 437 | A209 | 5c slate green | .35 | .10 ☐☐☐☐☐ |

1 5 1 9 1.98

111.4

A210

A209

A211

A212

A214

A213

A215

A217

A216

A218

Scott® No.	Illus No.	Description	Unused Price	Used Price	/ / / / / /

1965

Scott® No.	Illus No.	Description	Unused Price	Used Price	/ / / / / /
438	A210	5c Prussian blue	.35	.10	☒☒☐☐☐☐
439	A211	5c blue & red	.35	.10	☒☐☐☐☐☐
440	A212	5c brown	2 .35	.10	☒☐☐☐☐☐
441	A213	5c slate green	.35	.10	☒☒☐☐☐☐
442	A214	5c brown	5 .35	.10	☒☒☐☐☐☐
443	A215	3c olive	.25	.05	☒☒☐☐☐☐
443a	A215	Pane of 25	6.25	6.25	☒☐☐☐☐☐
443p	A215	Tagged	.25	.16	☒☒☐☐☐☐
443q	A215	As "a" tagged	4.50	4.50	☐☐☐☐☐☐
444	A215	5c violet blue	3 .30	.05	☒☒☐☐☐☐
444p	A215	Tagged	.35	.30	☒☒☐☐☐☐

1966

Scott® No.	Illus No.	Description	Unused Price	Used Price	/ / / / / /
445	A216	5c dk. violet blue	.35	.10	☒☒☐☐☐☐
446	A217	5c blue green	.35	.07	☒☒☐☐☐☒
447	A218	5c black, bl. & yel.	.35	.10	☒☒☐☐☐☐
448	A219	5c brown	.35	.07	☒☒☐☐☐☐
449	A220	5c dp. ultramarine	.35	.07	☒☒☐☐☐☐
450	A221	5c plum	.35	.06	☒☒☐☐☐☐
451	A222	3c carmine rose	.18	.05	☒☒☐☐☐☒ 3
451a	A222	Pane of 25	5.00	5.00	☒☐☐☐☐☐
451p	A222	Tagged	.25	.12	☒☒☐☐☐☐
451q	A222	As "a" tagged	6.00	6.00	☒☐☐☐☐☐
452	A222	5c orange	.30	.05	☒☒☐☐☐☐
452p	A222	Tagged	.35	.18	☒☒☐☐☐☐

1967

Scott® No.	Illus No.	Description	Unused Price	Used Price	/ / / / / /
453	A223	5c blue & red	2 .35	.05	☒☒☐☐☐☒ 3
453p	A223	Tagged	.35	.30	☐☐☐☐☐☐

1967-72

Scott® No.	Illus No.	Description	Unused Price	Used Price	/ / / / / /
454	A224	1c brown	.10	.04	☒☒☐☐☐☐
454a	A224	Booklet pane of 5 + label	.75		☒☐☐☐☐☐
454b	A224	Booklet pane of 5 (1#454, 4#459 + Label), perf. 10 ('68)	2.50	2.50	☐☐☐☐☐☐
454c	A224	Booklet pane of 10 (5#454 + 5#457) perf. 10 ('68)	2.50	2.50	☐☐☐☐☐☐
454d	A224	Perf. 10	.25	.25	☐☐☐☐☐☐
455	A224	2c green	.12	.04	☒☒☐☐☐☐
455a	A224	Bklt. pane (4#455, 4#456 with Gutter Btwn.)	2.50	2.50	☐☐☐☐☐☐
456	A224	3c dull purple	.18	.04	☒☒☐☐☐☐
457	A224	4c carmine rose	.25	.03	☒☒☐☐☐☐
457a	A224	Booklet pane of 5 + label	1.75	1.75	☒☐☐☐☐☐
457b	A224	Pane of 25 (5 × 5)	15.00		☒☐☐☐☐☐
457c	A224	Booklet pane of 25 + 2 labels, perf. 10 ('68)	6.50		☐☐☐☐☐☐
457d	A224	Perf. 10	.25	.25	☐☐☐☐☐☐

217

70.35

A219

A220

A221

A222

A224

A223

A225

A227

A226

A228

A229

A230

A231

A232

A234

A233

Scott® No.	Illus No.	Description	Unused Price	Used Price	/ / / / / /

1967-72

					M BLO U
458	A224	5c blue	.25	.03	☒ ☒ ☐ ☐ ☐
458a	A224	Booklet pane of 5 + label	6.00	6.00	☐ ☐ ☐ ☐ ☐
458b	A224	Pane of 20	35.00		☒ ☐ ☐ ☐ ☐
458c	A224	Bklt. pane of 20, perf. 10 ('68)	9.00		☐ ☐ ☐ ☐ ☐
458d	A224	Perf. 10	.45	.15	☐ ☐ ☐ ☐ ☐
459	A224	6c orange, perf. 10 ('68)	.40	.03	☒ ☒ ☐ ☐ ☐
459a	A224	Booklet pane of 25 + 2 labels, perf. 10 ('69)	10.00		☐ ☐ ☐ ☐ ☐
460	A224	6c black (I), perf. 12½ × 12 ('70)	.35	.03	☒ ☒ ☐ ☐ ☐
460a	A224	Bklt. pane of 25 + 2 Labels (I). perf. 10 ('70)	20.00	20.00	☐ ☐ ☐ ☐ ☐
460b	A224	As "a", perf. 12½ × 12 ('70)	20.00		☐ ☐ ☐ ☐ ☐
460c	A224	Type II, perf. 12½ × 12 ('70)	.35	.03	☒ ☐ ☐ ☐ ☐
460d	A224	As "c", booklet pane of 4 ('70)	6.00	6.00	☐ ☐ ☐ ☐ ☐
460e	A224	As "d", perf. 10 ('70)	9.00	6.00	☐ ☐ ☐ ☐ ☐
460f	A224	Type II, perf. 12 ('72)	.50	.15	☐ ☐ ☐ ☐ ☐
460g	A224	Type I, perf. 10	.70	.05	☐ ☐ ☐ ☐ ☐
460h	A224	Type II, perf. 10	1.00	.15	☐ ☐ ☐ ☐ ☐
461	A225	8c violet brown	2 .50	.25	☒ ☒ ☐ ☐ ☐
462	A225	10c olive green	.40	.04	☒ ☒ ☐ ☐ ☐
463	A225	15c dull purple	.75	.10	☒ ☒ ☐ ☐ ☐
464	A225	20c dark blue	1.00	.10	☒ ☒ ☐ ☐ ☐
465	A225	25c slate green	1.40	.10	☒ ☒ ☐ ☐ ☐
465A	A225	50c brown orange	3 5.00	.15	☒ ☐ ☐ ☐ ☒
465B	A225	$1 carmine rose	3 20.00	1.00	☒ ☐ ☐ ☐ ☐
		Tagged			
454p	A224	1c brown	.20	.15	☐ ☐ ☐ ☐ ☐
455p	A224	2c green	.20	.15	☐ ☐ ☐ ☐ ☐
456p	A224	3c dull purple	.30	.30	☐ ☐ ☐ ☐ ☐
457p	A224	4c carmine rose	.35	.25	☐ ☐ ☐ ☐ ☐
458p	A224	5c blue	.35	.20	☐ ☐ ☐ ☐ ☐
458bp	A224	Pane of 20	40.00	40.00	☐ ☐ ☐ ☐ ☐
459p	A224	6c orange, perf. 10 ('68)	.75	.50	☐ ☐ ☐ ☐ ☐
460p	A224	6c black (I), perf. 12½ × 12 ('70)	.45	.45	☐ ☐ ☐ ☐ ☐
460cp	A224	6c black (II), perf. 12½ × 12 ('70)	.45	.45	☐ ☐ ☐ ☐ ☐
460fp	A224	As "cp", perf. 12 ('72)	.35	.30	☐ ☐ ☐ ☐ ☐
462p	A225	10c olive green ('70)	1.00	.75	☐ ☐ ☐ ☐ ☐
463p	A225	15c dull purple ('70)	.85	.75	☐ ☐ ☐ ☐ ☐
464p	A225	20c dark blue ('70)	1.50	1.00	☐ ☒ ☐ ☐ ☐
465p	A225	25c slate green ('70)	2.00	1.50	☐ ☒ ☐ ☐ ☐

(handwritten: 459D X)

A235

A236

A237

A238

A239

A240

A241

A242

A243

A244

A246

A245

A247

A248

A249

A251

A250

A252

Scott® No.	Illus No.	Description	Unused Price	Used Price	/ / / / / /

1967-70 COILS   3LOY

466	A224	3c dull purple	— 1.00	.75 ☐☐☐☐☐
467	A224	4c carmine rose	.75	.60 ☐☐☒☐☐
468	A224	5c blue	1.00	.75 ☒☒☐☐☐
468A	A224	6c orange ('69)	.35	.10 ☒☒☐☐☐
468B	A224	6c black, die II ('70)	.35	.10 ☐☐☐☐☐

1967

469	A226	5c blue & red	.30	.10 ☒☒☐☐☐
470	A227	5c blk. & rose lilac	.30	.08 ☒☒☐☐☐
471	A228	5c dp. org. & purple	.30	.08 ☒☒☐☐☐
472	A229	5c red	3 .30	.08 ☒☒☐☐☐
473	A230	5c dp. ultramarine	.30	.08 ☒☒☐☐☐
474	A231	5c black	.40	.08 ☒☒☐☐☐
475	A232	5c slate green & salmon pink	.30	.08 ☒☒☐☐☐
476	A233	3c carmine	.15	.03 ☒☐☐☐☐ ☒ 22
476a	A233	Pane of 25	3.50	3.50 ☒☐☐☐☐
476p	A233	Tagged	.25	.15 ☒☒☐☐☐
476q	A233	As "a", tagged	5.00	5.00 ☐☐☐☐☐
477	A233	5c green	.25	.04 ☐☒☐☐☐
477p	A233	Tagged	.35	.25 ☒☒☐☐☐

1968

478	A234	5c grn., blk. & red	.60	.10 ☒☒☐☐☐
479	A235	5c dk & lt. blue, yellow & red	.30	.08 ☒☒☐☐☐
480	A236	5c multicolored	.30	.08 ☒☒☐☐☐
481	A237	5c multicolored	.30	.08 ☒☒☐☐☒
482	A238	5c dk. blue & multi.	.35	.15 ☒☒☐☐☐
483	A239	5c yel., black & red	.30	.15 ☒☒☐☐☐
484	A240	5c multicolored	.30	.15 ☒☒☐☐☐
485	A241	5c verm., buff & blk.	.30	.10 ☒☒☐☐☐
486	A242	15c slate	2.00	1.50 ☐☒☐☐☐
487	A243	5c multicolored	3 .30	.08 ☒☒☐☐☐
488	A244	5c brt. bl. & black	.25	.05 ☒☒☐☐☐
488a	A244	Blkt. pane of 10	2 2.50	☒☐☐☐☐
488p	A244	Tagged	.30	.25 ☐☐☐☐☐
488q	A244	As "a" tagged	3.00	☐☐☐☐☐
489	A244	6c dp. bister & black	.30	.05 ☒☒☐☐☐
489p	A244	Tagged	.35	.25 ☐☐☐☐☐

1969

490	A245	6c black, brt. blue & carmine	.30	.15 ☒☒☐☐☐
491	A246	6c yellow olive & dark brown	.30	.05 ☒☒☐☐☐
492	A247	50c multicolored	4.25	2.75 ☒☒☐☐☒
493	A248	6c dk. olive green	.30	.12 ☒☒☐☐☐
494	A249	15c red brn., yel. grn. & lt. ultra.	2.50	2.00 ☒☒☐☐☐
495	A250	6c dark blue & lt. red brown	.30	.10 ☒☒☐☐☐
496	A251	6c multicolored	.50	.08 ☒☒☐☐☐

10 7⁶⁸

A253

A255

A254

A256

A257

A258

A259

A260

A261

A262

A263

A265

A266

A267

A264

A268

A269

A270

222

Scott® No.	Illus No.	Description	Unused Price	Used Price	M	BLOX				U

1969

497	A251	10c ultra. & multi.	1.00	.60	☒	☒	☐	☐	☐	☐
498	A251	25c black & multi.	2.50	2.25	☐	☒	☐	☐	☐	☐
499	A252	6c ultra., org. brown & black	.35	.15	☒	☒	☐	☐	☐	☐
500	A253	6c ultra., brt. green & red	.30	.10	☒	☒	☐	☐	☐	☐
501	A254	6c yel. brown, brown & pale salmon	.30	.05	☒	☒	☐	☐	☐	☐
502	A255	5c blue & multi.	.25	.05	☒	☒	☐	☐	☐	☐
502a	A255	Bklt. pane of 10	2.50		☒	☐	☐	☐	☐	☐
502p	A255	Tagged	.25	.15	☐	☐	☐	☐	☐	☐
502q	A255	As "a," tagged	2.50		☐	☐	☐	☐	☐	☐
503	A255	6c red & multi.	.25	.05	☒	☒	☐	☐	☐	☐
503p	A255	Tagged	.30	.20	☐	☐	☐	☐	☐	☐
504	A256	6c multicolored	.35	.10	☒	☒	☐	☐	☐	☐

1970

505	A257	6c vio. blue & multi.	.30	.05	☒	☒	☐	☐	☐	☐
505p	A257	Tagged	.30	.05	☐	☐	☐	☐	☐	☐
506	A258	6c dk. red & black	.30	.07	☒	☒	☐	☐	☐	☐
507	A259	6c grn., lt. org. & bl.	.30	.10	☒	☐	☐	☐	☐	☐
508	A260	25c red emblem	4.00	3.00	☐	☐	☐	☐	☐	☐
508p	A260	Tagged	4.00	3.00	☐	☐	☐	☐	☐	☐
509	A261	25c violet emblem	4.00	3.00	☒	☐	☐	☐	☐	☐
509p	A261	Tagged	4.00	3.00	☐	☐	☐	☐	☐	☐
510	A261	25c green emblem	4.00	3.00	☐	☐	☐	☐	☐	☐
510p	A261	Tagged	4.00	3.00	☐	☐	☐	☐	☐	☐
511	A261	25c blue emblem	4.00	3.00	☒	☐	☐	☐	☐	☐
511p	A261	Tagged	4.00	3.00	☐	☐	☐	☐	☐	☐
512	A262	6c multicolored	.30	.10	☒	☒	☐	☐	☐	☐
513	A263	10c blue	1.00	.80	☒	☒	☐	☐	☐	☐
513p	A263	Tagged	1.00	.80	☒	☒	☐	☐	☐	☐
514	A263	15c lilac & dk. red	1.25	.90	☒	☒	☐	☐	☐	☐
514p	A263	Tagged	1.25	.90	☐	☐	☐	☐	☐	☐
515	A264	6c red & brt. blue	.30	.08	☒	☒	☐	☐	☐	☐
516	A265	6c brown	.30	.05	☐	☒	☐	☐	☐	☐
517	A266	6c red & black	.30	.10	☒	☒	☐	☐	☐	☐
518	A267	6c multicolored	.30	.07	☒	☒	☐	☐	☐	☐
519	A268	5c *Santa Claus*	.35	.07	☒	☐	☐	☐	☐	☐
520	A268	5c *Horse-drawn Sleigh*	.35	.07	☒	☐	☐	☐	☐	☐
521	A268	5c *Nativity*	.35	.07	☒	☐	☐	☐	☐	☐
522	A268	5c *Children Skiing*	.35	.07	☒	☒	☐	☐	☐	☐
523	A268	5c *Snowmen and Christmas Tree*	.35	.07	☒	☐	☐	☐	☐	☐
524	A269	6c *Christ Child*	.35	.07	☒	☐	☐	☐	☐	☐
525	A269	6c *Christmas Tree and Children*	.35	.07	☒	☒	☐	☐	☐	☐
526	A269	6c *Toy Store*	.35	.07	☒	☐	☐	☐	☐	☐
527	A269	6c *Santa Claus*	.35	.07	☒	☐	☐	☐	☐	☐
528	A269	6c *Church*	.35	.07	☒	☐	☐	☐	☐	☐
529	A270	10c *Christ Child*	.50	.25	☒	☒	☐	☐	☐	☐

A271

A272

A273

A274

A275

A277

A276

A278

A279

A282

A280

Scott® No.	Illus No.	Description	Unused Price	Used Price	M BLOX
530	A270	15c *Snowmobile and Trees*	1.25	1.25	☒ ☒ ☐ ☐ ☐ ☐
		Tagged			
519p	A268	5c multicolored	.35	.07	☐ ☐ ☐ ☐ ☐
520p	A268	5c multicolored	.35	.07	☐ ☐ ☐ ☐ ☐
521p	A268	5c multicolored	.35	.07	☐ ☐ ☐ ☐ ☐
522p	A268	5c multicolored	.35	.07	☐ ☐ ☐ ☐ ☐
523p	A268	5c multicolored	.35	.07	☐ ☐ ☐ ☐ ☐
524p	A269	6c multicolored	.35	.07	☐ ☐ ☐ ☐ ☐
525p	A269	6c multicolored	.35	.07	☐ ☐ ☐ ☐ ☐
526p	A269	6c multicolored	.35	.07	☐ ☐ ☐ ☐ ☐
527p	A269	6c multicolored	.35	.07	☐ ☐ ☐ ☐ ☐
528p	A269	6c multicolored	.35	.07	☐ ☐ ☐ ☐ ☐
529p	A270	10c multicolored	.50	.35	☐ ☐ ☐ ☐ ☐
530p	A270	15c multicolored	1.25	1.25	☐ ☐ ☐ ☐ ☐
1970					
531	A271	6c dk. green, yellow & black	2 .30	.05	☒ ☒ ☐ ☐ ☐
1971					
532	A272	6c multicolored	.30	.05	☒ ☒ ☐ ☐ ☐
533	A273	6c multicolored	.30	.05	☒ ☒ ☐ ☐ ☐
534	A274	6c red, org. & black	.30	.05	☒ ☒ ☐ ☐ ☐
535	A275	6c gray & multi.	.40	.10	☒ ☒ ☐ ☐ ☐
536	A275	6c gray & multi.	.40	.10	☒ ☒ ☐ ☐ ☐
537	A275	7c gray & multi.	.40	.10	☒ ☒ ☐ ☐ ☐
538	A275	7c gray & multi.	.40	.10	☒ ☒ ☐ ☐ ☐
539	A276	6c multicolored	.30	.15	☒ ☒ ☐ ☐ ☐
540	A277	6c buff, red & brown	.30	.15	☒ ☒ ☐ ☐ ☐
541	A278	15c black, red orange & yellow	2.50	2.25	☒ ☒ ☐ ☐ ☐
541p	A278	Tagged	2.50	2.25	☐ ☐ ☐ ☐ ☐
542	A279	6c blk., ultra. & red	.30	.10	☒ ☒ ☐ ☐ ☐
1971-72		*Perf. 12½x12*			
543	A280	7c slate green	.35	.05	☒ ☒ ☐ ☐ ☐
543a	A280	Booklet pane of 5 + label (#454,#456+3#543)	3.00	3.00	☒ ☐ ☐ ☐ ☐
543b	A280	Bklt. pane of 20 (4#454, 4#456, 12#453)	7.50	7.50	☐ ☐ ☐ ☐ ☐
543p	A280	Tagged	.50	.30	☐ ☐ ☐ ☐ ☐
544	A280	8c slate	.30	.03	☐ ☐ ☐ ☐ ☐
544a	A280	Bklt. pane of 6 (3#454, 1#460c, 2#544)	2.00		☒ ☐ ☐ ☐ ☐
544b	A280	Bklt. pane of 18 (6#454, 1#460c, 11#544)	5.00		☐ ☐ ☐ ☐ ☐
544c	A280	Bklt. pane of 10 (4#454, 1#460c, 5#544) ('72)	2.50		☒ ☐ ☐ ☐ ☐
544p	A280	Tagged	.50	.08	☐ ☐ ☐ ☐ ☐

BOOKLETS 1ᶠ(4)–3½(4)–7½(12)–7⁰⁰ ☒ 54⁰⁵

225

1ᶠ(c)–6ᶠ(i)–8ᶠ(11)–2⁰⁰ ☒

A283

A284

A285

A286

A287

A288

A289

A290

Scott® No.	Illus No.	Description	Unused Price	Used Price	/ / / / / /

1971-72

Scott® No.	Illus No.	Description	Unused Price	Used Price
544q	A280	As "a," tagged	1.50	
544r	A280	As "b," tagged	5.00	
544s	A280	As "c," tagged	2.00	

1971 Coil Stamps *Perf. 10 Horiz.*

549	A280	7c slate green	.40	.08
550	A280	8c slate	.40	.04
550p	A280	Tagged	.25	.04

1971

552	A282	7c multicolored	.30	.05
553	A283	7c multicolored	.65	.10
554	A284	6c dark blue	.25	.04
554p	A284	Tagged	.25	.04
555	A284	7c bright green	.30	.04
555p	A284	Tagged	.30	.04
556	A284	10c dp. car. & silver	.50	.45
556p	A284	Tagged	.50	.45
557	A284	15c lt. ultra., dp. car. & silver	1.00	1.00
557p	A284	Tagged	1.00	1.00
558	A285	7c black	.35	.10

1972

559	A286	8c deep red lilac	.35	.07
560	A287	8c red	.35	.07
560p	A287	Tagged	.35	.10
561	A288	8c red brown & multicolored	.35	.10
561p	A288	Tagged	.35	.15

1972-76

562	A289	8c *shown*	.50	.15
562p	A289	Tagged	.50	.20
563	A289	8c *Plains Indian artifacts*	.50	.15
563p	A289	Tagged	.50	.20
564	A290	8c *shown*	.50	.15
564p	A290	Tagged	.50	.20
565	A290	8c *Ceremonial sun dance costume*	.50	.15
565p	A290	Tagged	.50	.20
566	A289	8c *Algonkian artifacts*	.50	.15
567	A289	8c *"Micmac Indians"*	.50	.15
568	A290	8c *Thunderbird and belt*	.40	.15
569	A290	8c *Algonkian man and woman*	.40	.15
570	A289	8c *Nootka Sound, house, inside*	.35	.15
571	A289	8c *Artifacts*	.35	.15
572	A290	8c *Chief wearing Chilkat blanket*	.35	.15
573	A290	8c *Thunderbird from Kwakiutl house*	.35	.15

A291

A292

A292a

A293

A294

A295

A296

A297

A298

Scott® No.	Illus No.	Description	Unused Price	Used Price	/ / / / / /

1972-76

574	A289	8c *Montagnais-Naskapi artifacts*	.30	.12	☒ ☒ ☐ ☐ ☐
575	A289	8c *Dance of the Kutcha-Kutchin*	.30	.12	☒ ☐ ☐ ☐ ☐
576	A290	8c *Kutchin ceremonial costume*	.30	.12	☐ ☒ ☐ ☐ ☐
577	A290	8c *Ojibwa thunderbird and Naskapi pattern*	.30	.12	☐ ☐ ☐ ☐ ☐
578	A289	10c *Cornhusk mask, artifacts*	.30	.15	☒ ☒ ☐ ☐ ☐
579	A289	10c *Iroquoian Encampment, by George Heriot*	.30	.15	☒ ☐ ☐ ☐ ☐
580	A290	10c *Iroquoian thunderbird*	.30	.15	☒ ☒ ☐ ☐ ☐
581	A290	10c *Iroquoian man and woman*	2.30	.15	☒ ☐ ☐ ☐ ☐

1972 291 MINI SHEET 38.00 ☒

582	A291	15c *shown* PLT. ☒	3.00	3.00	☐ ☐ ☐ ☐ ☐
582p	A291	Tagged	3.00	3.00	☐ ☐ ☐ ☐ ☐
583	A291	15c *Bird's eye view of town*	3.00	3.00	☐ ☐ ☐ ☐ ☐
583p	A291	Tagged	3.00	3.00	☐ ☐ ☐ ☐ ☐
584	A291	15c *Aerial map photography*	3.00	3.00	☐ ☐ ☐ ☐ ☐
584p	A291	Tagged	3.00	3.00	☐ ☐ ☐ ☐ ☐
585	A291	15c *Contour lines*	3.00	3.00	☐ ☐ ☐ ☐ ☐
585p	A291	Tagged	3.00	3.00	☐ ☐ ☐ ☐ ☐

1972-76 Perf. 12x12½

586	A292	1c orange ('73)	.05	.03	☐ ☒ ☐ ☐ ☐ 2
586a	A292	Booklet pane of 6 (3#586, 1#591, 2#593) ('74)	.55		☐ ☐ ☐ ☐ ☐
586b	A292	Booklet pane of 18 (6#586, 1#591, 11#593) ('75)	2.10		☐ ☐ ☐ ☐ ☐
586c	A292	Booklet pane of 10 (2#586, 4#587, 4#593c) ('76)	1.60		☐ ☐ ☐ ☐ ☐
587	A292	2c green ('73)	5 .06	.03	☒ ☒ ☐ ☐ ☐
588	A292	3c brown ('73)	2 .10	.05	☒ ☒ ☐ ☐ ☐
589	A292	4c black ('73)	.15	2 .05	☐ ☒ ☐ ☐ ☐
590	A292	5c lilac ('73)	.20	2 .06	☐ ☒ ☐ ☐ ☐
591	A292	6c dark red ('73)	3 .22	.04	☒ ☒ ☐ ☐ ☐
592	A292	7c dark brown ('74)	.25	.06	☒ ☒ ☐ ☐ ☐
593	A292a	8c ultramarine ('73)	3 .25	.03	☒ ☒ ☐ ☐ ☐

Perf. 13x13½

| 593A | A292a | 10c dark car. ('76) | 2.30 | .03 | ☒ ☒ ☐ ☐ ☐ |

Perf. 12½x12

594	A293	10c multicolored	.30	.10	☒ ☒ ☐ ☐ ☐
595	A293	15c multicolored	.45	.15	☐ ☒ ☐ ☐ ☐
596	A293	20c multicolored	.65	.10	☒ ☐ ☐ ☐ ☐
597	A293	25c multicolored	.75	.10	☐ ☐ ☐ ☐ ☐
598	A293	50c multicolored	1.50	.15	☐ ☐ ☐ ☐ ☐

6758

A300

A299

A302

A301

A303

A306

A304

A307

A308

A305

A309

Scott® No.	Illus No.	Description	Unused Price	Used Price	`//////`

(handwritten above check columns: H BLOK u)

1972-76

599	A294	$1 multicolored ('73)	3.50	.75	☒☒☐☒☒
LOOA		*$1 VANCOUV Perf. 11 ERROR 7⁰ᵘ*			☒
600	A294	$1 multicolored	8.00	2.50	☐☐☐☐☐
601	A294	$2 multicolored	*5* 6.00	*2* 3.50	☒☒☐☐☐

1976-77 Perf. 13½

594a	A293	10c multicolored	*2* .35	.03	☒☒☐☐☐
595a	A293	15c multicolored	.55	*2* .10	☐☒☐☐☐
596a	A293	20c multicolored	.75	*2* .10	☐☒☐☐☐
597a	A293	25c multicolored	*3* .85	.10	☒☒☐☐☐
598a	A293	50c multicolored	*3* 1.50	.20	☒☒☐☐☐
599a	A294	$1 multicolored ('77)	*3* 3.50	.50	☒☒☐☐☐

1974-76 Coil Stamps Perf. 10 Vert.

| 604 | A292a | 8c ultramarine | .25 | .05 | ☐☐☐☐☐ |
| 605 | A292a | 10c dk. carmine ('76) | *19* .25 | .05 | ☒☒☐☐☐ |

1972

606	A295	6c red & multi.	.25	.04	☒☐☐☐☐
606p	A295	tagged	.25	.08	☐☐☐☐☐
607	A295	8c vio. bl. & multi.	.30	.04	☒☒☐☐☐
607p	A295	Tagged	.30	.10	☐☐☐☐☐
608	A296	10c green & multi.	.60	.50	☐☒☐☐☐
608p	A296	Tagged	.60	.50	☐☐☐☐☐
609	A296	15c yellow bister & multicolored	1.00	1.00	☒☒☐☐☐
609p	A296	Tagged	1.00	1.00	☐☐☐☐☐
610	A297	8c multicolored *DOOR VARIETY*	.45	.10	☒☒☒☐☐
610p	A297	Tagged	.45	.15	☐☐☐☐☐

1973

611	A298	8c silver, ultramarine & gold	.30	.08	☒☒☐☐☐
612	A299	8c dk. brown, orange & red	.30	.08	☒☒☐☐☐
613	A299	10c dk. blue & multi.	.50	.45	☒☒☐☐☐
614	A299	15c yel. grn. & multi.	.75	.75	☒☒☐☐☐
615	A300	8c multicolored	.30	.08	☒☒☐☐☐
616	A301	8c gold & black	.30	.08	☒☒☐☐☐
617	A302	15c multicolored	.75	.75	☒☒☐☐☐
618	A303	8c org. & red brown	.30	.08	☒☒☐☐☐
619	A304	8c multicolored	.30	.08	☐☐☐☐☐
620	A305	8c silver & multi.	.30	.15	☒☒☐☐☐
621	A305	15c gold & multi.	.85	.85	☐☒☐☐☐
622	A306	8c multicolored	.30	.08	☒☒☒☐☐
623	A307	8c silver & multi.	.25	.15	☒☒☐☐☐
624	A307	15c gold & multi.	.75	.75	☒☒☒☐☐
625	A308	6c *shown*	.20	.05	☒☒☐☐☐
626	A308	8c *Dove*	.25	.05	☒☒☒☐☐
627	A309	10c *shown*	.40	.40	☒☒☐☐☐
628	A309	15c *Shepherd and star*	.85	.85	☒☒☐☐☐

(handwritten bottom right: 2/5 —)

A311

A310

A312

A314

A313

A315

A316

A317

A318

A319

A320

A321

A322

A324

A323

A325

A326

232

Scott® No.	Illus No.	Description	Unused Price	Used Price	/ / / / / /

1974

Scott® No.	Illus No.	Description	Unused Price	Used Price	
629	A310	8c *shown*	.40	.15	☒ ☒ ☐ ☐ ☐ ☐
630	A310	8c *Joggers*	.40	.15	☒ ☐ ☐ ☐ ☐ ☐
631	A310	8c *Bicycling family*	.40	.15	☒ ☐ ☐ ☐ ☐ ☐
632	A310	8c *Hikers*	.40	.15	☒ ☐ ☐ ☐ ☐ ☐
633	A311	8c multicolored	.30	.08	☒ ☒ ☐ ☐ ☐ ☐
634	A312	8c *shown*	.50	.40	☒ ☒ ☐ ☐ ☐ ☐
635	A312	8c *Mail collector and truck*	.50	.40	☒ ☐ ☐ ☐ ☐ ☐
636	A312	8c *Mail handler*	.50	.40	☒ ☐ ☐ ☐ ☐ ☐
637	A312	8c *Mail sorters*	.50	.40	☒ ☐ ☐ ☐ ☐ ☐
638	A312	8c *Mailman*	.50	.40	☒ ☐ ☐ ☐ ☐ ☐
639	A312	8c *Rural mail delivery*	.50	.40	☒ ☐ ☐ ☐ ☐ ☐
640	A313	8c multicolored	.30	.08	☒ ☒ ☐ ☐ ☐ ☐
641	A314	8c multicolored	.30	.08	☒ ☒ ☐ ☐ ☐ ☐
642	A315	8c blk., red & silver	.30	.08	☒ ☒ ☐ ☐ ☐ ☐
643	A316	8c multicolored	.30	.08	☐ ☐ ☐ ☐ ☐ ☐
644	A317	8c *shown*	.45	.15	☒ ☐ ☐ ☐ ☐ ☐
645	A317	8c *Skiing*	.45	.15	☒ ☐ ☐ ☐ ☐ ☐
646	A317	8c *Skating*	.45	.15	☒ ☐ ☐ ☐ ☐ ☐
647	A317	8c *Curling*	.45	.15	☒ ☐ ☐ ☐ ☐ ☐
648	A318	8c vio., red & blue	.30	.08	☒ ☒ ☐ ☐ ☐ ☐
649	A318	15c vio., red & blue	.90	.90	☒ ☒ ☐ ☐ ☐ ☐
650	A319	6c multicolored	.20	.05	☒ ☒ ☐ ☐ ☐ ☐
651	A320	8c multicolored	.25	.05	☒ ☒ ☐ ☐ ☐ ☐
652	A319	10c multicolored	.50	.40	☒ ☒ ☐ ☐ ☐ ☐
653	A319	15c multicolored	.75	.75	☒ ☒ ☐ ☐ ☐ ☐
654	A321	8c multicolored	.30	.08	☒ ☒ ☐ ☐ ☐ ☐
655	A322	8c multicolored	.30	.08	☐ ☐ ☐ ☐ ☐ ☐

1975 656A / 657A MIN. SHTS ☒

Scott® No.	Illus No.	Description	Unused Price	Used Price	
656	A322	$1 multicolored	5.00	4.00	☐ ☒ ☐ ☐ ☐ ☐
657	A324	$2 multicolored	9.00	8.00	☒ ☒ ☐ ☐ ☐ ☐
658	A325	8c blue & multi.	.30	.10	☒ ☒ ☐ ☐ ☐ ☐
659	A326	8c brown & multi.	.30	.10	☒ ☐ ☐ ☐ ☐ ☐
660	A327	8c red & multi.	.30	.10	☐ ☒ ☐ ☐ ☐ ☐
661	A328	8c red & multi.	.30	.10	☐ ☒ ☐ ☐ ☐ ☐
662	A329	8c dk. brn., yel. & buff	.30	.15	☒ ☒ ☐ ☐ ☐ ☐
663	A330	8c dk. brn., yel. & buff	.30	.15	☒ ☐ ☐ ☐ ☐ ☐
664	A331	20c dk. bl. & multi.	.75	.70	☒ ☒ ☐ ☐ ☐ ☐
665	A331	25c maroon & multi.	.85	.80	☒ ☒ ☐ ☐ ☐ ☐
666	A332	50c multicolored	1.75	1.50	☒ ☒ ☐ ☐ ☐ ☐
667	A333	8c gray & multi.	.30	.08	☒ ☒ ☐ ☐ ☐ ☐
668	A334	8c dp. yel., gray & black	.30	.08	☒ ☒ ☐ ☐ ☐ ☐
669	A335	8c multicolored	.30	.08	☒ ☒ ☐ ☐ ☐ ☐
670	A336	8c *shown*	1.10	.30	☒ ☒ ☐ ☐ ☐ ☐
671	A336	8c *"Beaver"*	1.10	.30	☒ ☐ ☐ ☐ ☐ ☐
672	A336	8c *"Neptune"*	1.10	.30	☒ ☐ ☐ ☐ ☐ ☐
673	A336	8c *"Quadra"*	1.10	.30	☒ ☐ ☐ ☐ ☐ ☐

193 05

A327

A328

A329

A330

A331

A332

A334

A335

A333

A337

A336

A338

234

Scott® No.	Illus No.	Description	Unused Price	Used Price	/ / / / / /
1975					
674	A337	6c *shown*	.20	.07	☒☒☐☐☐☐
675	A337	6c *Skater*	.20	.07	☒☐☐☐☐☐
676	A338	8c *shown*	.25	.07	☒☒☐☐☐☐
677	A338	8c *Family and Christmas tree*	.25	.07	☒☐☐☐☐☐
678	A338	10c *Gift box*	.30	.30	☒☒☐☐☐☐
679	A339	15c *shown*	.60	.60	☒☒☐☐☐☐
680	A340	8c gray & multi.	.30	.08	☒☐☐☐☐☐
1976					
681	A341	8c black & multi.	.25	.07	☒☒☐☐☐☐
682	A341	20c black & multi.	.75	.75	☒☒☐☐☐☐
683	A341	25c black & multi.	.85	.85	☒☒☐☐☐☐
684	A342	20c gray & multi.	.75	.75	☒☒☐☐☐☐
685	A342	25c ocher & multi.	.85	.85	☒☒☐☐☐☐
686	A342	50c blue & multi.	1.50	1.50	☒☒☐☐☐☐
687	A343	$1 silver & multi.	4.00	3.50	☐☐☐☐☐☐
688	A343	$2 gold & multi.	8.00	7.50	☐☐☐☐☐☒
689	A344	20c multicolored	.75	.75	☒☒☐☐☐☐
690	A345	20c multicolored	.75	.75	☒☒☐☐☐☐
691	A346	10c multicolored	.30	.25	☒☒☐☐☐☐
692	A347	8c red & multi.	.25	.12	☒☒☐☐☐☐
693	A348	8c red & multi.	.25	.12	☒☐☐☐☐☐
694	A349	20c green & multi.	.75	.75	☒☒☐☐☐☐
695	A350	8c multicolored	.25	.10	☒☒☐☐☐☐
696	A351	8c multicolored	.25	.10	☒☐☐☐☐☐
697	A352	8c multicolored	.20	.06	☒☒☐☐☐☐
698	A352	10c multicolored	.25	.05	☒☒☐☐☐☐
699	A352	20c multicolored	.60	.60	☒☒☐☐☐☐
700	A353	10c black, lt. & dk. brown	.50	.45	☒☒☐☐☐☐
701	A353	10c black, lt. & dk. violet	.50	.45	☒☒☐☐☐☐
702	A353	10c black, lt. & dk. blue	.50	.45	☒☒☐☐☐☐
703	A353	10c black, lt. & dk. green	.50	.45	☒☒☐☐☐☐
1977					
704	A354	25c silver & multi.	.75	.60	☒☒☐☐☐☐
1977-79		*Perf. 12x12½*			
705	A355	1c multicolored	5 .05	.03	☒☒☐☐☐☐
707	A355	2c multicolored	.06	.03	☒☒☐☐☐☐
708	A355	3c multicolored	7 .06	.03	☒☒☐☐☐☐
709	A355	4c multicolored	5 .08	.04	☒☒☐☐☐☐
710	A355	5c multicolored	5 .10	2.05	☒☒☐☐☐☐
711	A355	10c multicolored	.20	.08	☒☒☐☐☐☐
		Perf. 12½x13			
712	A355	12c multi. ('78)	2 .24	2.03	☒☒☐☐☐☐
		Perf. 13x13½			
713	A356	12c blue & multi.	4 .24	.03	☒☒☐☐☐☐
713a	A356	Perf. 12×12½	.24	.03	☐☐☐☐☐☐

86,81

A339

A340

A341

A342

A344

A343

A345

A346

A347

A348

A349

A350

A353

A351

A352

A354

A355

A356

A357

A358

A359

237

A359a

A360

A361

A362

A363

A364

A365

A366

A368

A367

A370

A369

A371

Scott® No.	Illus No.	Description	Unused Price	Used Price	/ / / / / /
1977-79		*Perf. 13*			
714	A357	12c blue	.24	.03 ☐☐☐☐☐
715	A357	14c red ('78)	.28	.03 ☒☒☐☐☐
		Perf. 13x13½			
716	A356	14c red & blk. ('78)	.28	.03 ☐☐☐☐☐
716a	A356	Perf. 12×12½	.28	.03 ☐☐☐☐☐
716b	A356	As "a," bklt. pane of 25 + 2 labels ('78)	6.00	☐☐☐☐☐
		Perf. 13½			
717	A358	15c multi.	3 .30	.08 ☒☒☐☐☐
718	A358	20c multi.	2 .40	.10 ☒☒☐☐☐
719	A358	25c multi.	.50	2.12 ☒☒☐☐☐
720	A358	30c multi. ('78)	3 .60	.15 ☒☒☐☐☐
721	A358	35c multi ('79)	2 .70	.35 ☒☒☐☐☐
723	A359	50c multi. ('78)	2 1.00	.25 ☒☒☐☐☐
724	A359	75c multi. ('78)	2 1.50	.38 ☒☒☐☐☐
725	A359	80c multi. ('78)	2 1.60	.40 ☒☒☐☐☐
		Perf. 13			
726	A359a	$1 multi. ('79)	2 2.00	.75 ☒☒☐☐☐
727	A359a	$2 multi ('79)	2 4.00	1.50 ☒☒☐☐☐
1977-78		Coil Stamps	*Perf. 10 Vert.*		
729	A357	12c blue	16 .24	.03 ☒☒☐☐☐
730	A357	14c red ('78)	16 .28	.03 ☒☒☐☐☐
1977					
732	A360	12c multicolored	.24	.06 ☒☒☐☐☐
733	A361	12c black & multi.	.24	.10 ☒☐☐☐☐
734	A361	12c ocher & multi.	.24	.10 ☒☐☐☐☐
735	A362	12c vio. bl. & multi.	.24	2 .08 ☒☒☐☐☐
736	A363	12c multicolored	.24	2 .08 ☒☒☐☐☐
737	A364	12c blue & multi.	.24	2 .08 ☒☒☐☐☐
738	A365	12c dark blue	.24	2 .10 ☒☒☐☐☐
739	A366	12c brown	.24	.10 ☒☒☐☐☐
740	A367	25c multicolored	2 .50	2 .30 ☒☒☐☐☐
741	A368	10c multicolored	.20	2 .05 ☒☒☐☐☐
742	A368	12c multicolored	.24	2 .06 ☒☒☐☐☐
743	A368	25c multicolored	.50	2 .30 ☒☒☐☐☐
744	A369	12c *shown*	.24	8 .24 ☒☒☐☐☐
745	A369	12c *Tern schooner*	.24	.24 ☒☐☐☐☐
746	A369	12c *5-masted schooner*	.24	.24 ☒☐☐☐☐
747	A369	12c *Mackinaw boat*	.24	.24 ☒☐☐☐☐
748	A370	12c multicolored	.24	2 .12 ☒☒☐☐☐
749	A371	12c multicolored	.24	.12 ☒☐☐☐☐
750	A371	12c multicolored	.24	2 .12 ☒☒☐☐☐
751	A371	12c multicolored	.24	.12 ☒☐☐☐☐

A372

A373

A374

A375

A376

A377

A378

A379

A380

Scott® No.	Illus No.	Description	Unused Price	Used Price	/ / / / / /

1978

Scott® No.	Illus No.	Description	Unused Price	Used Price	/ / / / / /
752	A372	12c multicolored	.24	2 .08 □ ⊠ □ □ □
753	A373	12c gray & black	.24	3 .08 □ ⊠ □ □ □
754	A373	14c gray & blue	15 .28	⋅ .14 ⊠ ⊠ □ □ □
755	A373	30c gray & rose	.60	2 .30 ⊠ ⊠ □ □ □
756	A373	$1.25 gray & black	2 2.50	1.25 ⊠ ⊠ □ □ □
756a	A373	Souvenir sheet of 3	2 3.75	⊠ □ □ □ □
757	A374	14c silver & multi.	.28	.07 □ ⊠ □ □ □
758	A374	30c silver & multi.	.60	.30 □ □ □ □ □
759	A375	14c silver & multi.	.28	.07 ⊠ ⊠ □ □ □
760	A375	14c silver & multi.	.28	.07 ⊠ ⊡ □ □ □
761	A375	30c silver & multi.	.60	.30 ⊠ ⊠ □ □ □
762	A375	30c silver & multi.	.60	.30 ⊠ □ □ □ □
763	A376	14c multicolored	.28	2 .14 ⊠ ⊠ □ □ □
764	A377	14c multicolored	.28	.14 ⊠ ⊡ □ □ □
765	A378	14c multicolored	.28	.14 ⊠ ⊠ □ □ □
766	A379	14c multicolored	.28	.14 ⊠ ⊡ □ □ □
767	A380	14c multicolored	2 .28	.14 ⊠ ⊠ □ □ □
768	A381	14c multicolored	2 .28	2 .14 ⊠ ⊠ □ □ □
769	A382	14c multicolored	.28	.14 ⊠ ⊠ □ □ □
770	A383	14c multicolored	.28	.14 ⊠ ⊡ □ □ □
771	A382	14c multicolored	.28	.14 ⊠ ⊠ □ □ □
772	A383	14c multicolored	.28	.14 ⊠ ⊠ □ □ □
773	A384	12c multicolored	4 .24	3 .12 ⊠ ⊠ □ □ □
774	A384	14c multicolored	.28	.14 ⊠ ⊠ □ □ □
775	A384	30c multicolored	2 .60	.30 ⊠ ⊠ □ □ □
776	A385	14c *shown*	.28	4 .14 ⊠ ⊠ □ □ □
777	A385	14c *"St. Roch," 1928*	.28	.14 ⊠ ⊡ □ □ □
778	A385	14c *"Northern Light," 1928*	.28	.14 ⊠ ⊡ □ □ □
779	A385	14c *"Labrador," 1954*	.28	.14 ⊡ ⊡ □ □ □
780	A386	14c multicolored	.28	3 .14 □ ⊠ □ □ □

1977-79

Scott® No.	Illus No.	Description	Unused Price	Used Price	/ / / / / /
782	A355	5c multi	.10	.05 □ □ □ □ □
784	A356	17c green & black	3 .34	.03 ⊠ ⊠ □ □ □
785	A357	17c slate green	2 .34	.03 ⊠ ⊠ □ □ □

Booklet Stamps

Scott® No.	Illus No.	Description	Unused Price	Used Price	/ / / / / /
796	A355	1c multi	.03	.03 □ □ □ □ □
796a		Bklt. pane of 6(2 #796, 4 #713a)	1.10	□ □ □ □ □
797	A357	1c slate blue ('79)	.03	.03 □ □ □ □ □
797a		Bklt. of pane 6 (1 #797, 3 #800, 2 #784a)	1.00	□ □ □ □ □
798	A355	2c multi	.04	.03 □ □ □ □ □
798a		Bklt. pane of 7 (4 #798, 3 #716a, label)	1.00	□ □ □ □ □

Coil Stamps Perf.10 Vert.

Scott® No.	Illus No.	Description	Unused Price	Used Price	/ / / / / /
806	A357	17c slate green	.34	.03 □ □ □ □ □

A382

A381

A383

A385

A384

A386

A392

A393

SP1

SP2

Scott® No.	Illus No.	Description	Unused Price	Used Price	/ / / / / /
1979					
813	A392	17c multi	.34	.10 ☒☒☐☐☐☐
814	A392	35c multi	.70	.18 ☒☒☐☐☐☐
815	A393	17c multi	.34	.10 ☒☒☐☐☐☐
816	A393	17c multi	.34	.10 ☒☐☐☐☐☐

SEMI—POSTAL STAMPS

1974					
B1	A307	8c+2c bronze & multi.	.50	.50 ☐☐☐☐☐
B2	A307	10c+5c silver & multi.	.75	.75 ☐☐☐☐☐
B3	A307	15c+5c gold & multi.	1.00	1.00 ☐☐☐☐☐
1975					
B4	SP1	8c+2c multicolored	.50	.50 ☒☒☐☐☐
B5	SP1	10c+5c multicolored	.75	.75 ☒☒☐☐☐
B6	SP1	15c+5c multicolored	1.00	1.00 ☒☒☐☐☐
B7	SP2	8c+2c org. & multi.	.50	.50 ☒☒☐☐☐
B8	SP2	10c+5c org. & multi.	.75	.75 ☐☒☐☐☐
B9	SP2	15c+5c org. & multi.	1.00	1.00 ☒☒☐☐☐
1976					
B10	SP2	8c+2c bl. & multi.	.50	.50 ☒☒☐☐☐
B11	SP2	10c+5c bl. & multi.	.75	.75 ☒☒☐☐☐
B12	SP2	20c+5c bl. & multi.	1.25	1.25 ☒☒☐☐☐

AP1

AP2

AP3

AP4

AP5

AP6

APSD1

APSD2

SD1

AIR POST STAMPS

Scott® No.	Illus No.	Description	Unused Price	Used Price	/ / / / /
1928					
C1	AP1	5c brown olive	7.00	2.25	☒ ☐ ☐ ☐ ☐
1930					
C2	AP2	5c olive brown	25.00	16.00	☒ ☒ ☐ ☐ ☐
1932					
C3	AP1	6c on 5c brown olive	5.00	2.25	☒ ☒ ☐ ☐ ☐
C4	AP2	6c on 5c olive brn.	10.00	9.00	☒ ☒ ☐ ☐ ☐
1935					
C5	AP3	6c red brown	2.00	1.25	☒ ☒ ☐ ☐ ☒
1938		6 yLw Brwn			☒
C6	AP4	6c blue	1.75	.25	☒ ☒ ☐ ☐ ☐
1942-43					
C7	AP5	6c deep blue	3.00	1.00	☒ ☒ ☐ ☐ ☐
C8	AP5	7c deep blue ('43)	.75	.10	☒ ☒ ☐ ☐ ☐
1946					
C9	AP6	7c deep blue	.75	.10	☐ ☒ ☐ ☐ ☐
C9a		Booklet pane of 4	3.00	2.50	☒ ☐ ☐ ☐ ☐

AIR POST SPECIAL DELIVERY STAMPS

1942-43					
CE1	APSD1	16c brt. ultra.	2.25	2.25	☒ ☒ ☐ ☐ ☐
CE2	APSD1	17c bright ultramarine ('43)	3.00	3.00	☒ ☒ ☐ ☐ ☐
1946		Circumflex (∧) accent on second "E" of "EXPRES".			
CE3	APSD2	17c bright ultramarine	5.00	5.00	☒ ☒ ☐ ☐ ☐
1947		Corrected Die. Grave accent (ˋ) on the second "E" of "EXPRES".			
CE4	APSD2	17c bright ultramarine	5.00	5.00	☒ ☒ ☐ ☐ ☐

AIR POST OFFICIAL STAMPS

1949		Overprinted in Black **O. H. M. S.**			
CO1	AP6	7c deep blue	9.00	4.00	☐ ☐ ☐ ☐ ☐
1950		Same Overprinted **G**			
CO2	AP6	7c deep blue	15.00	12.50	☐ ☐ ☐ ☐ ☐

SPECIAL DELIVERY STAMPS

1898					
E1	SD1	10c blue green	35.00	6.50	☒ ☐ ☐ ☐ ☐
1922					
E2	SD2	20c carmine	45.00	6.00	☒ ☐ ☐ ☐ ☐
1927					
E3	SD3	20c orange	7.50	7.50	☒ ☒ ☐ ☐ ☐
1930					
E4	SD4	20c henna brown	45.00	12.50	☒ ☒ ☐ ☐ ☐
1933					
E5	SD5	20c henna brown	30.00	15.00	☒ ☐ ☐ ☐ ☐

SD2

SD4

SD3

SD5

SD6

SD7

SD8

SD9

R1

D1

D2

Scott® No.	Illus No.	Description	Unused Price	Used Price	/ / / / / /

M BLOX a

1935

| E6 | SD6 | 20c dark carmine | 7.50 | 6.00 | ☒ ☒ ☐ ☐ ☐ |

1938-39

| E7 | SD7 | 10c dark green ('39) | 6.00 | 2.75 | ☒ ☒² ☐ ☐ ☐ |
| E8 | SD7 | 20c dark carmine | 25.00 | 25.00 | ☒ ☐ ☐ ☐ ☐ |

1939

| E9 | SD7 | 10c on 20c dark carmine | 6.00 | 6.00 | ☒ ☒ ☐ ☐ ☐ |

1942

| E10 | SD8 | 10c green | 2.75 | 1.25 | ☐ ☒ ☐ ☐ ☐ |

1946

| E11 | SD9 | 10c green | 2.25 | .85 | ☒ ☒ ☐ ☐ ☐ |

SPECIAL DELIVERY OFFICIAL STAMPS
O.H.M.S.

1950

| EO1 | SD9 | 10c green | 20.00 | 20.00 | ☐ ☐ ☐ ☐ ☐ |

Same Overprinted **G**

| EO2 | SD9 | 10c green | 35.00 | 35.00 | ☐ ☐ ☐ ☐ ☐ |

REGISTRATION STAMPS

1875-88

F1	R1	2c orange	35.00	2.50	☐ ☐ ☐ ☐ ☐
F2	R1	5c dark green	40.00	2.50	☐ ☐ ☐ ☐ ☐
F3	R1	8c blue	225.00	200.00	☐ ☐ ☐ ☐ ☐

POSTAGE DUE STAMPS *Perf. 12.*

1906-28

J1	D1	1c violet	5.00	2.25	☐ ☐ ☐ ☐ ☐
J2	D1	2c violet	7.00	.75	☐ ☐ ☐ ☐ ☐
J2a		Thin paper	6.00	6.00	☐ ☐ ☐ ☐ ☐
J3	D1	4c violet ('28)	35.00	17.50	☐ ☐ ☐ ☐ ☐
J4	D1	5c violet	7.50	1.50	☐ ☐ ☐ ☐ ☐
J4a		Thin paper	5.00	5.00	☐ ☐ ☐ ☐ ☐
J5	D1	10c violet ('28))	25.00	7.50	☐ ☐ ☐ ☐ ☐

1930-32 *Perf. 11.*

J6	D2	1c dark violet	5.00	4.50	☐ ☐ ☐ ☐ ☐
J7	D2	2c dark violet	4.00	.75	☐ ☐ ☐ ☐ ☐
J8	D2	4c dark violet	6.00	4.00	☐ ☐ ☐ ☐ ☐
J9	D2	5c dark violet	6.50	5.00	☐ ☐ ☐ ☐ ☐
J10	D2	10c dark violet ('32)	65.00	6.50	☐ ☐ ☐ ☐ ☐

1933-34

J11	D3	1c dark violet ('34)	7.50	5.00	☐ ☐ ☐ ☐ ☐
J12	D3	2c dark violet	3.50	.85	☐ ☐ ☐ ☐ ☐
J13	D3	4c dark violet	6.50	4.50	☐ ☐ ☐ ☐ ☐
J14	D3	10c dark violet	7.50	3.50	☐ ☐ ☐ ☐ ☐

1935-65

| J15 | D4 | 1c dark violet | .15 | .10 | ☐ ☐ ☐ ☐ ☐ |
| J16 | D4 | 2c dark violet | .15 | .10 | ☐ ☐ ☐ ☐ ☐ |

D3

D4

D5

WT1

WT2

Scott® No.	Illus No.	Description	Unused Price	Used Price	//////
1935-65					
J16B	D4	3c dark violet ('65)	2.25	2.25 □□□□□
J17	D4	4c dark violet ('65)	.30	.10 □□□□□
J18	D4	5c dark violet ('48)	.40	.35 □□□□□
J19	D4	6c dark violet ('57)	1.50	1.25 □□□□□
J20	D4	10c dark violet	.35	.08 □□□□□
1967		Size: 20x17mm.			
J21	D5	1c carmine rose	.25	.25 □□□□□
J22	D5	2c carmine rose	.30	.30 □□□□□
J23	D5	3c carmine rose	.30	.30 □□□□□
J24	D5	4c carmine rose	.35	.35 □□□□□
J25	D5	5c carmine rose	2.50	2.50 □□□□□
J26	D5	6c carmine rose	.40	.40 □□□□□
J27	D5	10c carmine rose	.50	.40 □□□□□
1969-78		Size: 20x15¾mm.			
J28	D5	1c carmine rose ('70)	.20	.20 □□□□□
J28a		Perf. 12½ × 12 ('77)	.05	.05 □□□□□
J29	D5	2c carmine rose ('72)	.10	.10 □□□□□
J30	D5	3c carmine rose ('74)	.12	.12 □□□□□
J31	D5	4c carmine rose	.25	.25 □□□□□
J31a		Perf. 12½ × 12 ('77)	.12	.12 □□□□□
J32	D5	5c carmine rose, perf. 12½ × 12 ('77)	.10	.10 □□□□□
J32a		Perf. 12	20.00	20.00 □□□□□
J33	D5	6c carmine rose ('72)	.20	.20 □□□□□
J34	D5	8c carmine rose ('72)	.35	.25 □□□□□
J34a		Perf. 12½ × 12 ('78)	.16	.16 □□□□□
J35	D5	10c carmine rose	.35	.20 □□□□□
J35a		Perf. 12½ × 12 ('77)	.20	.15 □□□□□
J36	D5	12c carmine rose	.50	.30 □□□□□
J36a		Perf. 12½ × 12 ('77)	.24	.20 □□□□□
J37	D5	16c carmine rose ('74)	.50	.50 □□□□□
J38	D5	20c carmine rose ('77)	.40	.40 □□□□□
J39	D5	24c carmine rose ('77)	.48	.48 □□□□□
J40	D5	50c carmine rose ('77)	1.00	1.00 □□□□□

WAR TAX STAMPS

1915		Perf. 12			
MR1	WT1	1c green	1.75	.10 □□□□□
MR2	WT1	2c carmine	3.00	.12 □□□□□
1916					
MR3	WT2	2c+1c carmine (I)	5.00	.10 □□□□□
MR3a		2c+1c carmine (II)	50.00	2.00 □□□□□
MR4	WT2	2c+1c brown (II)	2.00	.05 □□□□□
MR4a		2c+1c brown (I)	50.00	5.00 □□□□□

Scott® No.	Illus No.	Description	Unused Price	Used Price	/ / / / / /
1916		*Perf. 12x8.*			
MR5	WT2	2c+1c car. (I)	15.00	15.00	☐☐☐☐☐
		Coil Stamps. *Perf. 8 Vertically.*			
MR6	WT2	2c+1c car. (I)	40.00	3.00	☐☐☐☐☐
MR7	WT2	2c+1c brown (II)	7.50	.50	☐☐☐☐☐
MR7a		2c+1c brown (I)	60.00	2.50	☐☐☐☐☐

OFFICIAL STAMPS

1949-50		**O.H.M.S.**			
O1	A97	1c green	2.00	1.75	☐☐☐☐☐
O2	A98	2e brown	10.00	9.00	☐☐☐☐☐
O3	A99	3c rose violet	2.00	1.25	☐☐☐☐☐
O4	A98	4c dark carmine	3.50	.60	☐☐☐☐☐
		O.H.M.S.			
O6	A108	10c olive	4.00	.60	☐☐☐☐▧
O7	A109	14c black brown	6.00	2.00	☐☐☐☐☐
O8	A110	20c slate black	15.00	2.00	☐☐☐☐▧
O9	A111	50c dark blue green	200.00	150.00	☐☐☐☐☐
O10	A112	$1 red violet	65.00	60.00	☐☐☐☐☐
1950					
O11	A124	50c dull green	35.00	20.00	☐☐☐☐☐
		O.H.M.S.			
O12	A119	1c green	.35	.35	☐☐☐☐☐
O13	A120	2c sepia	1.00	1.00	☐☐☐☐▧
O14	A121	3c rose violet	1.25	.50	☐☐☐☐▧
O15	A122	4c dark carmine	1.25	.15	☐☐☐☐☐
O15A	A123	5c deep blue	2.25	1.75	☐☐☐☐☐

G G G
(a) (b) (c)

O16	A119 (a) 1c green (#284)		.25	.12	☐☐☐☐▧
O17	A120 (a) 2c sepia (#285)		1.25	.80	☐☐☐☐☐
O18	A121 (a) 3c rose violet (#286)		1.25	.15	☐☐☐☐▧
O19	A122 (a) 4c dark carmine (#287)		1.25	.10	☐☐☐☐☐
O20	A123 (a) 5c deep blue (#288)		1.50	.85	☐☐☐☐▧
O21	A108 (b) 10c olive		3.00	.45	☐☐☐☐☐
O22	A109 (b) 14c blk. brown		8.50	1.75	☐☐☐☐☐
O23	A110 (b) 20c slate blk.		20.00	1.00	☐☐☐☐☐
O24	A124 (b) 50c dull green		10.00	5.00	☐☐☐☐☐
O25	A112 (b) $1 red violet		110.00	100.00	☐☐☐☐☐
O26	A125 10c black brown		1.50	.20	☐☐☐☐☐

Scott® No.	Illus No.	Description	Unused Price	Used Price	/ / / / / /
					M a

1950-51

| O27 | A126 | $1 bright ultramarine ('51) | 110.00 | 100.00 □□□□□ |

1951-52

| O28 | A120 | 2c olive green | .50 | .10 □□□□☒ |
| O29 | A122 | 4c org. verm. ('52) | .75 | .10 □□□□☒ |

1952

| O30 | A132 | 20c gray | 2.50 | .15 □□□□□ |

1952-53

| O31 | A136 | 7c blue | 4.00 | 1.00 □□□□☒ |
| O32 | A137 | $1 gray ('53) | 20.00 | 10.00 □□□□☒ |

1953-61

O33	A139 (a)	1c violet brown	.30	.10 □□□□□
O34	A139 (a)	2c green	.35	.10 □□□□□
O35	A139 (a)	3c carmine rose	.35	.07 □□□□□
O36	A139 (a)	4c violet	.50	.05 □□□□☒
O37	A139 (a)	5c ultramarine	.50	.10 □□□□☒
O38	A141 (b)	50c lt. green	6.00	1.25 □□□□□
O38a		Overprinted type "c" ('61)	4.00	1.75 □□□□□

1955-62

| O39 | A148 | 10c violet brown | 1.00 | .12 □□□□☒ |
| O39a | | Overprinted type "c" ('62) | 2.00 | 1.00 □□□□□ |

1955-56

O40	A144	1c violet brown ('56)	.30	.30 □□□□□
O41	A144	2c green ('56)	.40	.10 □□□□□
O43	A144	4c violet ('56)	1.00	.10 □□□□□
O44	A144	5c bright blue	.45	.05 ☒□□□☒

1956-62

| O45 | A159 | 20c green | 1.75 | .15 □□□□□ |
| O45a | | Overprinted type "c" ('62) | 6.00 | .50 □□□□□ |

1963

O46	A195	1c deep brown	.75	.75 □□□□□
O47	A195	2c green	.75	.75 □□□□□
O48	A195	4c carmine	.85	.85 □□□□□
O49	A195	5c violet blue	.50	.50 □□□□□
......	......			□□□□□
......	......			□□□□□
......	......			□□□□□
......	......			□□□□□
......	......			□□□□□
......	......			□□□□□
......	......			□□□□□
......	......			□□□□□
......	......			□□□□□

A1

A2

A3

A4

TWO CENTS
a

5.CENTS.5
b

A1

A2

A3

A4

A5

A6

A7

A8

BRITISH COLUMBIA AND
VANCOUVER ISLAND

Scott® No.	Illus No.	Description	Unused Price	Used Price	/ / / / / /
1860		*Imperf.*			
1	A1	2½p dull rose	2000.00		☐☐☐☐☐
		Perf. 14.			
2	A1	2½p dull rose	180.00	110.00	☐☐☐☐☐

VANCOUVER ISLAND.

1865		*Imperf.*			
3	A2	5c rose	15000.00	3000.00	☐☐☐☐☐
4	A3	10c blue	850.00	525.00	☐☐☐☐☐
		Perf. 14.			
5	A2	5c rose	175.00	110.00	☐☐☐☐☐
6	A3	10c blue	175.00	110.00	☐☐☐☐☐

BRITISH COLUMBIA.

1865					
7	A4	3p blue	45.00	45.00	☐☐☐☐☐
1867-69		*Perf. 14.*			
8	A4 (a)	2c on 3p brown (Bk)	52.50	52.50	☐☐☐☐☐
9	A4(b)	5c on 3p bright red (Bk) ('69)	70.00	70.00	☐☐☐☐☐
10	A4(b)	10c on 3p lilac rose (Bl)	700.00		☐☐☐☐☐
11	A4(b)	25c on 3p orange (V) ('69)	85.00	70.00	☐☐☐☐☐
12	A4(b)	50c on 3p violet (R)	250.00	600.00	☐☐☐☐☐
13	A4(b)	$1 on 3p green (G)	600.00		☐☐☐☐☐
1869		*Perf. 12½.*			
14	A4(b)	5c on 3p brt. red (Bk)	425.00	425.00	☐☐☐☐☐
15	A4(b)	10c on 3p lilac rose (Bl)	325.00	275.00	☐☐☐☐☐
16	A4(b)	25c on 3p org. (V)	275.00	225.00	☐☐☐☐☐
17	A4(b)	50c on 3p vio. (R)	325.00	225.00	☐☐☐☐☐
18	A4(b)	$1 on 3p grn. (G)	500.00	500.00	☐☐☐☐☐

NEW BRUNSWICK

1851		*Imperf.*			
1	A1	3p red	1000.00	250.00	☐☐☐☐☐
2	A1	6p olive yellow	2000.00	500.00	☐☐☐☐☐
3	A1	1sh bright red violet	5500.00	2250.00	☐☐☐☐☐
4	A1	1sh dull violet	5500.00	2250.00	☐☐☐☐☐
1860		*Perf. 12.*			
5	A2	5c brown	2250.00		☐☐☐☐☐
1860-63					
6	A3	1c red lilac	9.00	9.00	☐☐☐☐☐
7	A4	2c orange ('63)	6.00	6.00	☐☐☐☐☐
8	A5	5c yellow green	5.00	5.00	☐☐☐☐☐
9	A6	10c vermilion	15.00	15.00	☐☐☐☐☐
10	A7	12½c blue	25.00	25.00	☐☐☐☐☐
11	A8	17c black	20.00	20.00	☐☐☐☐☐

A1

A2

A3

A4

A5

A6

A7

A8

A9

A10

A11

A12

A14

A13

A15

A16

NEWFOUNDLAND

Scott® No.	Illus No.	Description	Unused Price	Used Price	//////
1857		Thick Porous Wove Paper with Mesh.		*Imperf.*	
1	A1	1p brown violet	50.00	50.00 □□□□□
2	A2	2p scarlet vermilion	3500.00	1800.00 □□□□□
3	A3	3p green	200.00	200.00 □□□□□
4	A4	4p scarlet vermilion	2250.00	1300.00 □□□□□
5	A1	5p brown violet	125.00	125.00 □□□□□
6	A5	6p scarlet vermilion	3000.00	1500.00 □□□□□
7	A6	6½p scarlet vermilion	900.00	900.00 □□□□□
8	A7	8p scarlet vermilion	175.00	175.00 □□□□□
9	A8	1sh scarlet vermilion	3500.00	1800.00 □□□□□
1860		Laid Paper.			
10	A8	1sh orange	16000.00	□□□□□
		Thin to Thick Wove Paper,	No Mesh.		
11	A2	2p orange	180.00	180.00 □□□□□
11A	A3	3p green	35.00	45.00 □□□□□
12	A4	4p orange	1100.00	500.00 □□□□□
12A	A1	5p violet brown	40.00	85.00 □□□□□
13	A5	6p orange	1250.00	400.00 □□□□□
15	A8	1sh orange	13500.00	3000.00 □□□□□
1861-62					
15A	A1	1p violet brown	80.00	80.00 □□□□□
16	A1	1p reddish brown	2000.00	□□□□□
17	A2	2p rose	100.00	100.00 □□□□□
18	A4	4p rose	15.00	22.50 □□□□□
19	A1	5p reddish brown	25.00	35.00 □□□□□
20	A5	6p rose	10.00	22.50 □□□□□
21	A6	6½p rose	35.00	90.00 □□□□□
22	A7	8p rose	35.00	140.00 □□□□□
23	A8	1sh rose	20.00	60.00 □□□□□
1865-94					
24	A9	2c green	25.00	12.50 □□□□□
25	A10	5c brown	180.00	110.00 □□□□□
26	A10	5c black ('68)	120.00	60.00 □□□□□
27	A11	10c black	70.00	17.50 □□□□□
28	A12	12c pale red brown	60.00	20.00 □□□□□
28a		White paper	15.00	15.00 □□□□□
29	A12	12c brown, *white* ('94)	15.00	15.00 □□□□□
30	A13	13c orange	25.00	25.00 □□□□□
31	A14	24c blue	15.00	15.00 □□□□□
1868-94					
32	A15	1c violet	20.00	20.00 □□□□□
32A	A15	1c brown lilac (re-engraved) ('71)	27.50	22.50 □□□□□

A17

A19

A20

A18

A21

A22

A23

A24

A25

A26

A27

A28

A29

A30

A31

A32

A33

A34

A35

A36

A37

Stamp of 1890 Surcharged
with Bars and
ONE CENT

a

ONE CENT ONE CENT

b *c*

256

Scott® No.	Illus No.	Description	Unused Price	Used Price	//////

1868-94

Scott® No.	Illus No.	Description	Unused Price	Used Price	
33	A16	3c vermilion ('70)	125.00	50.00	☐☐☐☐☐
34	A16	3c blue ('73)	150.00	10.00	☐☐☐☐☐
35	A16	6c dull rose ('70)	8.50	8.50	☐☐☐☐☐
36	A16	6c carmine lake ('94)	9.00	9.00	☐☐☐☐☐

1876-79

37	A15	1c brown lilac ('77)	35.00	20.00	☐☐☐☐☐
38	A9	2c green ('79)	35.00	20.00	☐☐☐☐☐
39	A16	3c blue ('77)	110.00	6.50	☐☐☐☐☐
40	A10	5c blue	70.00	6.50	☐☐☐☐☐

1880-96

41	A17	1c violet brown	10.00	7.50	☐☐☐☐☐
42	A17	1c gray brown	10.00	7.50	☐☐☐☐☐
43	A17	1c brown ('96)	17.50	17.50	☐☐☐☐☐
44	A17	1c deep green ('87)	4.00	3.00	☐☐☐☐☐
45	A17	1c green ('96)	6.00	6.00	☐☐☐☐☐
46	A19	2c yellow green	10.00	10.00	☐☐☐☐☐
47	A19	2c green ('96)	15.00	15.00	☐☐☐☐☐
48	A19	2c red orange ('87)	4.50	4.50	☐☐☐☐☐
49	A18	3c blue	10.00	3.00	☐☐☐☐☐
51	A18	3c umber brown ('87)	10.00	3.00	☐☐☐☐☐
52	A18	3c violet brown ('96)	25.00	22.50	☐☐☐☐☐
53	A20	5c pale blue	110.00	5.00	☐☐☐☐☐
54	A20	5c dark blue ('87)	50.00	4.25	☐☐☐☐☐
55	A20	5c brt. blue ('94)	15.00	4.25	☐☐☐☐☐

1887-96

56	A21	½c rose red	4.50	4.50	☐☐☐☐☐
57	A21	½c org. red ('96)	16.00	16.00	☐☐☐☐☐
58	A21	½c black ('94)	3.50	3.50	☐☐☐☐☐
59	A22	10c black	25.00	25.00	☐☐☐☐☐

1890

60	A23	3c slate	5.00	.60	☐☐☐☐☐

1897

61	A24	1c deep green	1.50	1.50	☐☐☐☐☐
62	A25	2c carmine lake	1.50	1.50	☐☐☐☐☐
63	A26	3c ultramarine	2.50	1.50	☐☐☐☐☐
64	A27	4c olive green	3.00	3.00	☐☐☐☐☐
65	A28	5c violet	3.50	3.00	☐☐☐☐☐
66	A29	6c red brown	3.00	3.00	☐☐☐☐☐
67	A30	8c red orange	9.00	6.00	☐☐☐☐☐
68	A31	10c black brown	11.00	5.50	☐☐☐☐☐
69	A32	12c dark blue	15.00	6.50	☐☐☐☐☐
70	A33	15c scarlet	15.00	6.50	☐☐☐☐☐
71	A34	24c gray violet	15.00	8.00	☐☐☐☐☐
72	A35	30c slate	25.00	17.50	☐☐☐☐☐
73	A36	35c red	42.50	35.00	☐☐☐☐☐
74	A37	60c black	7.50	5.00	☐☐☐☐☐

A38   A39   A40   A41

A42   A43   A44   A45

A46   A47   A48   A49

A50   A51   A52   A53

A54   A55   A56   A57

A58   A59   A60   A61

Scott® No.	Illus No.	Description	Unused Price	Used Price	/ / / / / /
1897					
75	A23(*a*)	1c on 3c gray lilac	9.00	9.00 ☐☐☐☐☐
76	A23(*b*)	1c on 3c gray lilac	50.00	50.00 ☐☐☐☐☐
77	A23(*c*)	1c on 3c gray lilac	300.00	250.00 ☐☐☐☐☐
1897-1901					
78	A38	½c olive green	2.50	2.50 ☐☐☐☐☐
79	A39	1c carmine rose	2.50	2.50 ☐☐☐☐☐
80	A39	1c yellow green ('98)	2.00	.25 ☐☐☐☐☐
81	A40	2c orange	2.00	2.00 ☐☐☐☐☐
82	A40	2c vermilion ('98)	4.00	.60 ☐☐☐☐☐
83	A41	3c orange ('98)	4.00	.50 ☐☐☐☐☐
84	A42	4c violet ('01)	12.00	3.00 ☐☐☐☐☐
85	A43	5c blue ('99)	12.00	2.25 ☐☐☐☐☐
1908					
86	A44	2c rose carmine	12.50	1.10 ☐☐☐☐☐
1910		*Perf. 12*			
87	A45	1c deep green, perf. 12×11	1.25	1.00 ☐☐☐☐☐
88	A46	2c carmine	2.50	.60 ☐☐☐☐☐
89	A47	3c brown olive	7.00	7.00 ☐☐☐☐☐
90	A48	4c dull violet	8.00	8.00 ☐☐☐☐☐
91	A49	5c ultra., perf. 14×12	4.25	2.75 ☐☐☐☐☐
92	A50	6c claret, type I (☉)	45.00	45.00 ☐☐☐☐☐
92A	A50	6c claret, type II (☉)	15.00	15.00 ☐☐☐☐☐
93	A51	8c pale brown	27.50	27.50 ☐☐☐☐☐
94	A52	9c olive green	25.00	25.00 ☐☐☐☐☐
95	A53	10c violet black	32.50	32.50 ☐☐☐☐☐
96	A54	12 lilac brown	30.00	30.00 ☐☐☐☐☐
97	A55	15c gray black	27.50	27.50 ☐☐☐☐☐
1911		*Perf. 14.*			
98	A50	6c brown violet	12.50	12.50 ☐☐☐☐☐
99	A51	8c bistre brown	32.50	32.50 ☐☐☐☐☐
100	A52	9c olive green	25.00	25.00 ☐☐☐☐☐
101	A53	10c violet black	55.00	55.00 ☐☐☐☐☐
102	A54	12c red brown	37.50	37.50 ☐☐☐☐☐
103	A55	15c slate green	37.50	37.50 ☐☐☐☐☐
1911					
104	A56	1c yellow green	1.50	.18 ☐☐☐☐☐
105	A57	2c carmine	1.50	.15 ☐☐☐☐☐
106	A58	3c red brown	12.50	12.50 ☐☐☐☐☐
107	A59	4c violet	10.00	10.00 ☐☐☐☐☐
108	A60	5c ultramarine	6.00	1.25 ☐☐☐☐☐
109	A61	6c black	12.50	12.50 ☐☐☐☐☐
110	A62	8c blue (paper colored through)	40.00	40.00 ☐☐☐☐☐
111	A63	9c blue violet	15.00	15.00 ☐☐☐☐☐
112	A64	10c dark green	20.00	20.00 ☐☐☐☐☐

A62

A63

A64

A65

A67

A66

A68

A70

A72

A73

A74

A71

A76

A77

A78

A75

A79

A81

A82

A83

A84

A85

A86

A87

A88

A80

A89

Scott® No.	Illus No.	Description	Unused Price	Used Price	/ / / / / /
1911					
113	A65	12c plum	20.00	20.00 ☐☐☐☐☐
114	A66	15c magenta	20.00	20.00 ☐☐☐☐☐
1919					
115	A67	1c green	1.25	.25 ☐☐☐☐☐
116	A68	2c scarlet	1.50	.35 ☐☐☐☐☐
117	A67	3c red brown	1.50	.25 ☐☐☐☐☐
118	A67	4c violet	2.00	1.00 ☐☐☐☐☐
119	A68	5c ultramarine	2.50	1.00 ☐☐☐☐☐
120	A67	6c gray	12.00	12.00 ☐☐☐☐☐
121	A68	8c magenta	9.00	9.00 ☐☐☐☐☐
122	A67	10c dark green	6.00	3.00 ☐☐☐☐☐
123	A68	12c orange	22.50	17.50 ☐☐☐☐☐
124	A67	15c dark blue	15.00	15.00 ☐☐☐☐☐
125	A67	24c bistre	20.00	20.00 ☐☐☐☐☐
126	A67	36c olive green	12.50	12.50 ☐☐☐☐☐
1920					
127	A35	2c on 30c slate	4.50	4.50 ☐☐☐☐☐
128	A33	3c on 15c scarl.(I) (Bars 10½mm)	75.00	75.00 ☐☐☐☐☐
129	A33	3c on 15c scarl.(II)(Bars 13½mm)	6.00	6.00 ☐☐☐☐☐
130	A36	3c on 35c red	5.00	5.00 ☐☐☐☐☐
1923-24					
131	A70	1c gray green	1.50	.25 ☐☐☐☐☐
131a		Booklet pane of 8	250.00	250.00 ☐☐☐☐☐
132	A71	2c carmine	1.50	.20 ☐☐☐☐☐
132a		Booklet pane of 8	110.00	110.00 ☐☐☐☐☐
133	A72	3c brown	1.50	.20 ☐☐☐☐☐
134	A73	4c brown violet	1.75	1.40 ☐☐☐☐☐
135	A74	5c ultramarine	2.75	1.75 ☐☐☐☐☐
136	A75	6c gray black	2.75	2.75 ☐☐☐☐☐
137	A76	8c dull violet	2.75	2.50 ☐☐☐☐☐
138	A77	9c slate green	15.00	15.00 ☐☐☐☐☐
139	A78	10c dark violet	2.75	1.75 ☐☐☐☐☐
140	A79	11c olive green	3.50	3.50 ☐☐☐☐☐
141	A80	12c lake	4.00	4.00 ☐☐☐☐☐
142	A81	15c deep blue	6.50	6.50 ☐☐☐☐☐
143	A82	20c red brown ('24)	6.00	5.00 ☐☐☐☐☐
144	A83	24c black brown ('24)	32.50	32.50 ☐☐☐☐☐
1928					
145	A84	1c deep green	1.00	.60 ☐☐☐☐☐
146	A85	2c deep carmine	1.50	.60 ☐☐☐☐☐
147	A86	3c brown	1.75	.40 ☐☐☐☐☐
148	A87	4c lilac rose	2.25	1.75 ☐☐☐☐☐
149	A88	5c slate green	3.25	2.25 ☐☐☐☐☐
150	A89	6c ultramarine	2.75	2.75 ☐☐☐☐☐

A90

A91

A92

A93

A94

A95

A96

Wmk 224

A97

A98

A99

A100

A101

A102

A103

A104

A105

A106

Scott® No.	Illus No.	Description	Unused Price	Used Price	—Checklist—
1928					
151	A90	8c light red brown	4.25	4.25	☐☐☐☐☐
152	A91	9c myrtle green	5.00	5.00	☐☐☐☐☐
153	A92	10c dark violet	4.50	3.50	☐☐☐☐☐
154	A93	12c brown carmine	3.00	3.00	☐☐☐☐☐
155	A91	14c red brown	4.25	4.25	☐☐☐☐☐
156	A94	15c dark blue	5.50	5.50	☐☐☐☐☐
157	A95	20c gray black	4.00	3.25	☐☐☐☐☐
158	A93	28c gray green	13.50	13.50	☐☐☐☐☐
159	A96	30c olive brown	4.50	4.50	☐☐☐☐☐
1929		**Unwmkd.**			
160	A75	3c on 6c gray black (II) (R)	2.75	2.75	☐☐☐☐☐
163	A84	1c green	1.50	.50	☐☐☐☐☐
164	A85	2c deep carmine	1.50	.25	☐☐☐☐☐
165	A86	3c deep red brown	1.75	.20	☐☐☐☐☐
166	A87	4c magenta	2.25	1.00	☐☐☐☐☐
167	A88	5c slate green	2.25	1.10	☐☐☐☐☐
168	A89	6c ultramarine	7.00	7.00	☐☐☐☐☐
169	A92	10c dark violet	3.00	1.75	☐☐☐☐☐
170	A94	15c deep blue ('30)	22.50	20.00	☐☐☐☐☐
171	A95	20c gray black ('31)	37.50	18.00	☐☐☐☐☐
1931		**Wmkd. Coat of Arms (224)**			
172	A84	1c green	1.50	1.00	☐☐☐☐☐
173	A85	2c red	2.25	1.25	☐☐☐☐☐
174	A86	3c red brown	2.25	1.00	☐☐☐☐☐
175	A87	4c rose	3.00	1.50	☐☐☐☐☐
176	A88	5c greenish gray	5.50	5.50	☐☐☐☐☐
177	A89	6c ultramarine	12.50	12.50	☐☐☐☐☐
178	A90	8c lt. red brown	12.50	12.50	☐☐☐☐☐
179	A92	10c dark violet	6.50	6.00	☐☐☐☐☐
180	A94	15c deep blue	20.00	20.00	☐☐☐☐☐
181	A95	20c gray black	25.00	5.50	☐☐☐☐☐
182	A96	30c olive brown	17.50	17.50	☐☐☐☐☐
1932-37					
183	A97	1c green	1.25	.35	☐☐☐☐☐
183a		Booklet pane of 4, Perf. 13	40.00		☐☐☐☐☐
184	A97	1c gray black	.25	.08	☐☐☐☐☐
184a		Booklet pane of 4, Perf. 13½	30.00		☐☐☐☐☐
184b		Booklet pane of 4, Perf. 14	30.00		☐☐☐☐☐
185	A98	2c rose	1.00	.25	☐☐☐☐☐
185a		Booklet pane of 4, Perf. 13	12.50		☐☐☐☐☐
186	A98	2c green	.75	.08	☐☐☐☐☐
186a		Booklet pane of 4, Perf. 13½	7.00		☐☐☐☐☐
186b		Booklet pane of 4, Perf. 14	7.50		☐☐☐☐☐

A107   A108

A111   A109   A110

A112   A113   A114   A115

A116   A117   A118   A119

A120   A121   A122   A123

A124

No. C9 Overprinted
Bars and

SCOTT 211

A125

Scott® No.	Illus No.	Description	Unused Price	Used Price	/ / / / / /
1932-37					
187	A99	3c orange brown	.75	.20 ☐☐☐☐☐
187a		Booklet pane of 4, Perf. 13½	30.00	☐☐☐☐☐
187b		Booklet pane of 4, Perf. 14	30.00	☐☐☐☐☐
187c		Booklet pane of 4, Perf. 13	40.00	☐☐☐☐☐
188	A100	4c deep violet	3.25	1.00 ☐☐☐☐☐
189	A100	4c rose lake	.45	.15 ☐☐☐☐☐

Two Dies of the 5c.
Die I—Antlers even, or equal in height.
Die II—Antler under letter "T" higher.

190	A101	5c violet brown, perf. 13½ (Die I)	3.75	1.00 ☐☐☐☐☐
191	A101	5c deep violet, perf. 13½ (Die II)	.85	.10 ☐☐☐☐☐
191a		5c deep violet, perf. 13½ (Die I)	6.00	.45 ☐☐☐☐☐
192	A102	6c dull blue	7.50	7.50 ☐☐☐☐☐
193	A103	10c olive black	1.00	.75 ☐☐☐☐☐
194	A104	14c intense black	2.00	2.00 ☐☐☐☐☐
195	A105	15c magenta	2.00	2.00 ☐☐☐☐☐
196	A106	20c gray green	2.00	.75 ☐☐☐☐☐
197	A107	25c gray	2.25	2.00 ☐☐☐☐☐
198	A108	30c ultramarine	14.00	14.00 ☐☐☐☐☐
199	A108	48c red brown (('37)	5.00	4.00 ☐☐☐☐☐
1932					
208	A109	7c red brown	1.00	1.00 ☐☐☐☐☐
209	A110	8c orange red	1.10	.90 ☐☐☐☐☐
210	A111	24c light blue	2.25	2.00 ☐☐☐☐☐
1933					
211	AP6	15c brown	6.00	6.00 ☐☐☐☐☐
212	A112	1c gray black	1.00	.75 ☐☐☐☐☐
213	A113	2c green	1.25	.75 ☐☐☐☐☐
214	A114	3c yellow brown	1.50	1.25 ☐☐☐☐☐
215	A115	4c carmine	1.50	.50 ☐☐☐☐☐
216	A116	5c dull violet	2.00	1.25 ☐☐☐☐☐
217	A117	7c blue	10.00	10.00 ☐☐☐☐☐
218	A118	8c orange red	7.00	7.00 ☐☐☐☐☐
219	A119	9c ultramarine	7.50	7.50 ☐☐☐☐☐
220	A120	10c red brown	7.50	4.50 ☐☐☐☐☐
221	A121	14c black	15.00	15.00 ☐☐☐☐☐
222	A122	15c claret	16.00	16.00 ☐☐☐☐☐
223	A123	20c deep green	9.00	6.00 ☐☐☐☐☐
224	A124	24c violet brown	20.00	20.00 ☐☐☐☐☐
225	A125	32c gray	20.00	20.00 ☐☐☐☐☐
1935					
226	CD301	4c bright rose	1.25	.75 ☐☐☐☐☐
227	CD301	5c violet	1.25	1.00 ☐☐☐☐☐

CD301

CD302

A126

A127

A128

A129

A130

A131

A132

A133

A134

A135

A136

A139

A141

A142

Scott® No.	Illus No.	Description	Unused Price	Used Price	/ / / / / /
1935					
228	CD301	7c dark blue	1.75	1.75 ☐☐☐☐☐
229	CD301	24c olive green	4.00	4.00 ☐☐☐☐☐
1937					
230	CD302	2c deep green	.60	.60 ☐☐☐☐☐
231	CD302	4c carmine rose	.60	.40 ☐☐☐☐☐
232	CD302	5c dark violet	1.00	1.00 ☐☐☐☐☐
1937					
233	A126	1c gray black	.35	.25 ☐☐☐☐☐
234	A127	3c orange brown	1.50	.50 ☐☐☐☐☐
235	A128	7c blue	1.50	1.50 ☐☐☐☐☐
236	A129	8c orange red	1.50	1.50 ☐☐☐☐☐
237	A130	10c olive gray	3.00	3.00 ☐☐☐☐☐
238	A131	14c black	2.50	2.50 ☐☐☐☐☐
239	A132	15c rose lake	2.75	2.75 ☐☐☐☐☐
240	A133	20c green	2.00	2.00 ☐☐☐☐☐
241	A134	24c turquoise blue	2.75	2.75 ☐☐☐☐☐
242	A135	25c gray	2.75	2.75 ☐☐☐☐☐
243	A136	48c dark violet	3.00	3.00 ☐☐☐☐☐
1938					
245	A139	2c green	1.25	.15 ☐☐☐☐☐
246	A139	3c dark carmine	1.25	.20 ☐☐☐☐☐
247	A139	4c light blue	1.50	.15 ☐☐☐☐☐
248	A139	7c dk. ultramarine	1.25	1.25 ☐☐☐☐☐
1939					
249	A141	5c violet blue	1.00	1.00 ☐☐☐☐☐
250	A141	2c on 5c vio. blue (Br)	1.25	1.25 ☐☐☐☐☐
251	A141	4c on 5c vio. blue (R)	1.00	1.00 ☐☐☐☐☐
1941					
252	A142	5c dull blue	.40	.35 ☐☐☐☐☐
1941-44		*Perf. 12½.* **Wmk. 224**			
253	A97	1c dark gray	.25	.10 ☐☐☐☐☐
254	A139	2c deep green	.30	.08 ☐☐☐☐☐
255	A139	3c rose carmine	.35	.08 ☐☐☐☐☐
256	A139	4c blue	.70	.08 ☐☐☐☐☐
257	A101	5c violet (Die I)	.70	.18 ☐☐☐☐☐
258	A139	7c vio. blue ('42)	1.10	1.10 ☐☐☐☐☐
259	A110	8c red	.85	.70 ☐☐☐☐☐
260	A103	10c brownish black	.85	.60 ☐☐☐☐☐
261	A104	14c black	1.60	1.35 ☐☐☐☐☐
262	A105	15c pale rose violet	1.75	1.50 ☐☐☐☐☐
263	A106	20c green	1.50	1.25 ☐☐☐☐☐
264	A111	24c deep blue	2.00	1.75 ☐☐☐☐☐
265	A107	25c slate	2.00	1.75 ☐☐☐☐☐
266	A108	48c red brn. ('44)	3.00	2.00 ☐☐☐☐☐

A143

A144

A145

AP6

AP7

AP8

AP9

AP10

AP11

AP12

AP13

AP14

D1

Scott® No.	Illus No.	Description	Unused Price	Used Price	/ / / / / /
1943					
267	A143	30c carmine	1.50	1.25 ☐☐☐☐☐
1946					
268	A143	2c on 30c carmine	.35	.35 ☐☐☐☐☐
1947					
269	A144	4c light blue	.35	.10 ☐☐☐☐☐
270	A145	5c rose violet	.35	.25 ☐☐☐☐☐

AIR POST STAMPS

1919		Trans-Atlantic			
C1	A67	3c red brown	16000.00	15000.00 ☐☐☐☐☐
C2	A33	$1 on 15c scarlet	150.00	150.00 ☐☐☐☐☐
1921		Airmail to Halifax, N.S.			
C3	A36	35c red	125.00	125.00 ☐☐☐☐☐
1927		De Pinedo			
C4	A37	60c black	25000.00	7500.00 ☐☐☐☐☐
1930		"Columbia"			
C5	A67	50c on 36c olive green	6000.00	6000.00 ☐☐☐☐☐
1931		Unwmkd.			
C6	AP6	15c brown	7.00	7.00 ☐☐☐☐☐
C7	AP7	50c green	15.00	15.00 ☐☐☐☐☐
C8	AP8	$1 blue	40.00	40.00 ☐☐☐☐☐
1931		Wmkd. Coat of Arms (224)			
C9	AP6	15c brown	6.00	6.00 ☐☐☐☐☐
C10	AP7	50c green	22.50	22.50 ☐☐☐☐☐
C11	AP8	$1 blue	60.00	60.00 ☐☐☐☐☐
1932					
C12	AP8	$1.50 on $1 blue	300.00	300.00 ☐☐☐☐☐
1933					
C13	AP9	5c light brown	11.00	11.00 ☐☐☐☐☐
C14	AP10	10c yellow	16.00	16.00 ☐☐☐☐☐
C15	AP11	30c blue	30.00	30.00 ☐☐☐☐☐
C16	AP12	60c green	47.50	47.50 ☐☐☐☐☐
C17	AP13	75c bistre	50.00	50.00 ☐☐☐☐☐
C18	AP13	$4.50 on 75c	500.00	500.00 ☐☐☐☐☐
1943					
C19	AP14	7c bright ultramarine	.40	.30 ☐☐☐☐☐

POSTAGE DUE STAMPS

1939-49		Unwmkd.			
J1	D1	1c yellow green	1.50	1.50 ☐☐☐☐☐
J2	D1	2c vermilion	2.50	2.50 ☐☐☐☐☐
J3	D1	3c ultramarine	3.00	3.00 ☐☐☐☐☐
J4	D1	4c yellow orange	4.00	4.00 ☐☐☐☐☐
J5	D1	5c pale brown	2.25	2.25 ☐☐☐☐☐
J6	D1	10c dark violet	2.25	2.25 ☐☐☐☐☐

A1

A2

A3

A5

A6

A1

A2

A3

A4

A5

A6

A7

A8

A9

A10

A11

A12

A13

Scott® No.	Illus No.	Description	Unused Price	Used Price	/ / / / / /

1939-49 *Perf. 11* **Wmk. 224**

J7	D1	10c dark violet	5.00	5.00 ☐☐☐☐☐

NOVA SCOTIA

1851-53 *Imperf.*

1	A1	1p red brown ('53)	800.00	275.00 ☐☐☐☐☐
2	A2	3p blue	275.00	75.00 ☐☐☐☐☐
3	A2	3p dark blue	325.00	75.00 ☐☐☐☐☐
4	A2	6p yellow green	1350.00	275.00 ☐☐☐☐☐
5	A2	6p dark green	2100.00	550.00 ☐☐☐☐☐
6	A2	1sh reddish violet	5500.00	2000.00 ☐☐☐☐☐
7	A2	1sh dull violet	5500.00	2000.00 ☐☐☐☐☐

1860-63 *Perf. 12.*

8	A3	1c black	3.50	3.50 ☐☐☐☐☐
9	A3	2c lilac	4.00	4.00 ☐☐☐☐☐
10	A3	5c blue	100.00	6.00 ☐☐☐☐☐
10a		Yellowish paper	85.00	6.00 ☐☐☐☐☐
11	A5	8½c green	3.50	12.00 ☐☐☐☐☐
11a		White paper	4.00	7.00 ☐☐☐☐☐
12	A5	10c vermilion	5.00	5.00 ☐☐☐☐☐
13	A6	12½c black	15.00	15.00 ☐☐☐☐☐

PRINCE EDWARD ISLAND

1861 *Perf. 9*

1	A1	2p dull rose	175.00	125.00 ☐☐☐☐☐
2	A2	3p blue	400.00	225.00 ☐☐☐☐☐
3	A3	6p yellow green	600.00	325.00 ☐☐☐☐☐

1862-65 *Perf. 11, 11½, 12 and Compound*

4	A4	1p yellow orange	20.00	20.00 ☐☐☐☐☐
5	A1	2p rose	5.00	5.00 ☐☐☐☐☐
6	A2	3p blue	6.00	6.00 ☐☐☐☐☐
7	A3	6p yellow green	50.00	50.00 ☐☐☐☐☐
8	A5	9p violet	25.00	25.00 ☐☐☐☐☐

1868

9	A6	4p black	5.00	12.00 ☐☐☐☐☐

1870

10	A7	4½p brown	30.00	30.00 ☐☐☐☐☐

1872

11	A8	1c brown orange	3.50	6.00 ☐☐☐☐☐
12	A9	2c ultramarine	7.50	20.00 ☐☐☐☐☐
13	A10	3c rose	12.50	12.50 ☐☐☐☐☐
14	A11	4c green	3.00	8.00 ☐☐☐☐☐
15	A12	6c black	3.00	8.00 ☐☐☐☐☐
16	A13	12c violet	3.00	15.00 ☐☐☐☐☐

Scott® No.	Illus No.	Description	Unused Price	Used Price	/ / / / / /
......	......	......			☐☐☐☐☐
......	......	......			☐☐☐☐☐
......	......	......			☐☐☐☐☐
......	......	......			☐☐☐☐☐
......	......	......			☐☐☐☐☐
......	......	......			☐☐☐☐☐
......	......	......			☐☐☐☐☐
......	......	......			☐☐☐☐☐
......	......	......			☐☐☐☐☐
......	......	......			☐☐☐☐☐
......	......	......			☐☐☐☐☐
......	......	......			☐☐☐☐☐
......	......	......			☐☐☐☐☐
......	......	......			☐☐☐☐☐
......	......	......			☐☐☐☐☐
......	......	......			☐☐☐☐☐
......	......	......			☐☐☐☐☐
......	......	......			☐☐☐☐☐
......	......	......			☐☐☐☐☐
......	......	......			☐☐☐☐☐
......	......	......			☐☐☐☐☐
......	......	......			☐☐☐☐☐
......	......	......			☐☐☐☐☐
......	......	......			☐☐☐☐☐
......	......	......			☐☐☐☐☐
......	......	......			☐☐☐☐☐
......	......	......			☐☐☐☐☐
......	......	......			☐☐☐☐☐
......	......	......			☐☐☐☐☐
......	......	......			☐☐☐☐☐
......	......	......			☐☐☐☐☐
......	......	......			☐☐☐☐☐
......	......	......			☐☐☐☐☐
......	......	......			☐☐☐☐☐
......	......	......			☐☐☐☐☐
......	......	......			☐☐☐☐☐
......	......	......			☐☐☐☐
......	......	......			☐☐☐☐
......	......	......			☐☐☐☐
......	......	......			☐☐☐☐
......	......	......			☐☐☐☐
......	......	......			☐☐☐☐

Scott® No.	Illus No.	Description	Unused Price	Used Price	/ / / / / /
......	....				☐☐☐☐☐
......	....				☐☐☐☐☐
......	....				☐☐☐☐☐
......	....				☐☐☐☐☐
......	....				☐☐☐☐☐
......	....				☐☐☐☐☐
......	....				☐☐☐☐☐
......	....				☐☐☐☐☐
......	....				☐☐☐☐☐
......	....				☐☐☐☐☐
......	....				☐☐☐☐☐
......	....				☐☐☐☐☐
......	....				☐☐☐☐☐
......	....				☐☐☐☐☐
......	....				☐☐☐☐☐
......	....				☐☐☐☐☐
......	....				☐☐☐☐☐
......	....				☐☐☐☐☐
......	....				☐☐☐☐☐
......	....				☐☐☐☐☐
......	....				☐☐☐☐☐
......	....				☐☐☐☐☐
......	....				☐☐☐☐☐
......	....				☐☐☐☐☐
......	....				☐☐☐☐☐
......	....				☐☐☐☐☐
......	....				☐☐☐☐☐
......	....				☐☐☐☐☐
......	....				☐☐☐☐☐
......	....				☐☐☐☐☐
......	....				☐☐☐☐☐
......	....				☐☐☐☐☐
......	....				☐☐☐☐☐
......	....				☐☐☐☐☐
......	....				☐☐☐☐☐
......	....				☐☐☐☐☐
......	....				☐☐☐☐☐
......	....				☐☐☐☐☐
......	....				☐☐☐☐☐
......	....				☐☐☐☐☐
......	....				☐☐☐☐☐
......	....				☐☐☐☐☐
......	....				☐☐☐☐☐
......	....				☐☐☐☐☐
......	....				☐☐☐☐☐
......	....				☐☐☐☐☐
......	....				☐☐☐☐☐
......	....				☐☐☐☐☐
......	....				☐☐☐☐☐

A2

A1

A3

A4

A5

A6

A7

A9

A8

A10

A12

A11

A13

A15

A14

UNITED NATIONS

Scott® No.	Illus No.	Description	Unused Price	Used Price	/ / / / / /
1951					
1	A1	1c magenta	.04	.04	☐☐☐☐☐
2	A2	1½ blue green	.04	.04	☐☐☐☐☐
3	A3	2c purple	.08	.07	☐☐☐☐☐
4	A4	3c magenta & blue	.10	.08	☐☐☐☐☐
5	A5	5c blue	.15	.12	☐☐☐☐☐
6	A1	10c chocolate	.60	.30	☐☐☐☐☐
7	A4	15c violet & blue	.75	.40	☐☐☐☐☐
8	A6	20c dark brown	2.25	1.25	☐☐☐☐☐
9	A4	25c olive gray & blue	1.50	1.25	☐☐☐☐☐
10	A2	50c indigo	27.50	13.00	☐☐☐☐☐
11	A3	$1 red	7.00	4.00	☐☐☐☐☐
1952					
12	A7	5c blue	1.75	.65	☐☐☐☐☐
13	A8	3c deep green	.50	.30	☐☐☐☐☐
14	A8	5c blue	5.50	.70	☐☐☐☐☐
1953					
15	A9	3c dark red brown & rose brown	.30	.75	☐☐☐☐☐
16	A9	5c indigo & blue	9.00	2.00	☐☐☐☐☐
17	A10	3c black brown	1.00	.35	☐☐☐☐☐
18	A10	5c dark blue	10.00	2.25	☐☐☐☐☐
19	A11	3c dark gray	.65	.40	☐☐☐☐☐
20	A11	5c dark green	6.75	1.00	☐☐☐☐☐
21	A12	3c bright blue	1.00	.40	☐☐☐☐☐
22	A12	5c rose red	12.50	1.25	☐☐☐☐☐
1954					
23	A13	3c dark green & yellow	2.50	.40	☐☐☐☐☐
24	A13	8c indigo & yellow	5.00	1.50	☐☐☐☐☐
25	A14	3c brown	.75	.50	☐☐☐☐☐
26	A14	8c magenta	15.00	2.00	☐☐☐☐☐
27	A15	3c dark blue violet	17.50	2.50	☐☐☐☐☐
28	A15	8c red	1.00	.75	☐☐☐☐☐
29	A16	3c red orange	37.50	6.00	☐☐☐☐☐
30	A16	8c olive green	1.00	1.00	☐☐☐☐☐
1955					
31	A17	3c blue	20.00	1.25	☐☐☐☐☐
32	A17	8c rose carmine	6.00	2.25	☐☐☐☐☐
33	A18	3c lilac rose	8.00	1.25	☐☐☐☐☐
34	A18	8c light blue	.50	.50	☐☐☐☐☐
35	A19	3c deep plum	15.00	1.85	☐☐☐☐☐
36	A19	4c dull green	.45	.35	☐☐☐☐☐
37	A19	8c bluish black	.80	.60	☐☐☐☐☐

A17

A16

A18

A19

A20

A21

A23

A22

A24

A26

A27

A28

A25

A29

A30

A31

A32

A33

Scott® No.	Illus No.	Description	Unused Price	Used Price	/ / / / / /
1955					
38	A19	Sheet of three Imperf.	350.00	100.00 ☐☐☐☐☐
38a		3c deep plum	25.00	12.00 ☐☐☐☐☐
38b		4c dull green	25.00	12.00 ☐☐☐☐☐
38c		8c bluish black	25.00	12.00 ☐☐☐☐☐
39	A20	3c ultramarine	.35	.25 ☐☐☐☐☐
40	A20	8c green	5.75	1.10 ☐☐☐☐☐
1956					
41	A21	3c turquoise blue	2.00	.60 ☐☐☐☐☐
42	A21	8c deep carmine	4.00	1.25 ☐☐☐☐☐
43	A22	3c bright greenish blue	.20	.20 ☐☐☐☐☐
44	A22	8c golden brown	5.75	1.60 ☐☐☐☐☐
45	A23	3c dark blue	.10	.10 ☐☐☐☐☐
46	A23	8c gray olive	.35	.30 ☐☐☐☐☐
47	A24	3c plum	10.00	.08 ☐☐☐☐☐
48	A24	8c dark blue	.20	.15 ☐☐☐☐☐
1957					
49	A25	3c violet blue	.10	.08 ☐☐☐☐☐
50	A25	8c dark carmine rose	.20	.15 ☐☐☐☐☐
51	A26	3c light blue	.10	.08 ☐☐☐☐☐
52	A26	8c rose carmine	.20	.15 ☐☐☐☐☐
		Re-engraved		
53	A26	3c blue	.10	.10 ☐☐☐☐☐
54	A26	8c rose carmine	.35	.35 ☐☐☐☐☐
55	A27	3c orange brown	.10	.07 ☐☐☐☐☐
56	A27	8c dark blue green	.20	.15 ☐☐☐☐☐
57	A28	3c red brown	.10	.07 ☐☐☐☐☐
58	A28	8c black	.20	.15 ☐☐☐☐☐
1958					
59	A29	3c olive	.10	.07 ☐☐☐☐☐
60	A29	8c blue	.20	.15 ☐☐☐☐☐
61	A30	3c violet blue	.10	.07 ☐☐☐☐☐
62	A30	8c rose claret	.20	.15 ☐☐☐☐☐
63	A31	4c red orange	.10	.06 ☐☐☐☐☐
64	A31	8c bright blue	.20	.12 ☐☐☐☐☐
65	A32	4c dark blue green	.10	.10 ☐☐☐☐☐
66	A32	8c vermilion	.25	.20 ☐☐☐☐☐
67	A33	4c yellow green	.10	.10 ☐☐☐☐☐
68	A33	8c red brown	.25	.20 ☐☐☐☐☐
1959					
69	A34	4c light lilac rose	.15	.10 ☐☐☐☐☐
70	A34	8c aquamarine	.30	.25 ☐☐☐☐☐
71	A35	4c blue	.20	.20 ☐☐☐☐☐
72	A35	8c red orange	.40	.35 ☐☐☐☐☐
73	A36	4c bright red	.15	.15 ☐☐☐☐☐
74	A36	8c dark olive green	.35	.30 ☐☐☐☐☐

A35

A34

A36

A38

A37

A42

A40

A39

A47

A44

A46

A45

A43

A49

A48

Scott® No.	Illus No.	Description	Unused Price	Used Price	/ / / / / /

1959

75	A37	4c olive & red	.12	.10 ☐☐☐☐☐
76	A37	8c olive & bright greenish blue	.30	.20 ☐☐☐☐☐

1960

77	A38	4c rose lilac & blue	.12	.10 ☐☐☐☐☐
78	A38	8c dull green & brown	.25	.20 ☐☐☐☐☐
79	A39	4c deep claret, blue green & dull yellow	.12	.10 ☐☐☐☐☐
80	A39	8c olive green, blue & rose	.25	.20 ☐☐☐☐☐
81	A40	4c grn., dk. blue & org.	.12	.10 ☐☐☐☐☐
82	A40	8c yellow green, black & orange	.25	.20 ☐☐☐☐☐
83	A41	4c blue	.10	.08 ☐☐☐☐☐
84	A41	8c gray	.20	.15 ☐☐☐☐☐
85	A41	Sheet of two Imperf.	11.00	4.50 ☐☐☐☐☐
85a		4c blue	1.00	.75 ☐☐☐☐☐
85b		8c gray	1.00	.75 ☐☐☐☐☐
86	A42	4c multicolored	.12	.10 ☐☐☐☐☐
87	A42	8c multicolored	.25	.20 ☐☐☐☐☐

1961

88	A43	4c yellow, orange brown & black	.12	.10 ☐☐☐☐☐
89	A43	8c yellow, green & black	.30	.20 ☐☐☐☐☐
90	A44	4c bright bluish green	.12	.10 ☐☐☐☐☐
91	A44	7c terra cotta & yellow	.25	.20 ☐☐☐☐☐
92	A45	30c multicolored	.65	.30 ☐☐☐☐☐
93	A46	4c blue, red & citron	.30	.20 ☐☐☐☐☐
94	A46	11c green, lilac & orange verm.	.90	.45 ☐☐☐☐☐
95	A47	4c ultra., orange, yellow & brown	.15	.15 ☐☐☐☐☐
96	A47	11c emerald, orange, yellow & brown	.50	.35 ☐☐☐☐☐
97	A48	3c brown, gold, orange & yellow	.10	.08 ☐☐☐☐☐
98	A48	4c brown, gold, blue & emerald	.15	.15 ☐☐☐☐☐
99	A48	13c dp. green, gold, purple & pink	.50	.40 ☐☐☐☐☐

1962

100	A49	4c bright blue	.20	.15 ☐☐☐☐☐
101	A49	7c orange brown	.40	.30 ☐☐☐☐☐
102	A50	4c orange, yel., grn. & black	.25	.15 ☐☐☐☐☐
103	A50	11c grn., yel., brn. & indigo	.55	.35 ☐☐☐☐☐
104	A51	1c vermilion, blue, black & gray	.15	.08 ☐☐☐☐☐
105	A52	3c lt. green, Prussian blue, yellow & gray	.10	.10 ☐☐☐☐☐

A50

A51

A52

A53

A54

A56

A55

A57

A58

A60

A59

A61

A62

A63

Scott® No.	Illus No.	Description	Unused Price	Used Price	/ / / / / /
1962					
106	A53	5c dk. carmine rose	.50	.30 ☐☐☐☐☐
107	A54	11c dk. & lt. blue & gold	.22	.18 ☐☐☐☐☐
108	A55	5c black, lt. blue & blue	.25	.20 ☐☐☐☐☐
109	A55	15c black, gray olive & blue	1.75	.55 ☐☐☐☐☐
110	A56	4c olive, orange, black & yellow	.35	.20 ☐☐☐☐☐
111	A56	11c bl. green, orange, black & yellow	1.40	.55 ☐☐☐☐☐
112	A57	4c violet blue	.15	.15 ☐☐☐☐☐
113	A57	11c rose claret	.50	.35 ☐☐☐☐☐
1963					
114	A58	5c pale grn., maroon, dark blue & Prussian blue	.20	.15 ☐☐☐☐☐
115	A58	11c yellow, maroon, dark blue & Prussian blue	.50	.40 ☐☐☐☐☐
116	A59	5c vermilion, green & yellow	.20	.15 ☐☐☐☐☐
117	A59	11c vermilion, deep claret & yel.	.50	.40 ☐☐☐☐☐
118	A60	25c blue, grn. & gray	1.25	.85 ☐☐☐☐☐
119	A61	5c vio. bl. & multi.	.20	.15 ☐☐☐☐☐
120	A61	11c green & multi.	.50	.40 ☐☐☐☐☐
121	A62	5c green, gold, red & yellow	.20	.15 ☐☐☐☐☐
122	A62	11c car., gold, blue & yellow	.50	.40 ☐☐☐☐☐
1964					
123	A63	5c blue, olive, ocher & yellow	.20	.15 ☐☐☐☐☐
124	A63	11c blue, dk. green, emerald & yel.	.50	.40 ☐☐☐☐☐
1964-71					
125	A64	2c lt. & dk. blue, org. & yellow green	.06	.06 ☐☐☐☐☐
126	A65	7c dk. blue, orange brown & black	.18	.14 ☐☐☐☐☐
127	A66	10c blue grn., olive green & black	.25	.18 ☐☐☐☐☐
128	A67	50c multicolored	1.50	.90 ☐☐☐☐☐
1964					
129	A68	5c blk., red & yel.	.15	.12 ☐☐☐☐☐
130	A68	11c blk., olive & yel.	.45	.40 ☐☐☐☐☐
131	A69	5c rose red & black	.15	.12 ☐☐☐☐☐
132	A69	11c emerald & black	.55	.40 ☐☐☐☐☐
133	A70	5c dk. red & dk. brn.	.15	.12 ☐☐☐☐☐
134	A71	4c multicolored	.12	.10 ☐☐☐☐☐
135	A71	5c multicolored	.15	.12 ☐☐☐☐☐
136	A71	11c multicolored	.30	.25 ☐☐☐☐☐
1965					
137	A72	5c multicolored	.15	.12 ☐☐☐☐☐
138	A72	11c multicolored	.30	.25 ☐☐☐☐☐
139	A73	5c org., olive & blk.	.15	.12 ☐☐☐☐☐
140	A73	11c yel. grn., bl. grn. & black	.30	.25 ☐☐☐☐☐

A64

A65

A66

A67

A68

A69

A70

A71

A72

A73

A74

A75

A76

A77

A78

A79

A80

A81

A83

A82

A84

A86

A85

A87

A89

A92

A88

A90

A93

A91

A94

Scott® No.	Illus No.	Description	Unused Price	Used Price	/ / / / / /
1965					
141	A74	5c multicolored	.15	.12 ☐☐☐☐☐
142	A74	11c multicolored	.30	.25 ☐☐☐☐☐
143	A75	5c dark blue	.15	.12 ☐☐☐☐☐
144	A75	15c lilac rose	.40	.25 ☐☐☐☐☐
145	A75	Sheet of two	1.25	1.00 ☐☐☐☐☐
1965-66					
146	A76	1c vermilion, blue, black & gray	.03	.03 ☐☐☐☐☐
147	A77	15c olive bister, dull yel., black & deep claret	.35	.25 ☐☐☐☐☐
148	A78	20c dk. blue., blue, red & yellow	.50	.35 ☐☐☐☐☐
149	A79	25c lt. & dark blue	.60	.45 ☐☐☐☐☐
150	A80	$1 sapphire & aqua	2.50	1.80 ☐☐☐☐☐
151	A81	4c multicolored	.10	.08 ☐☐☐☐☐
152	A81	5c multicolored	.12	.10 ☐☐☐☐☐
153	A81	11c multicolored	.30	.22 ☐☐☐☐☐
1966					
154	A82	5c multicolored	.15	.12 ☐☐☐☐☐
155	A82	15c multicolored	.40	.35 ☐☐☐☐☐
156	A83	5c multicolored	.15	.12 ☐☐☐☐☐
157	A83	11c multicolored	.30	.22 ☐☐☐☐☐
158	A84	5c multicolored	.15	.12 ☐☐☐☐☐
159	A84	11c multicolored	.30	.22 ☐☐☐☐☐
160	A85	15c multicolored	.40	.30 ☐☐☐☐☐
161	A86	4c pink & multi.	.10	.08 ☐☐☐☐☐
162	A86	5c pale grn. & multi.	.12	.10 ☐☐☐☐☐
163	A86	11c ultra. & multi.	.30	.22 ☐☐☐☐☐
1967					
164	A87	5c multicolored	.12	.10 ☐☐☐☐☐
165	A87	11c multicolored	.30	.25 ☐☐☐☐☐
166	A88	1½ ultra, black, org. & ocher	.10	.10 ☐☐☐☐☐
167	A53	5c red brown, brown & orange yellow	.10	.08 ☐☐☐☐☐
168	A89	5c dk. bl. & multi.	.12	.10 ☐☐☐☐☐
169	A89	11c brn. lake & multi.	.30	.25 ☐☐☐☐☐
170	A90	4c red & red brown	.15	.15 ☐☐☐☐☐
171	A90	5c blue & red brown	.20	.20 ☐☐☐☐☐
172	A91	8c multicolored	.35	.35 ☐☐☐☐☐
173	A90	10c green & red brn.	.60	.60 ☐☐☐☐☐
174	A90	15c dk. brn. & red brown	1.25	1.25 ☐☐☐☐☐
175	A92	5c multicolored	.10	.06 ☐☐☐☐☐
176	A92	15c multicolored	.30	.20 ☐☐☐☐☐
177	A93	6c multicolored	.12	.08 ☐☐☐☐☐
178	A93	13c multicolored	.26	.15 ☐☐☐☐☐
179	A94	Sheet of six	.75	.60 ☐☐☐☐☐
179a	A94	6c multi., 41×46mm.	.12	.08 ☐☐☐☐☐

UNITED NATIONS • 6c

A95

A96

A97

A98

A99

A100

A101

A103

A102

A105

A104

A106

A108

A107

A109

A110

A111

Scott® No.	Illus No.	Description	Unused Price	Used Price	/ / / / / /
1967					
179b	A94	6c multi., 24 × 46mm.	.12	.08 ☐☐☐☐☐
179c	A94	6c multi., 41 × 33½mm.	.12	.08 ☐☐☐☐☐
179d	A94	6c multi., 36 × 33½mm.	.12	.08 ☐☐☐☐☐
179e	A94	6c multi., 29 × 33½mm.	.12	.08 ☐☐☐☐☐
179f	A94	6c multi., 41 ½ × 47mm.	.12	.08 ☐☐☐☐☐
180	A95	6c multicolored	.15	.08 ☐☐☐☐☐
1968					
181	A96	6c multicolored	.12	.08 ☐☐☐☐☐
182	A96	13c multicolored	.26	.15 ☐☐☐☐☐
183	A97	6c blue & multi.	.15	.12 ☐☐☐☐☐
184	A97	75c rose lake & multi.	8.00	5.00 ☐☐☐☐☐
185	A98	6c multicolored	.12	.08 ☐☐☐☐☐
186	A98	13c multicolored	.26	.15 ☐☐☐☐☐
187	A99	6c multicolored	.20	.10 ☐☐☐☐☐
188	A100	6c green & multi	.12	.10 ☐☐☐☐☐
189	A100	20c lilac & multi	.40	.35 ☐☐☐☐☐
190	A101	6c brt. blue, deep ultra & gold	.25	.20 ☐☐☐☐☐
191	A101	13c rose red, dk. red & gold	.35	.35 ☐☐☐☐☐
1969					
192	A102	6c yellow green & multicolored	.15	.12 ☐☐☐☐☐
193	A102	13c bluish lilac & multicolored	.35	.30 ☐☐☐☐☐
194	A103	6c lt. blue, vio. blue & light green	.15	.12 ☐☐☐☐☐
195	A103	15c pink, cream & red brown	.35	.30 ☐☐☐☐☐
196	A104	13c brt. blue, black & gold	.26	.13 ☐☐☐☐☐
197	A105	6c brt. green, ultra. & gold	.15	.12 ☐☐☐☐☐
198	A105	13c crimson, lilac & gold	.35	.30 ☐☐☐☐☐
199	A106	6c blue, dp. blue, yellow & gold	.15	.12 ☐☐☐☐☐
200	A106	20c orange verm., magenta, yellow & gold	.50	.40 ☐☐☐☐☐
201	A107	6c blue & multi.	.15	.12 ☐☐☐☐☐
202	A107	13c red & multi.	.35	.30 ☐☐☐☐☐
1970					
203	A108	6c vio. blue & multi.	.15	.12 ☐☐☐☐☐
204	A108	25c claret & multi.	.75	.60 ☐☐☐☐☐
205	A109	6c dk. blue & multi.	.15	.12 ☐☐☐☐☐
206	A109	13c dp. plum & multi.	.35	.30 ☐☐☐☐☐
207	A110	6c blue & black	.15	.12 ☐☐☐☐☐
208	A110	13c olive & black	.35	.30 ☐☐☐☐☐
209	A111	6c red, gold, dk. & light blue	.15	.12 ☐☐☐☐☐
210	A111	13c dk. blue, gold, green & red	.35	.35 ☐☐☐☐☐
211	A112	25c dark blue, gold & light blue	.65	.60 ☐☐☐☐☐
212		Sheet of 3 Imperf.	1.50	1.25 ☐☐☐☐☐
212a	A111	6c multi.	.12	.10 ☐☐☐☐☐
212b	A111	13c multi.	.26	.20 ☐☐☐☐☐
212c	A112	25c multi.	.50	.35 ☐☐☐☐☐

A112

A113

A114

A115

A116

A117

A119

A118

A120

A121

A122

A123

A125

A124

A126

Scott® No.	Illus No.	Description	Unused Price	Used Price	/ / / / / /
1970					
213	A113	6c gold & multi.	.15	.12 ☐☐☐☐☐	
214	A113	13c silver & multi.	.40	.35 ☐☐☐☐☐	
1971					
215	A114	6c blue & multi.	.15	.12 ☐☐☐☐☐	
216	A115	6c brown, ocher & black	.15	.12 ☐☐☐☐☐	
217	A115	13c ultra., greenish blue & black	.35	.30 ☐☐☐☐☐	
218	A116	13c brown red, gold & green	.30	.25 ☐☐☐☐☐	
219	A117	20c brown orange & multicolored	.50	.40 ☐☐☐☐☐	
220	A118	8c yellow green & multicolored	.20	.15 ☐☐☐☐☐	
221	A119	13c blue & multi.	.35	.30 ☐☐☐☐☐	
222	A120	8c vio. bl. & multi.	.16	.12 ☐☐☐☐☐	
223	A121	60c ultra. & multi.	1.20	.90 ☐☐☐☐☐	
224	A122	8c olive & multi.	.20	.15 ☐☐☐☐☐	
225	A122	21c ultra. & multi.	.50	.40 ☐☐☐☐☐	
1972					
226	A123	95c blue & multi.	1.90	1.50 ☐☐☐☐☐	
227	A124	8c dull rose, black, blue & gray	.20	.15 ☐☐☐☐☐	
228	A125	15c black & multi.	.35	.25 ☐☐☐☐☐	
229	A126	8c multicolored	.20	.15 ☐☐☐☐☐	
230	A126	15c multicolored	.40	.35 ☐☐☐☐☐	
231	A127	21c yel. brn. & multi.	.50	.40 ☐☐☐☐☐	
232	A128	8c gold, brown & golden brown	.25	.15 ☐☐☐☐☐	
233	A128	15c gold, brown & blue green	.45	.35 ☐☐☐☐☐	
1973					
234	A129	8c blue & multi.	.30	.15 ☐☐☐☐☐	
235	A129	15c lilac rose & multi.	.50	.35 ☐☐☐☐☐	
236	A130	8c multicolored	.25	.15 ☐☐☐☐☐	
237	A130	15c multicolored	.45	.35 ☐☐☐☐☐	
238	A131	8c ol. bis. & multi.	.20	.15 ☐☐☐☐☐	
239	A131	21c gray bl. & multi.	.50	.40 ☐☐☐☐☐	
240	A132	8c emerald & multi.	.25	.15 ☐☐☐☐☐	
241	A132	15c brt. rose & multi.	.60	.35 ☐☐☐☐☐	
242	A133	8c dp. car. & multi.	.25	.15 ☐☐☐☐☐	
243	A133	21c bl. grn. & multi.	.60	.40 ☐☐☐☐☐	
1974					
244	A134	10c ultra. & multi.	.35	.20 ☐☐☐☐☐	
245	A134	21c bl. grn. & multi.	.75	.40 ☐☐☐☐☐	
246	A135	10c multicolored	.30	.20 ☐☐☐☐☐	
247	A136	10c gold & multi.	.25	.20 ☐☐☐☐☐	
248	A136	18c ultra. & multi.	.45	.35 ☐☐☐☐☐	
249	A137	2c dk. & light blue	.04	.03 ☐☐☐☐☐	
250	A138	10c multicolored	.20	.15 ☐☐☐☐☐	
251	A139	18c multicolored	.36	.25 ☐☐☐☐☐	
252	A140	10c lt. bl. & multi.	.25	.20 ☐☐☐☐☐	

A127

A129

A128

A131

A130

A132

A133

A134

A135

A136

A138

A137

A139

A140

A141

A142

A143

290

A145

A144

A146

A147

A148

A149

United Nations 50c

A151

30c

A150

A152

A154

A153

A155

A156

A157

A158

A159

A160

A161

A162

A163

A164

A165

A166

A168

A167

A169

Scott® No.	Illus No.	Description	Unused Price	Used Price	//////
1974					
253	A140	18c lilac & multi.	.55	.35 ☐☐☐☐☐	
254	A141	10c green & multi.	.30	.20 ☐☐☐☐☐	
255	A141	26c multicolored	.75	.55 ☐☐☐☐☐	
1975					
256	A142	10c multicolored	.30	.20 ☐☐☐☐☐	
257	A142	26c multicolored	.75	.55 ☐☐☐☐☐	
258	A143	10c multicolored	.30	.20 ☐☐☐☐☐	
259	A143	18c multicolored	.55	.35 ☐☐☐☐☐	
260	A144	10c multicolored	.25	.20 ☐☐☐☐☐	
261	A144	26c pur. & multi.	.65	.50 ☐☐☐☐☐	
262	A144	Sheet of 2 Imperf.	1.25	☐☐☐☐☐	
262a	A144	10c olive bister & multi	.20	☐☐☐☐☐	
262b	A144	26c purple & multicolored	.52	☐☐☐☐☐	
263	A145	10c multicolored	.25	.20 ☐☐☐☐☐	
264	A145	18c multicolored	.40	.35 ☐☐☐☐☐	
265	A146	13c ultramarine	.35	.25 ☐☐☐☐☐	
266	A146	26c rose carmine	.65	.50 ☐☐☐☐☐	
1976					
267	A147	3c multicolored	.06	.05 ☐☐☐☐☐	
268	A148	4c multicolored	.08	.06 ☐☐☐☐☐	
269	A149	9c multicolored	.18	.15 ☐☐☐☐☐	
270	A150	30c bl., emerald & black	.60	.50 ☐☐☐☐☐	
271	A151	50c multicolored	1.00	.75 ☐☐☐☐☐	
272	A152	13c blue, grn. & blk.	.30	.25 ☐☐☐☐☐	
273	A152	26c green & multi.	.60	.50 ☐☐☐☐☐	
274	A153	13c multicolored	.30	.25 ☐☐☐☐☐	
275	A153	31c multicolored	.70	.60 ☐☐☐☐☐	
276	A154	13c multicolored	.30	.25 ☐☐☐☐☐	
277	A154	25c green & multi.	.50	.50 ☐☐☐☐☐	
278	A155	13c blue & multi.	1.00	1.00 ☐☐☐☐☐	
279	A155	31c green & multi.	9.00	5.00 ☐☐☐☐☐	
280	A156	13c multicolored	.30	.25 ☐☐☐☐☐	
1977					
281	A157	13c citron & multi.	.26	.13 ☐☐☐☐☐	
282	A157	31c brt. grn. & multi.	.62	.30 ☐☐☐☐☐	
283	A158	13c yel. & multi.	.26	.13 ☐☐☐☐☐	
284	A158	25c salmon & multi.	.50	.25 ☐☐☐☐☐	
285	A159	13c pur. & multi.	.26	.13 ☐☐☐☐☐	
286	A159	31c dp. bl. & multi.	.62	.30 ☐☐☐☐☐	
287	A160	13c black & yel.	.26	.13 ☐☐☐☐☐	
288	A160	25c black & verm.	.50	.25 ☐☐☐☐☐	
289	A161	13c yellow bister & multi.	.26	.13 ☐☐☐☐☐	
290	A161	18c dull green & multi.	.36	.18 ☐☐☐☐☐	
1978					
291	A162	1c gold, brn. & red	.03	.03 ☐☐☐☐☐	
292	A163	25c multicolored	.50	.25 ☐☐☐☐☐	

A170

A171

A172

A174

A173

A175

AP1

AP3

AP2

AP4

Scott® No.	Illus No.	Description	Unused Price	Used Price	//////
1978					
293	A164	$1 multicolored	2.00	1.00 □□□□□
294	A165	13c rose & black	.26	.13 □□□□□
295	A165	31c blue & black	.62	.30 □□□□□
296	A166	13c multicolored	.26	.13 □□□□□
297	A166	18c multicolored	.36	.18 □□□□□
298	A167	13c multicolored	.26	.13 □□□□□
299	A167	25c multicolored	.50	.25 □□□□□
300	A168	13c multicolored	.26	.13 □□□□□
301	A168	18c multicolored	.36	.18 □□□□□
302	A169	13c multicolored	.26	.13 □□□□□
303	A169	31c multicolored	.62	.30 □□□□□
1979					
304	A170	5c multicolored	.10	.05 □□□□□
305	A171	14c multicolored	.28	.14 □□□□□
306	A172	15c multicolored	.30	.15 □□□□□
307	A173	20c multicolored	.40	.20 □□□□□
308	A174	15c multicolored	.30	.15 □□□□□
309	A174	20c multicolored	.40	.20 □□□□□
310	A175	15¢ multicolored	.30	.15 □□□□□
311	A175	31¢ multicolored	.62	.30 □□□□□
....	....			□□□□□
....	....			□□□□□
....	....			□□□□□
....	....			□□□□□
....	....			□□□□□
....	....			□□□□□
....	....			□□□□□
....	....			□□□□□
....	....			□□□□□
....	....			□□□□□
....	....			□□□□□
....	....			□□□□□
....	....			□□□□□
....	....			□□□□□
....	....			□□□□□
....	....			□□□□□
....	....			□□□□□
....	....			□□□□□
....	....			□□□□□
....	....			□□□□□
....	....			□□□□□
....	....			□□□□□
....	....			□□□□□
....	....			□□□□□
....	....			□□□□□

AP6

AP5

AP8

AP7

AP9

AP10

AP12

AP13

AP11

AP15

AP16

AP14

AP19

AP18

AP17

AP20

AIR POST STAMPS

Scott® No.	Illus No.	Description	Unused Price	Used Price	/ / / / / /
1951					
C1	AP1	6c henna brown	.15	.15 ☐☐☐☐☐
C2	AP1	10c bright blue green	.35	.35 ☐☐☐☐☐
C3	AP2	15c deep ultra.	1.50	1.00 ☐☐☐☐☐
C4	AP2	25c gray black	8.00	5.00 ☐☐☐☐☐
1957					
C5	AP3	4c maroon	.10	.08 ☐☐☐☐☐
1959					
C6	AP3	5c rose red	.15	.10 ☐☐☐☐☐
C7	AP4	7c ultramarine	.20	.15 ☐☐☐☐☐
1963-64					
C8	AP5	6c black, blue & yellow green	.12	.10 ☐☐☐☐☐
C9	AP6	8c yellow, olive green & red	.16	.12 ☐☐☐☐☐
C10	AP7	13c ultra., aqua, gray & carmine	.30	.22 ☐☐☐☐☐
C11	AP8	15c vio., buff, gray & pale green ('64)	.40	.30 ☐☐☐☐☐
C12	AP9	25c yel., org., gray, bl. & red ('64)	1.60	.90 ☐☐☐☐☐
1968					
C13	AP10	20c multicolored	.45	.35 ☐☐☐☐☐
1969					
C14	AP11	10c org. verm., org., yel. & black	.30	.25 ☐☐☐☐☐
1972					
C15	AP12	9c lt. blue, dk. red & violet blue	.18	.15 ☐☐☐☐☐
C16	AP13	11c blue & multi.	.22	.15 ☐☐☐☐☐
C17	AP14	17c yel., red & org.	.34	.25 ☐☐☐☐☐
C18	AP15	21c silver & multi.	.42	.35 ☐☐☐☐☐
1974					
C19	AP16	13c multicolored	.35	.25 ☐☐☐☐☐
C20	AP17	18c multicolored	.45	.35 ☐☐☐☐☐
C21	AP18	26c blue & multi.	.65	.50 ☐☐☐☐☐
1977					
C22	AP19	25c greenish blue & multi.	.50	.25 ☐☐☐☐☐
C23	AP20	31c magenta	.62	.30 ☐☐☐☐☐
......	......			☐☐☐☐☐
......	......			☐☐☐☐☐
......	......			☐☐☐☐☐
......	......			☐☐☐☐☐
......	......			☐☐☐☐☐
......	......			☐☐☐☐☐
......	......			☐☐☐☐☐
......	......			☐☐☐☐☐
......	......			☐☐☐☐☐
......	......			☐☐☐☐☐

A1

A2

A3

A4

A5

A6

A7

A8

A9

A10

A11

A12

298

Scott® No.	Illus No.	Description	Unused Price	Used Price	/ / / / / /
1969-70					
1	A88	5c purple & multi.	.05	.03	☐☐☐☐☐
2	A52	10c salmon & multi.	.12	.10	☐☐☐☐☐
3	A66	20c black & multi.	.24	.15	☐☐☐☐☐
4	A1	30c dk. blue & multi.	.35	.30	☐☐☐☐☐
5	A77	50c ultra. & multi.	.60	.40	☐☐☐☐☐
6	A54	60c dk. brown, salmon & gold ('70)	.75	.45	☐☐☐☐☐
7	A104	70c red, black & gold ('70)	.85	.40	☐☐☐☐☐
8	AP8	75c carmine rose & multi	.90	.55	☐☐☐☐☐
9	A78	80c blue green, red & yellow ('70)	.95	.60	☐☐☐☐☐
10	A45	90c blue & multi. ('70)	1.10	.65	☐☐☐☐☐
11	A79	1fr lt. & dark green	1.20	.75	☐☐☐☐☐
12	A67	2fr bl. & multi. ('70)	2.40	2.00	☐☐☐☐☐
13	A97	3fr olive & multi.	3.50	2.50	☐☐☐☐☐
14	A3	10fr deep blue ('70)	12.00	9.00	☐☐☐☐☐
1971					
15	A114	30c green & multi.	.35	.30	☐☐☐☐☐
16	A115	50c carmine, dp. orange & black	.85	.75	☐☐☐☐☐
17	A116	50c dark purple, gold & green	1.10	.75	☐☐☐☐☐
18	A117	75c green & multi.	2.25	1.25	☐☐☐☐☐
19	A118	30c blue & multi.	.60	.40	☐☐☐☐☐
20	A119	50c multicolored	1.00	.75	☐☐☐☐☐
21	A122	1.10fr car. & multi.	2.00	1.50	☐☐☐☐☐
1972					
22	A2	40c olive & multi.	.50	.25	☐☐☐☐☐
23	A124	40c yel. green, black, rose & gray	1.50	1.00	☐☐☐☐☐
24	A125	80c black & multi.	1.75	1.25	☐☐☐☐☐
25	A126	40c multicolored	.90	.65	☐☐☐☐☐
26	A126	80c multicolored	1.80	1.35	☐☐☐☐☐
27	A127	1.10fr red & multi.	2.50	1.80	☐☐☐☐☐
28	A128	40c gold, brn. & red	1.00	.65	☐☐☐☐☐
29	A128	80c gold, brn. & ol.	2.00	1.25	☐☐☐☐☐
1973					
30	A129	60c vio. & multi.	1.00	.75	☐☐☐☐☐
31	A129	1.10fr olive & multi.	1.75	1.40	☐☐☐☐☐
32	A130	60c blue & multi.	1.25	.80	☐☐☐☐☐
33	A131	80c multicolored	1.40	.90	☐☐☐☐☐
34	A132	60c red & multi.	1.25	.80	☐☐☐☐☐
35	A133	40c ultra. & multi.	.60	.50	☐☐☐☐☐
36	A133	80c olive & multi.	1.25	.90	☐☐☐☐☐
1974					
37	A134	60c violet & multi.	.90	.65	☐☐☐☐☐
38	A134	80c brown & multi.	1.20	.90	☐☐☐☐☐

Scott® No.	Illus No.	Description	Unused Price	Used Price	//////
1974					
39	A135	30c multicolored	.40	.30 ☐☐☐☐☐
40	A135	60c multicolored	.90	.60 ☐☐☐☐☐
41	A136	60c dk. red & multi.	.90	.60 ☐☐☐☐☐
42	A136	1fr green & multi.	1.50	1.00 ☐☐☐☐☐
43	A140	60c grn. & multi.	.90	.60 ☐☐☐☐☐
44	A140	80c brown & multi.	1.20	.80 ☐☐☐☐☐
45	A141	1.30fr blue & multi.	2.00	1.50 ☐☐☐☐☐
1975					
46	A142	60c multicolored	.90	.60 ☐☐☐☐☐
47	A142	90c multicolored	1.35	.90 ☐☐☐☐☐
48	A143	60c multicolored	.90	.60 ☐☐☐☐☐
49	A143	90c multicolored	1.35	.90 ☐☐☐☐☐
50	A144	60c green & multi.	.90	.60 ☐☐☐☐☐
51	A144	90c violet & multi.	1.35	.90 ☐☐☐☐☐
52	A144	Sheet of 2 Imperf.	2.25	2.00 ☐☐☐☐☐
52a	A144	60c green & multicolored	.40	☐☐☐☐☐
52b	A144	90c violet & multicolored	.60	☐☐☐☐☐
53	A145	50c multicolored	.60	.40 ☐☐☐☐☐
54	A145	1.30fr multicolored	1.65	.90 ☐☐☐☐☐
55	A146	60c greenish blue	.90	.60 ☐☐☐☐☐
56	A146	70c bright violet	1.05	.70 ☐☐☐☐☐
1976					
57	A152	90c multicolored	1.30	.90 ☐☐☐☐☐
58	A153	1.10fr multicolored	1.65	1.20 ☐☐☐☐☐
59	A154	40c multicolored	.50	.40 ☐☐☐☐☐
60	A154	1.50fr vio. & multi.	1.75	1.50 ☐☐☐☐☐
61	A3	80c tan & multi.	6.00	4.00 ☐☐☐☐☐
62	A3	1.10fr lt. grn. & multi.	8.00	5.00 ☐☐☐☐☐
63	A156	70c multicolored	.90	.70 ☐☐☐☐☐
1977					
64	A157	80c red & multi.	1.00	.80 ☐☐☐☐☐
65	A4	80c ultra. & multi.	.95	.75 ☐☐☐☐☐
66	A4	1.10fr dk. car. & multi.	1.30	1.00 ☐☐☐☐☐
67	A5	80c blue & multi.	.95	.75 ☐☐☐☐☐
68	A5	1.10fr emerald & multi.	1.30	1.00 ☐☐☐☐☐
69	A6	40c multicolored	.50	.40 ☐☐☐☐☐
70	A6	1.10fr multicolored	1.30	1.00 ☐☐☐☐☐
71	A7	80c dk. car. & multi.	.95	.70 ☐☐☐☐☐
72	A7	1.10fr Prus. blue & multicolored	1.30	1.00 ☐☐☐☐☐
1978					
73	A8	35c multicolored	.40	.30 ☐☐☐☐☐
74	A9	80c yel. & multi.	.95	.70 ☐☐☐☐☐
75	A9	1.10fr lt. green & multi.	1.30	1.00 ☐☐☐☐☐
76	A166	80c multicolored	.95	.70 ☐☐☐☐☐
77	A10	70c multicolored	.85	.60 ☐☐☐☐☐

Scott® No.	Illus No.	Description	Unused Price	Used Price	//////
1978					
78	A10	80c multicolored	.95	.70	☐☐☐☐☐
79	A11	70c multicolored	.85	.60	☐☐☐☐☐
80	A11	1.10fr multicolored	1.30	1.00	☐☐☐☐☐
81	A169	80c multicolored	.95	.70	☐☐☐☐☐
1979					
82	A12	80c multicolored	.95	.70	☐☐☐☐☐
83	A12	1.50fr multicolored	1.75	1.35	☐☐☐☐☐
84	A13	80c multi	.95	.70	☐☐☐☐☐
85	A13	1.10fr multi	1.30	1.00	☐☐☐☐☐
......					☐☐☐☐☐
......					☐☐☐☐☐
......					☐☐☐☐☐
......					☐☐☐☐☐
......					☐☐☐☐☐
......					☐☐☐☐☐
......					☐☐☐☐☐
......					☐☐☐☐☐
......					☐☐☐☐☐
......					☐☐☐☐☐
......					☐☐☐☐☐
......					☐☐☐☐☐
......					☐☐☐☐☐
......					☐☐☐☐☐
......					☐☐☐☐☐
......					☐☐☐☐☐
......					☐☐☐☐☐
......					☐☐☐☐☐
......					☐☐☐☐☐
......					☐☐☐☐☐
......					☐☐☐☐☐
......					☐☐☐☐☐
......					☐☐☐☐☐
......					☐☐☐☐☐
......					☐☐☐☐☐
......					☐☐☐☐☐
......					☐☐☐☐☐
......					☐☐☐☐☐
......					☐☐☐☐☐
......					☐☐☐☐☐
......					☐☐☐☐☐

Scott® No.	Illus No.	Denom	Description	Unused Price	Used Price	/ / / / / /
......	......					□□□□□
......	......					□□□□□
......	......					□□□□□
......	......					□□□□□
......	......					□□□□□
......	......					□□□□□
......	......					□□□□□
......	......					□□□□□
......	......					□□□□□
......	......					□□□□□
......	......					□□□□□
......	......					□□□□□
......	......					□□□□□
......	......					□□□□□
......	......					□□□□□
......	......					□□□□□
......	......					□□□□□
......	......					□□□□□
......	......					□□□□□
......	......					□□□□□
......	......					□□□□□
......	......					□□□□□
......	......					□□□□□
......	......					□□□□□
......	......					□□□□□
......	......					□□□□□
......	......					□□□□□
......	......					□□□□□
......	......					□□□□□
......	......					□□□□□
......	......					□□□□□
......	......					□□□□□
......	......					□□□□□
......	......					□□□□□
......	......					□□□□□
......	......					□□□□□
......	......					□□□□□
......	......					□□□□□
......	......					□□□□□
......	......					□□□□□
......	......					□□□□□
......	......					□□□□
......	......					□□□□

Scott® No.	Illus No.	Denom	Description	Unused Price	Used Price	/ / / / /
......	......					☐☐☐☐☐
......	......					☐☐☐☐☐
......	......					☐☐☐☐☐
......	......					☐☐☐☐☐
......	......					☐☐☐☐☐
......	......					☐☐☐☐☐
......	......					☐☐☐☐☐
......	......					☐☐☐☐☐
......	......					☐☐☐☐☐
......	......					☐☐☐☐☐
......	......					☐☐☐☐☐
......	......					☐☐☐☐☐
......	......					☐☐☐☐☐
......	......					☐☐☐☐☐
......	......					☐☐☐☐☐
......	......					☐☐☐☐☐
......	......					☐☐☐☐☐
......	......					☐☐☐☐☐
......	......					☐☐☐☐☐
......	......					☐☐☐☐☐
......	......					☐☐☐☐☐
......	......					☐☐☐☐☐
......	......					☐☐☐☐☐
......	......					☐☐☐☐☐
......	......					☐☐☐☐☐
......	......					☐☐☐☐☐
......	......					☐☐☐☐☐
......	......					☐☐☐☐☐
......	......					☐☐☐☐☐
......	......					☐☐☐☐☐
......	......					☐☐☐☐☐
......	......					☐☐☐☐☐
......	......					☐☐☐☐☐
......	......					☐☐☐☐☐
......	......					☐☐☐☐☐
......	......					☐☐☐☐☐
......	......					☐☐☐☐☐
......	......					☐☐☐☐☐
......	......					☐☐☐☐☐
......	......					☐☐☐☐☐
......	......					☐☐☐☐☐
......	......					☐☐☐☐☐
......	......					☐☐☐☐☐
......	......					☐☐☐☐☐
......	......					☐☐☐☐☐
......	......					☐☐☐☐☐

Scott® No.	Illus No.	Description	Unused Price	Used Price	//////
......	......	....			☐☐☐☐☐
......	......	....			☐☐☐☐☐
......	......	....			☐☐☐☐☐
......	......	....			☐☐☐☐☐
......	......	....			☐☐☐☐☐
......	......	....			☐☐☐☐☐
......	......	....			☐☐☐☐☐
......	......	....			☐☐☐☐☐
......	......	....			☐☐☐☐☐
......	......	....			☐☐☐☐☐
......	......	....			☐☐☐☐☐
......	......	....			☐☐☐☐☐
......	......	....			☐☐☐☐☐
......	......	....			☐☐☐☐☐
......	......	....			☐☐☐☐☐
......	......	....			☐☐☐☐☐
......	......	....			☐☐☐☐☐
......	......	....			☐☐☐☐☐
......	......	....			☐☐☐☐☐
......	......	....			☐☐☐☐☐
......	......	....			☐☐☐☐☐
......	......	....			☐☐☐☐☐
......	......	....			☐☐☐☐☐
......	......	....			☐☐☐☐☐
......	......	....			☐☐☐☐☐
......	......	....			☐☐☐☐☐
......	......	....			☐☐☐☐☐
......	......	....			☐☐☐☐☐
......	......	....			☐☐☐☐☐
......	......	....			☐☐☐☐☐
......	......	....			☐☐☐☐☐
......	......	....			☐☐☐☐☐
......	......	....			☐☐☐☐☐
......	......	....			☐☐☐☐
......	......	....			☐☐☐☐
......	......	....			☐☐☐☐
......	......	....			☐☐☐☐
......	......	....			☐☐☐☐
......	......	....			☐☐☐☐
......	......	....			☐☐☐☐
......	......	....			☐☐☐☐
......	......	....			☐☐☐☐
......	......	....			☐☐☐☐